COMPUTER SUPPORTED COOPERATIVE WORK

Steve Easterbrook (Ed.)

CSCW: Cooperation or Conflict?

Springer-Verlag
London Berlin Heidelberg New York
Paris Tokyo Hong Kong
Barcelona Budapest

Steve Easterbrook, PhD
School of Cognitive and Computing Sciences
University of Sussex
Falmer, Brighton BN1 9QH, UK

Series Editors

Dan Diaper, PhD
Department of Computer Science
University of Liverpool
PO Box 147, Liverpool L69 3BX, UK

Colston Sanger
GID Ltd
69 King's Road
Haslemere, Surrey GU27 2QG, UK

ISBN-13: 978-3-540-19755-3   e-ISBN-13: 978-1-4471-1981-4
DOI: 10. 978-1-4471-1981-4

British Library Cataloguing in Publication Data
CSCW: Cooperation or Conflict?. – (Computer Supported Cooperative Work
Series)
 I. Easterbrook, Steven Michael
 II. Series
 004.01

Library of Congress Cataloging-in-Publication Data
CSCW : cooperation or conflict? / S.M. Easterbrook, ed.
    p. cm.. – (Computer supported cooperative work)
    Includes bibliographical references and indexes.

    1. Work groups–Data processing.   2. Microcomputer workstations.
 I. Easterbrook, S.M. (Steven Michael), *1965–* . II. Series.
 HD66.C77   1992
 306.3'6–dc20   92-202405

Typeset from authors' disks by Fox Design, Bramley, Guildford, Surrey
34/3830–543210 Printed on acid-free paper

Preface

The word *cooperative* in computer supported cooperative work (CSCW) is frequently taken for granted. It is assumed that people who use a CSCW system want to cooperate and can actually do so without difficulty. This assumption ignores the possibility of conflict, and hence the management and resolution of conflict are not supported. In some cases, a CSCW environment might not even allow conflicts to be articulated, causing misunderstanding and frustration.

This book is the result of a one-day meeting held at the Department of Trade and Industry (DTI) in London, on 23rd October 1991. The aim of the meeting was to arrive at an understanding of what it is that people actually do when they say they are cooperating, and in particular, an understanding of the role of conflict. A range of views and experiences of the role of conflict in collaborative work were presented at the meeting, covering both examination of conflict in related disciplines and case studies of conflict in real situations. The chapters of this book are fuller accounts of the work presented during the meeting. Each provides a different view of the nature of conflict in collaborative work, and each draws out, to some degree, the implications for the design of CSCW systems.

As the remainder of the book will show, our understanding of conflict is still at an early stage. In general, the designers of the first generation of CSCW systems have assumed that the social conventions that allow us to work together will carry over to a new medium. For many of these systems, this assumption makes sense. It is not yet clear how these systems will affect working practices; it is not even clear how they might be used. Indeed, CSCW is often presented as an enabling technology: like the telephone, it provides a service, which may in turn offer new opportunities for collaborative work where none existed before. In this sense, CSCW is a solution looking for a problem.

As CSCW matures, the driving force is changing. As well as being an investigation into the opportunities offered by the technology, CSCW is becoming a study of the nature of collaborative work. As with any new technology, success and acceptance will depend on producing systems that address real needs. Hence, those needs must be understood so that the available technologies can be matched to them.

Collaborative work is a complex activity involving an intricate pattern of interactions, governed by social norms and contingencies. Collaboration is not always easy, even between consenting participants, as it requires effort to maintain the relationship between participants, to negotiate the nature of the common task, and to make progress on this task. Conflict seems to be an inevitable part of this activity, sometimes reducing stagnation and promoting change, while at other times disrupting successful cooperation.

This book is the first to examine conflict from a CSCW perspective. As a pioneer in the field, it offers a unique glimpse at current research into the area, and establishes the importance of the issue. The field is still young, and the picture may seem rather fragmented. In many ways this is to be expected: it is hard to pin down a precise meaning for the term "conflict", and it is equally hard to isolate and study the conditions that shape conflict from their social and organizational settings. Rather than providing a single, unified view of conflict, the book presents a number of separate viewpoints. Each sheds light on some particular aspects of the phenomenon, and each adds to our understanding.

This multiplicity of views is itself typical of conflict in collaborative work: there are clearly advantages in the richness offered by these alternative conceptions of the issues, but reconciling these conceptions is hard, if not impossible. A reconciliation that accommodates all the detail and subtlety of each view is likely to get bogged down in the morass of inconsistencies; while any consistent summary may be so generalized as to be vacuous. For this reason, I will not attempt to distil any definitive statements about the nature of conflict: if I liken the viewpoints to pieces of a jigsaw, then there are still many pieces missing, and forcing the existing pieces to fit together would require me to distort them. Instead, I will let each chapter speak for itself.

I have attempted to organize the chapters to form a progression, starting with a literature survey, followed by examinations of conflict situations and analytical techniques, through to experimental work with CSCW systems. Some of the chapters fall into more than one of these categories, and to some extent, all of them provide theoretical frameworks for the study of conflict.

Chapter 1 introduces the book, with an extensive survey of the literature on conflict, drawing on areas such as small group behaviour, organizational psychology, bargaining, negotiation and game theory. The survey is presented using a series of assertions about conflict in collaborative work, to challenge common misconceptions and assumptions. In this way, the chapter provides both a summary of important findings, and pointers to the literature for more information. Although it is a rather long chapter, the assertions can be read in isolation from one another, and the cross-referencing makes it more of a hypertext to explore, rather than a straight read. The chapter ends with an analysis of assumptions made about conflict in existing CSCW systems.

The next three chapters focus on conflict in specific areas: in the systems design process, in scientific research and in small group planning. Chapter 2 treats user resistance as symptomatic of conflicts in the process of information system design. In surveying a number of research paradigms in information systems research, Wastell concludes that systems design is a complex, "protean" process, in which conflict is endemic. The common prescription for user resistance, that of participative design, fails as a panacea, as it is too simplistic.

In Chapter 3, Susan Leigh Star discusses how the scientific community manages to cooperate, even in the absence of common perspectives and common languages. Scientific work is by its very nature heterogeneous: scientists use different methods of analysis and abstraction, have different goals, and have different audiences to satisfy. One way in which cooperation is achieved is through what Star terms "boundary objects". These are objects that are both plastic enough to be adaptable to local contingencies, and coherent enough not to lose their identity through such adaption. A typology of such objects is presented.

The use of conflict as a mechanism for cognitive change is the subject of Chapter 4. Joiner presents a model of inter-individual conflict based on discourse analysis, identifying focus as a major issue. Differences in focus lead to conflict, and the model distinguishes three areas in which conflict may occur: dialogue focus, task focus and task representation. The latter two may lead to learning, as the participants attempt to resolve their differences. The model has implications for the role of conflict in computer supported cooperative learning (CSCL) environments.

Chapters 5 and 6 offer two different analytic techniques for identifying conflict in organizations, both based on concepts from organization theory. Chapter 5, by Hutchison and Rosenberg, begins with observations of conflicts arising from the introduction of expert system technology into organizations, and provides an analysis of these conflicts. They examine the overt and covert structures of organizations, and use systemic nets as an analytical tool. These nets can be annotated to expose the covert structure, and hence reveal possible conflicts.

An alternative analysis of organizations is offered in Chapter 6, which uses stratified systems theory to examine design work in the construction industry. By dividing the work into a number of levels according to the conceptual sophistication of the tasks, conflicts can be identified in the interactions between the levels. Thomas and Riddick make the important point that conflict should not be topicalized, but is part of the nature of work. A fuller understanding of the nature of work and the nature of organizations is needed before we can build better CSCW systems.

The final two chapters discuss experimental CSCW systems, through which conflicts in collaborative work are explored. In Chapter 7, Hughes describes an experiment with shared work-spaces, identifying mutual awareness as a necessity for coordinated actions and coordinated views. In Chapter 8, Condon points out that without clear cues about such matters as ownership of information, attempts to resolve conflicts between participants only lead to conflicts between people and the system. Hence the frustrated cry: "The computer won't let me!"

Finally, although the work presented in this book is of great importance to CSCW, the implications for the design of CSCW systems are still emerging. This book is only the beginning: a first step towards understanding how conflict arises and is handled in collaborative work. Although we may further this study with experimental systems, the design of real systems based on sound principles is some way off. At a subsequent workshop we plan to sketch out some of those principles; in the meantime, this book provides many clues about what those principles would have to cover.

Brighton   Steve Easterbrook
January 1992

Contents

Contents

3 Cooperation Without Consensus in Scientific Problem Solving: Dynamics of Closure in Open Systems
S.L. Star 93

4 Resolution of Inter-Individual Conflicts: A Mechanism of Learning in Joint Planning
R. Joiner 107

8 The Computer Won't Let Me: Cooperation, Conflict and the Ownership of Information

Contributors

Eevi Beck

School of Cognitive and Computing Sciences, University of Sussex, Falmer, Brighton BN1 9QH, UK

Chris Condon

Bremer Institut für Betriebstechnik und angewandte Arbeitswissenschaftan der Universität Bremen, Hochschulring 20, Postfach 330560, D2800 Bremen 33, Germany

Steve Easterbrook

School of Cognitive and Computing Sciences, University of Sussex, Falmer, Brighton BN1 9QH, UK

James Goodlet

School of Cognitive and Computing Sciences, University of Sussex, Falmer, Brighton BN1 9QH, UK

Phil Hughes

BNR Europe Limited, London Road, Harlow, Essex CM17 9NA, UK

Chris Hutchison

School of Information Systems, Kingston Polytechnic, Penryn Road, Kingston upon Thames, Surrey KT1 2EE, UK

Richard Joiner

Psychology Department, Hatfield Polytechnic, Hatfield, Herts AL10 9AB, UK

Lydia Plowman

School of Cognitive and Computing Sciences, University of Sussex, Fulmer, Brighton BN1 9QH, UK

Joanna Riddick

Psychology Department, Hatfield Polytechnic, Hatfield, Herts AL10 9AB, UK

Duska Rosenberg

Department of Computer Sciences, Brunel University, Uxbridge UB8 3PH, Middlesex, UK

Mike Sharples

School of Cognitive and Computive Sciences, University of Sussex, Falmer, Brighton BN1 9QH, UK

Susan Leigh Star

Department of Sociology, University of Illinois, 326 Lincoln Hall, 702 South Wright Street, Urbana, IL 61801, USA

Peter Thomas

Department of Computer Science, Brunel University, Uxbridge UB8 3PH, Middlesex, UK

Dave Wastell

Department of Computer Science, University of Manchester, Oxford Road, Manchester M13 9PL, UK

Charles Wood

School of Cognitive and Computing Sciences, University of Sussex, Falmer, Brighton BN1 9QH, UK

Chapter 1

A Survey of Empirical Studies of Conflict

*S. M. Easterbrook, E. E. Beck, J. S. Goodlet, L. Plowman,
M. Sharples and C. C. Wood*

1.1 Introduction

Conflict is a common phenomenon in interactions both between individuals, and between groups of individuals. As computer-supported cooperative work (CSCW) is concerned with the design of systems to support such interactions, an examination of conflict, and the various ways of dealing with it, would clearly be of benefit. This chapter surveys the literature that is most relevant to the CSCW community, covering many disciplines that have addressed particular aspects of conflict.

The chapter is organized around a series of assertions, representing both commonly held beliefs about conflict, and hypotheses and theories drawn from the literature. In many cases no definitive statement can be made about the truth or falsity of an assertion: the empirical evidence – both supporting and opposing – is examined, and pointers are provided to further discussion in the literature. One advantage of organizing the survey in this way is that it need not be read in order. Each assertion forms a self-contained essay, with cross-references to related assertions.

Hence, treat the chapter as a resource to be dipped into rather than read in sequence. This introduction sets the scene by defining conflict, and providing a rationale for studying conflict in relation to CSCW. The assertions are presented in Section 1.2, and form the main body of the chapter. Finally, Section 1.3 relates the assertions to current work on CSCW systems.

1.1.1 Relevance to CSCW

Research in CSCW embraces disciplines such as human psychology and social science. Unfortunately, there may be good reasons why the results of work in these areas cannot be applied to CSCW: they might not provide appropriate answers; they might not even tackle the kinds of question asked by designers of CSCW systems. These problems are compounded because researchers in CSCW are unlikely to have a background in all the fields that might provide relevant results, making access to the literature difficult.

This chapter attempts to bridge the gap for one particular topic, by providing a guide to the literature on conflict. Rather than simply surveying the relevant disciplines, the literature is presented in relation to a series of assertions representing beliefs about conflict. This format serves both as a pointer into the literature, and to provide (partial) answers to questions which may arise in the development of CSCW. We also hope to challenge some myths which otherwise may become embedded in implemented systems, as underlying assumptions about the nature of conflict in collaborative work.

In attempting to justify the relevance to CSCW of an examination of conflict, one could equally well ask why it should not be relevant. CSCW is concerned with enabling people to work together. Whether or not conflict is inherent in collaborative work, and whether or not conflict is detrimental to collaboration, it is indisputable that conflicts sometimes develop between people engaged in collaborative activities. If CSCW is about facilitating working together, it must be built on an understanding of collaborative work. This must include an understanding of how collaboration may break down, and how collaborative work can continue even in the presence of conflict. Handling conflict is one of the factors that determines whether a group of people can work together successfully.

We believe that the question of conflict between members of a group is highly relevant to any organization of group work. To assume absence of conflicts is naive. Inherent differences between individuals' experiences, personalities and commitment make the *potential* for conflict inherent to any group of people.

A CSCW system or other such technology necessarily influences styles of cooperation, by making some things easier and other things harder to do, or by changing or reinforcing power relationships and patterns of interaction between collaborators. This is the case even if the designers did not deliberately set out to influence styles of cooperation. If designers ignore issues of conflict in the explicit part of the design, then their underlying assumptions about conflict, or its absence, become embedded in the system. These assumptions may influence the style of cooperation in unplanned ways, for instance by restricting the means that collaborators have of dealing with conflict.

It is clear then, that any assumptions made about conflict in the design of CSCW systems need to be made explicit. Once made explicit, the assumptions can be validated against an understanding of the nature of conflict, including the causes and development of conflict, the expression (or lack of expression) of conflict, and the potential for resolution. We suggest that such an understanding can best be gained by building on work already done on the subject, as described in the literature.

1.1.2 Perspectives on Conflict

1.1.2.1 Definitions of Conflict

A fundamental aspect of collaborative work is that individuals are not identical, and will approach the same task with differences in their expectations, goals and preferred styles of working. They will have different amounts of time to commit to the resolution of a problem, and even different notions of what the problem is. These differences will at times lead to conflict.

It is easy to cite situations in which most people would agree that there is a conflict (for example, a strike, a lawsuit, a war). It is not so easy to define conflict. When it comes to what exactly constitutes conflict in the general sense, there are many different views. Pondy (1967) points out that the word "conflict" has been used in the literature to describe variously antecedent conditions of conflictual behaviour, affective states of individuals, cognitive states of individuals, and various types of conflictful behaviour. Fink (1968) notes that the many different uses of the term "conflict" in the literature reflect the many different conceptual frameworks for studying conflict. Much of Fink's paper is devoted to the terminological and conceptual confusion surrounding the study of social conflict, from which he concludes that "scientific knowledge about social conflict has not yet moved to a level of analytical precision superior to that of common sense" (p. 430). A plethora of terms in common usage are cited in support of this point, none of which have precise definitions: conflict, competition, tensions, disputes, opposition, antagonism, quarrel, disagreement, controversy, violence, conflict resolution, mode of resolution.

In the past, some authors have used the term "conflict" in specific ways, for example as the opposite to "cooperation" (cf. the title of this book), as the opposite to "competition" (Mack 1965), or even as a particular species of struggle (Coser 1956). In contrast, others advocate use of the term "conflict" in a more general sense: according to Dahrendorf (1959) "All relations between sets of individuals that involve an incompatible difference of objective [are] relations of social conflict" (p. 135).

More recent views seem to agree that a broad definition has the advantage of subsuming a range of phenomena from psychological antagonism through to overt struggle. For example, Putnam and Poole (1987) give the following definition: "the interaction of interdependent people who perceive opposition of goals, aims, and values, and who see the other party as potentially interfering with the realization of these goals ... [This] definition highlights three general characteristics of conflict: interaction, interdependence, and incompatible goals" (p. 552). Thus, although there is no consensus on the definition of conflict, the preferred view seems to be that conflict should be defined as broadly as possible.

In this chapter, we adopt this broader definition of conflict. This avoids the problem of imposing an arbitrary division, in that any interference or potential interference is treated as conflict, no matter how the parties deal with it. Using this definition, conflict is not the opposite of cooperation, but a phenomenon that may arise whether people are cooperating or not. Successful cooperation depends on how the conflicts are handled.

1.1.2.2 Classifications of Conflict

Given such a broad view of what may constitute conflict, it is useful to distinguish different types of conflict, so that analytical study becomes tractable. A number of different survey papers have been published, each providing its own classification scheme. Some concentrate on the stages of a conflict, others on structural or affective aspects, or on the outcome.

Pondy (1967) identifies three conceptual models to deal with the major classes of conflict in formal organizations:

1. Bargaining model: conflict among interest groups which are in competition for scarce resources.

2. Bureaucratic model: conflicts between a superior and a subordinate, or along any vertical dimension in the organizational hierarchy.

3. Systems model: conflict among parties in a lateral or functional relationship, and in particular, the problems of coordination.

Pondy's model of the development of conflict episodes is described further under Assertion L (see p. 30).

Fink's survey provides a number of different classifications used in the study of social conflict (Fink 1968). For example, he cites an eighteen-level classification derived from Chase (1951), which begins with personal quarrels, family versus family, and feuds between clans, passes through racial and religious conflicts, and culminates with cultural conflicts, cold war, and East versus West. He compares this with similar classifications, which distinguish fewer levels, and also with Dahrendorf (1959), who provides a two-dimensional classification, with the social unit (roles, groups, sectors, societies and nations) on one axis and structural relationship (equal versus equal, superordinate versus subordinate, whole versus part) on the other (see Fig. 1.1). Fink populates this scheme with examples of each of the fifteen combinations, and then groups these fifteen into six main types: role conflicts, competition (between equal groups or equal sectors), proportion struggle (between equal societies), class conflicts (between

Social Units	Equal vs. equal	Superordinate vs. subordinate	Whole vs. part
Roles	1 (family role vs. occupational role)	2 (occupational role vs. union role)	3 (social personality vs. family role)
Groups	4 (boys vs. girls in school class	5 (father vs. children)	6 (nuclear family vs. extended family)
Sectors	7 (air force vs. army)	8 (management vs. union)	9 (department vs. university)
Societies	10 (Protestants vs. Catholics)	11 (free men vs. slaves)	12 (state vs. criminal gang)
Suprasocietal relations	13 (Soviet bloc vs. western bloc)	14 (Soviet Union vs. Hungary)	15 (Common Market vs. UK)

Fig. 1.1. The classification scheme for social conflict suggested by Dahrendorf (1959), showing the groupings identified by Fink. Adapted from Fink (1968).

superordinates and subordinates), minority conflict and deviation (between a part and the whole), and international conflicts.

Putnam and Poole (1987) review the research on conflict from a communicational perspective. Communication is treated as one of the five components of "conflict situations", the others being actor attributes (e.g. beliefs, skills, cognitive style), conflict issues, relationship variables (e.g. trust, power, interdependency), and contextual factors (e.g. organizational norms, history of conflict). The review is partitioned according to the level at which conflict occurs: interpersonal, bargaining and negotiation, intergroup, and interorganizational. The interpersonal analysis focuses on dyadic conflict between constituents with asymmetric power division (e.g. manager–minion), while the bargaining and negotiation level covers aspects of coalition formation, and so could be viewed as intragroup conflict.

As can be seen from these surveys, it is traditional to partition the space of conflicts according to the organizational level at which they occur, and, to a lesser extent, according to whether the relationship between the parties involved is horizontal or vertical with regard to an organizational hierarchy. These classifications clearly reflect the divisions used in social psychology, where empirical studies are necessarily restricted to particular levels. Indeed, Thomas (1976) criticizes such studies for focusing on only a small set of variables, although he does point out that this is understandable for an applied field.

Other classifications are clearly possible. Thomas divides his review into two areas, centred around two general models of conflict: a process model and a structural model. The process model focuses upon the sequence of events within a conflict episode, and is intended to be of use when intervening directly in the stream of events of an ongoing episode. The structural model focuses upon the conditions which shape conflict behaviour in a relationship, and is intended to help in restructuring a situation to facilitate various behaviour patterns. Similarly, Patchen (1970), in reviewing formal models of bargaining, identifies four types of model:

1. Negotiation models, which are used to predict whether two parties will reach agreement, and what the terms of that agreement might be.

2. Cognitive models, which attempt to explain how parties try to influence one another in terms of cognitive elements, including subjective utilities and perceived probabilities.

3. Learning models, which focus on interaction as a learning process.

4. Reaction process models, which describe each action in terms of a reaction to the last action of the other party, according to various characteristics of each party.

In contrast, McGrath (1984), in his book on small group behaviour, examines the literature in relation to the type of task engaged in by groups. He identifies eight types of task, grouped into four categories: generating, choosing, executing and negotiating (see Fig. 1.2). The negotiating category covers those tasks where conflict is prevalent, and McGrath identifies two such tasks: resolving conflicts of viewpoint ("cognitive conflict") and resolving conflicts of interest ("mixed-motive task conflict"). There is also a category covering conflicts of power, including competitions and battles, which McGrath places in the executing category. There is also a distinction between tasks that do not force a competition between group members, and those that directly pit the members against one another, and although tasks involving conflicts of interest or power are clearly in the latter group, cognitive conflicts seem to be in a grey area in between. The later chapters of McGrath review the literature for each of the task types. Cognitive conflicts, for example, are studied in social judgement theory, which we introduce under Assertion F (see p. 22). Mixed-motive tasks have been studied in game theory (see p. 9), in which the motives of participants are manipulated by awarding different payoffs for particular outcomes.

Finally, in addition to the levels of conflict discussed above, Putnam and Poole (1987) categorize the research according to which descriptive model is applied to the conflict, and they identify five such models: "psychologi-

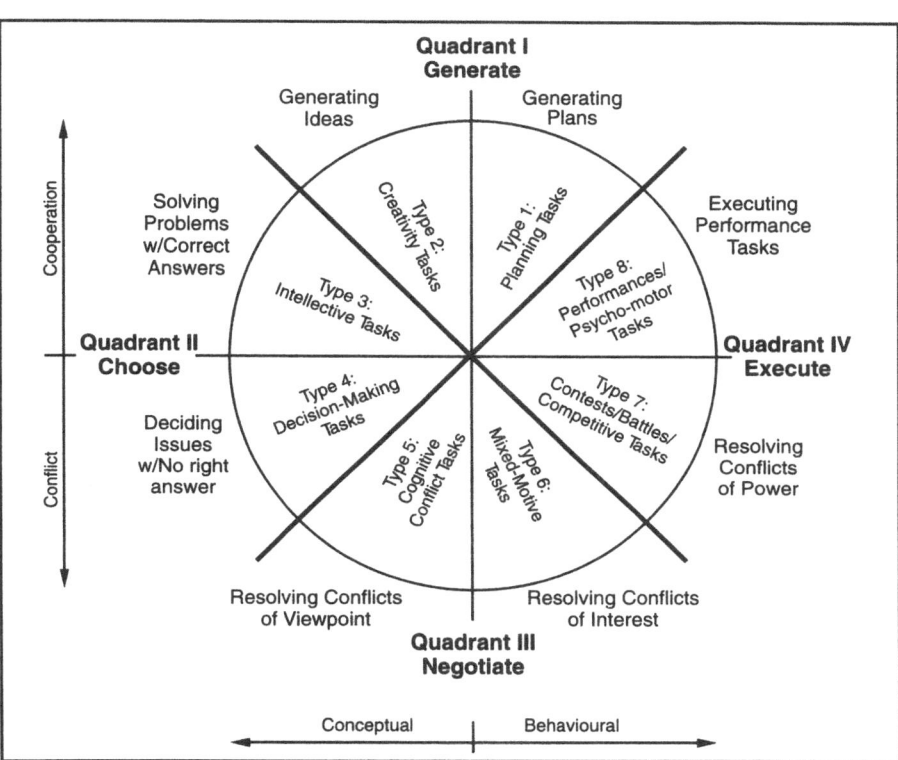

Fig. 1.2. The "Group Task Circumplex", adapted from McGrath (1984). Note that McGrath uses this typology merely to organize a review of the literature, without making any strong claims about its empirical validity.

cal", "interpretive-symbolic", "systems-interaction", "mechanistic" and "critical theory". The psychological approach treats conflict as semantic misunderstanding or difference in perceptions and cognitive abilities of conflicting parties, and includes research on bargaining and stereotyping of an opponent's position. The interpretive-symbolic perspective considers ways in which group ideologies are formed and the organizational impact on shared meanings. The systems-interaction approach considers conflict cycles and phases of conflict development, and analyses patterns of messages that evolve into a communication system and result in reciprocity of conflict behaviours and "locking-in". The mechanistic view emphasizes communication channels and transmission of messages. The fifth perspective, critical theory, is related to the interpretive-symbolic approach. This focuses on the structures of meaning that embody and reinforce domination. "Communication enters into critical theory as the cumulative effect of multiple messages that form consensual meanings, constitute the hidden structures, and provide critical insights into the subtle patterns of domination" (p. 554).

1.1.3 The Literature

The literature surveyed in this chapter is drawn from a number of areas of research. We have concentrated mainly on empirical work in the survey, because we are primarily concerned with providing evidence for or against the assertions. However, the empirical work is often driven by theoretical concerns, which may vary according to the field of research from which it is drawn. Hence it is useful to have an overview of the concerns of the different areas on which we draw, in order to provide a context for the survey. In this section we give a brief overview of each of the main fields we have examined.

1.1.3.1 Disciplines

The *sociology* of conflict is concerned, in part, with how social order is challenged and maintained. There are fundamental differences in perspective on society and social order. An individualist perspective is that social order is maintained by the consent which individuals give to institutions to set regulations, in return for the protection of the individuals' rights and well-being. A pluralist perspective is that the framework of societal rules is maintained in the "general interest" of the society as a whole, to contain disorder and to adjudicate the claims of rival groups. From a Marxist perspective it is the ruling class, using the instruments of the state, which imposes order and suppresses dissent. In each of these perspectives social order is achieved, at least in the short term, but never without conflict. From an individualist perspective, the drive to maximize advantage over others will lead to competitive tension. From a pluralist perspective, different social groups have differing goals and competing claims for scarce resources. A Marxist sees endemic conflict in the fundamentally opposed interests of the ruling and working classes. There is disagreement over how deep is the stability of societies and how strong is the desire of individuals and social groups to maintain social order. Hall (1982), for example, suggests that "the social order is always really quite precarious. It rests on a very delicate set of balances". Strauss (1978) points out that, in fact, most social conflicts are resolved by cooperative means, often unconsciously, and that, despite this, very little attention is paid to these cooperative mechanisms.

Social psychology studies the cognitive aspects of social interactions, and is particularly concerned with small group behaviour, while the applied field of *organizational psychology* is partly concerned with team-work within organizations, and how communication and coordination of teams can be effected. Early work tended to assume all conflict was undesirable, and so should be eliminated, although empirical studies in the last few decades have demonstrated that conflict is an inevitable feature of group interaction. Moreover, Robbins (1974), among others, has advocated that conflict management should include not just resolution of conflict, but stimulation of conflict too. This is a result of observations that conflict has a useful role in organizations, in providing a stimulus to innovation, as it involves questioning and evaluating received wisdom. It is also a major weapon against stagnation and resistance to change.

Cognitive science is concerned with developing computational models of the processes, systems and principles that make behaviour possible. Much of the research to date has been concerned with representing the knowledge of single experts or idealized knowledge (what a person *ought to know*) and so has been little concerned with interpersonal or mental conflict. Recent developments in cognitive science have included the construction of logics to model beliefs and assumptions (Ramsay 1988) and the development of computational models of multiple minds and social groupings. Distributed artificial intelligence (DAI) questions the assumption that a single self-consistent knowledge base can demonstrate intelligence (Huhns 1987). Conflicting knowledge is handled by allowing different agents to develop and maintain alternative hypotheses, with the premise that intelligence is an emergent feature of cooperative behaviour. However, most DAI systems assume benevolent agents working towards the same goal. Rosenschein (1985) notes that in real-world situations, perfect cooperation never happens, as the goals of any two agents will never coincide exactly. While conflict can arise in the process of acquiring knowledge from human experts, knowledge-based systems rely on a consistent "knowledge base" for their inference mechanisms to work. If that knowledge is acquired from human experts then any inconsistencies in understanding or interpretation must be resolved (Easterbrook 1991).

1.1.3.2 Theoretical Paradigms

Bargaining theory is an attempt to produce descriptive models of bargaining processes, and is especially concerned with commerce and politics. Patchen (1970) surveys models of bargaining theory and notes that the more complete models include wider concerns than bids and outcomes, including how participants influence each other's behaviour, and factors such as the cost of various actions and the cost of delaying agreement. Bargaining theory frequently makes use of the joint outcome space (Thomas 1976) as a tool for illustrating how the parties perceive the options in a conflict (see Fig. 1.6, under Assertion V, p. 43). Note that there may be possibilities not perceived by the participants, which provide better resolutions. Bargaining theory does not indicate how these might be found, concentrating instead on the process of bidding and counter-bidding.

Game theory is defined as the theory of rational decision in conflict situations (Rapoport 1974). Participants are regarded as players, and game theory examines the strategies used by the players in the process of trying to achieve particular outcomes. In contrast to the joint outcome space, game theory often makes use of the payoff matrix (see Fig. 1.3). This reflects the assumption that the set of outcomes is known (though not necessarily finite), and that associated with each outcome is a calculable payoff for each player. Limitations of game theory include the restricted sets of available actions, and the assumption that the payoffs for any action are known with certainty by all players. However, game theory does produce some useful information about the kinds of strategy that can be used to induce cooperation and how various strategies reward the players (Axelrod 1984).

		Prisoner B	
		Not Confess	*Confess*
Prisoner A	*Not Confess*	1 year each	10 years for A and 3 months for B
	Confess	3 months for A and 10 years for B	8 years each

Fig. 1.3. The payoff matrix for the prisoner's dilemma. Each player must decide, in isolation from the other, whether to confess to a crime that the judge is sure they both committed. By confessing, each will implicate the other; their joint best strategy is for both to keep quiet.

Decision theory offers a prescriptive approach to decision making, via analysis of sets of pre-specified alternatives. The interesting problems in this context are concerned with resolving multiple conflicting objectives (Keeney and Raiffa 1976). Decision theory assumes a single entity is making a choice, in contrast to conflict where there is more than one entity, each with a different perspective. It has a role in conflict resolution in helping participants to evaluate bids, to justify such evaluations, and to persuade the other participant(s) that a solution is satisfactory.

Group decision making is the normative study of how individual preferences can be combined into a group decision. Luce and Raiffa (1957) defined the problem as that of finding a method, or welfare function, for combining individual preference rankings into a social preference, which satisfies properties such as fairness and representativeness. Work on group decision making extends decision theory to cope with more than one decision maker, but still suffers from the assumption that all the options are known.

1.1.4 Background on the Assertions

As we have mentioned, the main body of this chapter is structured around a series of assertions about conflict. Each assertion is labelled with a letter, to facilitate cross-referencing, and we have grouped the assertions into a number of categories, roughly corresponding to the phases of a conflict episode. Before we present the assertions, some explanation of their origins may be useful.

The assertions are phrased in a variety of ways: some are intended to be contentious, while others seem relatively innocuous. In each case we have tried to give an impression of what the literature has to say on the matter, weighing up the evidence both for and against the assertion. In this section we explain some of the rationale for the assertions we have chosen, and our reasons for attempting to answer them. To our surprise, it proved difficult to provide definite answers even to some of the most ingenuous assertions, and some of the most obvious strawmen. The last part of this section discusses why this was so.

1.1.4.1 Where They Come From

The assertions we have used arose from several sources during our investigations of the literature. Some were generated by writing down our initial preconceptions about conflict, and hence represent our own assumptions derived from the folklore, or filtered through from some previous exposure to the literature. We include these deliberately, as we suspect they may be shared by others working in CSCW. For example the assertion "styles of handling conflict vary with gender" seemed obvious when we wrote it, but analysis of the literature revealed some confusion on this issue (see Assertion W, p. 46). In some cases our preconceptions were challenged, while in others they were confirmed.

The bulk of the assertions were unearthed during our literature search, and represent those questions and hypotheses considered in the various fields we have examined. For example, "anonymity and physical separation contribute to conflict" summarizes the theme of a hot debate in the empirical study of the effects of computer-mediated communication (CMC), and has been used to explain some peculiarities in the use of electronic mail (e-mail) (Lea and Spears 1991, see Assertion H, p. 24).

Some of the assertions appeared relatively late in the writing of this chapter, when it became apparent that there were important issues in the literature which we had overlooked, as they had not fitted into any of the assertions we had. In some ways these are the most interesting: if they did not emerge from our initial brainstorming sessions, nor from our first trawl of the literature, then they might equally well be overlooked by others involved in the design of CSCW systems. An example of this type is the assertion on saving face (Assertion Y, p. 50). There is literature on the role of face-saving in conflict resolution (Brown 1977), and there are important implications for CSCW. For instance, CSCW systems may make the outcome of a conflict more explicit, and hence reduce the opportunity for face-saving.

Finally, there are some assertions which we wanted to include, but for which we could find nothing in the literature. Although it is possible that we have overlooked entire areas of the literature, our suspicion is there are some important issues that have not been explored previously, and we flag these in our conclusion as possible areas for future research.

1.1.4.2 Why They Should Be Answered

The assertions we have covered encapsulate at least some of the questions about conflict that need to be addressed in CSCW. Hence, simply stating them in this chapter may help designers to question their own assumptions about the role of conflict, and recognize whether they make any of the assumptions we describe. This will lead to an increased awareness of these issues in relation to the design of CSCW systems.

However, simply stating the assumptions is insufficient in many cases: they need to be questioned and dissected. CSCW needs prescriptive results, and trying to establish the truth of the assertions goes some way towards providing specific guidelines for the design of CSCW systems. In this chapter, we provide an analysis based on existing literature. Further work is needed to examine the applicability of this analysis in respect of CSCW systems, and the domains to which they are applied.

1.1.4.3 Why They Are Difficult to Answer

Having established the relevance of the assertions, and the genuine need for answers to them, it turns out that we cannot provide definitive answers for most of them. There are a number of reasons for this.

First and foremost, many of the assertions themselves are ambiguous. Taken at surface value, they appear to offer common-sense principles, which explains their appearance in the literature as hypotheses about group interaction, and as assumptions underlying CSCW systems. When examined closely, many of the assertions resist the attempt to pin down a precise meaning. Part of this problem is terminological: different authors use different definitions of key terms, and different fields of study put emphasis on different aspects of a definition. An immediate example of this is the problem of defining the term "conflict" itself. Selecting a broad meaning for the term does not help here, as few assertions are general enough to apply to all the many manifestations of conflict. Examination of the assertion must then involve asking to which type of conflict is reference being made.

The simplicity of many of the assertions also causes problems. Although it is tempting to look for simplistic relationships between cause and effect, these rarely exist in the social sciences. There are also methodological problems: conflict is a complex phenomenon, and it is hard to devise experiments that isolate particular variables. Many of the results are open to interpretation. There are at times assumptions hidden in the work which makes it impossible to interpret each piece of research without access to the assumptions of the researchers. Part of these assumptions may rest in the culture of the area from which the paper comes, and consideration of the audience to which it is addressed.

1.2 Assertions about Conflict

In this section we present the assertions about conflict. We have clustered them into a number of categories according to the aspect of conflict to which they refer: the factors that affect whether conflict will arise (occurrence), the specific causes of conflict (causes), the role that conflict may play in group interactions (utility), the processes involved in an individual conflict episode (development), approaches to handling conflict, including resolution techniques (management), and the outcomes and long-term effects of conflict (results). These categories are not intended to be exhaustive, nor even clearly defined, but simply provide a convenient way of organizing our discussion of different aspects of conflict.

1.2.1 Occurrence of Conflict

A Conflict is inevitable

Whether or not conflict at large is inevitable depends on how you view the fabric of society. Marx attempted to show that conflict was a necessary outcome of antagonisms between social classes. In a capitalist society the interests of the ruling class, to buy the labour of workers in order to make profit, is incompatible with the needs of the proletariat. Conflict, it is argued, is not random, but a systematic product of the structure of society. It is a necessary part of class consciousness and social change "without conflict, no progress: that is the law which civilization has followed to the present day" (Marx 1847, p. 80, cited in Dahrendorf 1959, p. 9).

To Dahrendorf also, conflict is endemic in society, but it arises primarily from the structure of authority. Every society is founded on inequalities in power and authority, resulting in the coercion of some members by others: "the authority structure of entire societies as well as particular institutional orders within societies (such as industry) is ... the structural determinant of class formation and class conflict" (Dahrendorf 1959, p. 136). Conflict between social classes is just one aspect of "the differential distribution of positions of authority in societies and their institutional orders".

A more subtle analysis of conflict, based on Hall (1982), is to view it as a clash of ideologies. Ideologies are "sets of ideas, concepts, images and propositions which we use to represent to ourselves – and thus make sense of – how society works and our relationship to it" (Hall 1982, p. 14). They colour all aspects of social life from voting patterns to interpersonal relations and they are developed through social practice. Ideologies reflect the opinions of individuals and groups, and societies have ruling ideologies around which the social institutions cohere. The liberal-democratic ideology of western European and North American societies recognizes a plurality of interests and assumes that individuals will compete to maximize their own interests. This competition is fostered and controlled by a range of institutions that have evolved to ensure "fairness" and stability, from the law courts, to arbitration procedures for industrial disputes, to chairpersons and agreed agendas at meetings.

The surface appearance of liberal-democratic institutions is one of stability and minimization of conflict. But to benefit from the institutions it is necessary to accept the dominant ideology, to "play the game", with its assumptions that there will be "winners" and "losers", both in particular competitions and in society as a whole. Those who, through choice or circumstance, reject the liberal-democratic ideology come into conflict with the entire weight of institutionalized procedure. The fact that people adopt the liberal-democratic position explains popular consent for harsh measures, such as wage cuts, and the acceptance of authority and arbitration to manage disputes. The fact that liberal democracy is an ideology, one which favours social order and inequalities of wealth and power, explains the larger conflicts of interest and outlook in society. This analysis explains why conflict is inevitable in (liberal-democratic) society and, furthermore, it suggests that those people who do not subscribe to the dominant ideology of the society or group will be regarded as deviant and may be a source of conflict. However, the analysis cannot predict the onset of conflict in any particular setting.

Experimental studies with small groups, such as Brehmer (1976), have shown that although conflict within any given group may not be inevitable, it is very likely to occur: even when there are no differences in the goals, interests and motivations of the collaborators, their individual prior experiences will give them different cognitive viewpoints on issues. Pendell (1990) also found experimental evidence that deviant behaviour and conflict are normal elements of small group decision making. Deviant behaviour is not necessarily related to conflict, but the perceived deviants who did initiate conflict were "opinion deviants", who presented incompatible views and tested others' opinions and solutions.

In conclusion, although we cannot say that conflict is inevitable for every particular situation, the structure of society is such that conflict forms a integral part of it. Conflict is inevitable in society at large. Similarly, although conflict may not be inevitable for every possible group, the tensions that lead to conflict are apparent in most groups. Furthermore, there may be particular types of group for which conflict *is* inevitable: for example, Unger (1990) suggests that conflict is inevitable in group psychotherapy because of the nature of the group and its task.

B *The more cohesive the group, the less conflict there is*

Cohesiveness can be defined as sense of *we-ness*, "a dynamic process that is reflected in the tendency for a group to stick together and remain united in the pursuit of its goals and objectives" (Carron 1982), although Mudrack (1989a) warns that some studies have used different definitions. Owen (1985) cites research that indicates members of highly cohesive groups are more satisfied, more effective, and communicate more frequently and more positively than members of low cohesive groups. Hence, it would seem that cohesiveness reduces conflict.

Weinberg et al. (1981) found that lack of cohesion ("problems resulting in maintenance of the group" p. 84) was the greatest cause of conflict in 70% of 125 naturally occurring groups encountering some interaction problems, but they accept that "lack of cohesion" is such a broad category that it subsumes a number of potential conflicts: "one could argue that cohesion is an umbrella problem, containing within it several other categories" and that "cohesion is not really the most common problem, merely the broadest category" (p. 90). They cite Shaw (1976) on the role of leadership in creating cohesion through the coordination of individual contributions.

However, there are disadvantages to cohesion. Evans and Jarvis (1980) suggest that "too cohesive a group may cause members to be more concerned with the group itself than with the purpose for which the group exists". Although there may be less conflict, the group may be less productive. Wood (1989) provides a specific example. The unsuccessful group described in her case study (see Assertion E, p. 21) were more committed to the group as a group than to the task, and she suggests that "when a norm of cohesiveness exists, members are well advised to ensure that they are not preserving the group at the expense of the work at hand" (pp. 444–445).

Hence cohesiveness can be taken too far. *Group-think* is a term that describes how individuals in certain types of cohesive group engage in self-censorship of deviations from the majority decision, to preserve the group's (or their own) cohesiveness and confidence in the decision (Janis 1972). Gero (1985) provides experimental evidence of group-think, and states in conclusion "I would again emphasize the importance of disagreement to the outcome of group decisions. ... If disagreement is suppressed, the conditions of group-think may develop and threaten the quality of the group's decision". We discuss group-think further, and ways of reducing it, under Assertion J, p. 28.

Finally, the cohesion of a group is closely related to its composition, and hence is also related to the level of conflict. Collaros and Anderson (1969) found that heterogeneous teams (in terms of skills and abilities) experience more conflict at first in their interaction processes. Although such heterogeneity may be necessary to reach creative problem solutions, too much diversity of expertise may inhibit those who feel more or less knowledgeable. On the other hand, Dyson et al. (1976) show that homogeneous groups are more likely to make high-risk decisions, a phenomenon generally known as "shift-to-risk" or "risk-shift". This is closely related to groupthink. Bass (1980) suggests that where task accomplishment depends on "smooth, conflict-free, coordinated efforts among the members" (pp. 467–468) then homogeneous membership should prove more productive, but if the creative solution of a complex problem is more important than speedy, smooth interaction, then a heterogeneous group is more desirable.

C Occurrence of conflict varies with the development of the group

The classic model of group development is presented in Tuckman (1965). This model identifies four phases in development of a group, which have been labelled as *forming*, *storming*, *norming* and *performing*. The phases describe behaviour of the group members in relation both to the group structure and to the task. The first phase describes the initial formation of a group, and involves orientation for the task and testing of the group structure. The second phase, storming, was derived from empirical observations of group interactions which consistently reveal a sharp rise in negative reactions in the second meeting of the group. Phase three involves the creation of group norms and the strengthening of cohesion, while real progress on the task comes in phase four, performing. Tuckman and Jensen (1977) add a fifth stage: *adjourning*.

Although Tuckman's model originated from studies of therapy groups, it has been successfully applied to other types of interaction; Tuckman (1965) distinguishes training groups, laboratory groups and natural groups. Many studies have supported the model. For example, Maples (1988) attempted to identify subjective characteristics of each phase from diaries kept by group members. In particular, she found that storming was marked by concern, conflict, confrontation and criticism, and that these characteristics were absent from the other phases.

Such empirical investigations of the model appear to show that occurrence of conflict reaches a peak at an early stage in group development, after which the group gains cohesion and the level of conflict subsides. Hence, the model relates conflict not only to lack of cohesiveness, but also implies that both are tied in with the maturity of the group. What the model does not indicate is whether this applies only to a particular type of conflict, or even just to a particular reaction to conflict. The model has its origins in the interaction process analysis developed by Bales (1950), and the empirical studies which support it measure only the social-emotional responses of group members. Hence, it is possible that what the model is really showing is that the group learns to deal with conflict and suppress emotional responses. If this is the case then the model says very little about the underlying level of conflict throughout group development.

Although the utility of Tuckman's model has been questioned, the view that groups move through discernible developmental phases is widely held. Cissna (1984) reviews the handful of studies which did not find developmental phases, but notes methodological and conceptual problems with all of them and concludes that the negative evidence is unconvincing. On the other hand, he points out that there are likely to be aspects of groups which do not develop, while other aspects do, that groups may develop in idiosyncratic ways (there is far more evidence to support the notion of group development in general than there is to support any particular model of development), and even that some types of groups do not change. He suggests that it is more useful to identify significant differences and similarities in group development among various types of groups, and to relate variations in developmental processes to group outcomes such as cohesiveness.

In contrast to generalized models of group development such as Tuckman's, Gemmill and Wynkoop (1991) present a model of the psychodynamics of a group transformation. The model is concerned with second order change – disorderly, discontinuous change – as opposed to first order change, which is orderly and gradual. For small groups, second order change results in a transformation of attitudes on focal issues. The model describes how members unconsciously accept covert roles to dramatize the central conflicts of the group, to reflect negative attributes ("scapegoat") and positive attributes ("charismatic prophet"). The process by which these roles are accepted and integrated is known as reparation.

The model has a number of phases and transitions as follows (see Fig. 1.4): the first phase is "hanging on" which involves intellect only; once the defensive boundary has collapsed, the "working through" phase is reached, involving emotions only; expanding the emotional boundary leads to "letting go", with a confluence of intellect and emotions; and taking self-responsibility leads to "moving beyond", in which intellect and emotions are integrated. The final transition is the infusion of new meaning. At any of the transition points, the group may fail to make the transition and seek regressive solutions. The model is presented as a downward vortex, spiralling around the central issue, which acts as a focus to offset the defensive pull toward regressive solutions. The entire model is presented partly to explain empirical observations of the individual phases, and partly to investigate the theoretical proposition that when faced with a difficult issue, the group members either react with a sense of denial and seek a regressive solution or choose to deal with the uncertainty. The model is normative in the sense that it indicates in which direction the group should move in order to develop.

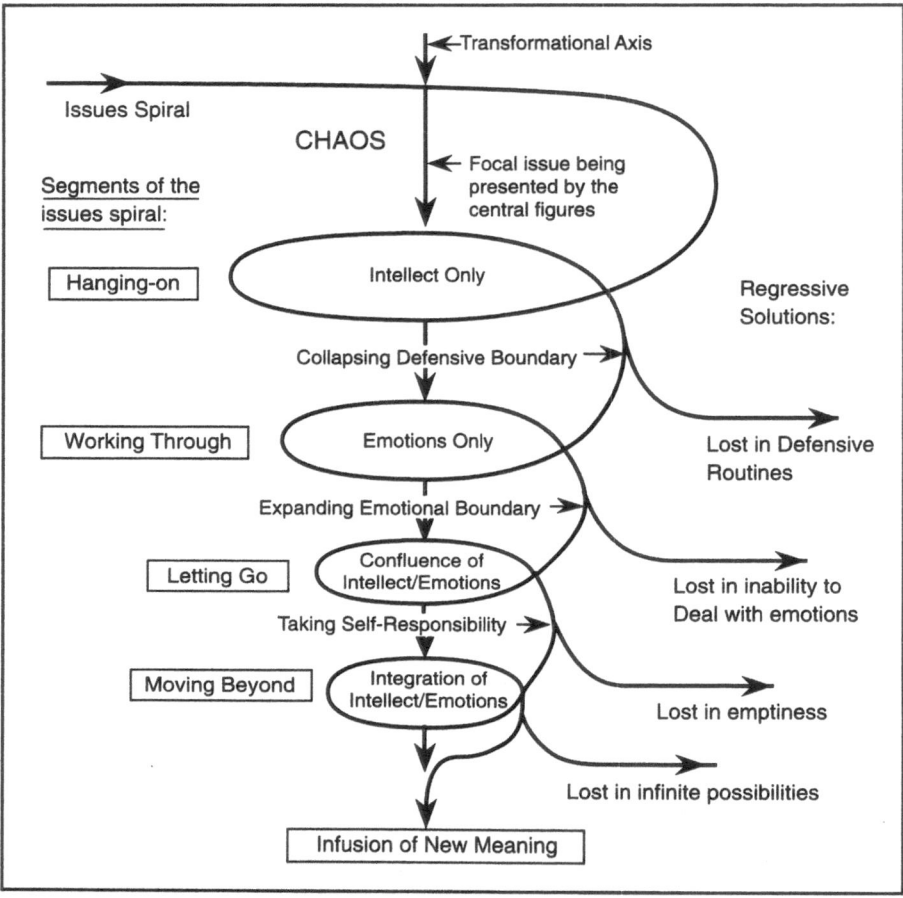

Fig. 1.4. The vortex of transformation in small groups, adapted from Gemmill and Wynkoop (1991).

Regardless of the validity of either of these models of group develop-ment, one would expect the longevity to have a bearing on the cohesiveness and on the level of conflict. Ford et al. (1977) consider the issue of group tradition or lifespan and its impact upon various measures of group performance. Their results present no conclusive evidence that established groups perform a decision-making task better than *ad hoc* groups but they suggest that further research should consider the impact of different intervention techniques, such as the nominal group technique (Moore 1987), for groups with varying lifespans.

D *The more communication there is between people, the more opportunities there are for conflict*

Communication is carried out for a purpose within a developing context, and it can vary in both amount and quality. Weinberg et al. (1981) found that in 22% of groups encountering interaction problems there were problems with communication patterns. This category included difficulties caused by inadequate networks, unclear speech patterns and inattentive listening.

There is no one-to-one relationship between communication and organizational conflict. Simple formulae such as "more communication will reduce conflict" or "ambiguities in communication lead to conflict" have been refuted in various empirical studies (Putnam and Poole 1987). Putnam and Poole concentrate on communication, as it is so fundamental to conflict: the very "activity of having or managing a conflict occurs through communication" (p. 550). They point out that the mechanistic view of communication, with its emphasis on channels and transmission of messages, is central to many studies of conflict. This, they argue, leads to research in which the medium or mode of communication is manipulated, and different types of networks investigated.

Research on the effects of different communication networks is reviewed by McGrath (1984). Centralized communication nets (where all communication has to travel via a central person at the hub of a wheel) have been found to be very efficient for transmission of information. But if the task is complex and not reliant simply on information, then the wheel loses its relative task efficiency advantage, and the onus of solving the problem falls to the person at the hub of the wheel. In the "circle" each member is connected to two other members, but no one member is more central than the others. Although information cannot be routed to one node as efficiently, each group member feels equally central. It is the level of satisfaction with the structure that is more likely to affect conflict than the efficiency of the arrangement. For example, McGrath points out that in a circle group, all members have a relatively high satisfaction, as does the person at the hub in a wheel group. On the other hand, peripheral members of a wheel report much dissatisfaction.

The bandwidth of communication available seems to have a greater influence. McGrath points out that the amount of communication and amount of influence in the group is much lower in restricted bandwidth communications than in face-to-face groups. Different modes of communication, such as face-to-face, electronically mediated audio-visual, or text only, provide different bandwidths, with face-to-face communication providing the richest interactions. One finding is that the narrower the bandwidth, the more task-focused the interaction becomes, since interpersonal and social aspects are not conveyed, due to the absence of non-verbal cues. In some circumstances, the interpersonally rich conditions may produce "noise" that distracts from the task, and under such conditions the relatively lean modalities may deliver more efficient task performance – provided the leanness does not eliminate necessary cues – but there will be no pattern of interpersonal relations and members will not be very interpersonally satisfied. McGrath concludes that "group members *prefer* relatively rich communication modes, need them for some tasks, and do better in them for some – but not all – tasks" (p. 181, original emphasis).

It could be argued that the opportunity for conflict increases with the communication bandwidth, as there is more opportunity to perceive both conflict of values and motivation, and affective conflict. However, this is not found to be the case. High bandwidth media (e.g. face-to-face) permit group members to exercise "regulatory functions" in their interaction, thus achieving a better success rate in conflict resolution (fewer abandoned discourses), suppressing the use of high-risk conflict strategies such as bluffing (Crott et al. 1980), and decreasing the readiness to harm one's opponent (Milgram 1965). Presumably there would be less miscommunication as well: Curtis et al. (1988) observed that textual documentation is ineffective for communication among software development teams, as it does not resolve misunderstandings. One further problem with low bandwidth communication is that the relative anonymity may lead to de-individuation (neutralization of individuals' distinguishing characteristics), which may make group members more critical and more probing and hence generate more conflict. We discuss de-individuation further under Assertion H, p. 24.

The concentration on networks and bandwidths obscures the possibility that it may matter more *what* is communicated than how. Saine and Bock (1973, cited in Putnam 1983) found that groups which fail to agree on procedural matters spend time on procedural issues than on substantive issues. Agreement on procedural issues guides the task activity of the group and facilitates the integration of substantive issues.

We could examine the inverse of this assertion: "the less communication there is, the fewer opportunities there are for conflict". If conflict is a communicational activity, then this is trivially true. However, Pood (1980) suggests that disagreements and competitive and violent behaviours are not actually conflicts, but are communicational responses to conflict. Examples of extreme conflict involving very little communication can be found. Inter-racial prejudice is one such example, and is the concern of the "contact hypothesis", which states that interaction between individuals from different groups will reduce intergroup tension (Hewstone and Brown 1986). Although authors such as Pettigrew (1986) have criticized the contact hypothesis as being so loose and general as to be untestable, it nevertheless contains an element of truth for particular types of group.

Finally, we might also observe that a decrease in communication may serve to intensify a conflict. Thomas (1976) points out that if a party uses communication to manipulate or control another party (or is suspected of doing so), then trust is reduced to the point that communications from that party cease to be believed, or even listened to. This pattern has been observed in labour relations. Such breakdowns in communication allow the conflicting parties to maintain distorted stereotypical views of one another, and to feed their hostility. Thomas cites as examples maintenance of army morale by preventing fraternization with the enemy, and political assassins, who fantasise that their targets are devils.

Overall it would seem that the assertion is not supported by the evidence. In fact, conflict *can* be reduced by better communication, where "better" refers not just to the pattern and the bandwidth of communication, but to the effectiveness of the communication. In Section 1.3.1.3 we discuss this last point further, in relation to problems with the use of video links in CSCW systems.

E *Clearly defined roles reduce conflict*

Baker (1981) reviews work on the division of labour in small groups and distinguishes two key concepts – *differentiation* and *specialization* – both of which provide measures of interdependence of the group members. Task differentiation describes the extent to which the work is divided into a large number of subtasks relative to the size of the group. Task specialization is the degree to which tasks are able to be performed by a small subset of the group. The latter is a better measure of interdependence, because "as task specialization increases, the group becomes dependent on fewer individuals for the completion of each task" (p. 96). Baker comments that an increase in task specialization leads to more cohesion, but that this simultaneously leads to more actor specialization, which reduces cohesion and tends to isolate individuals. Actor specialization, in this context, is defined as the extent to which group members spend all their time on particular tasks. He suggests that plenty of face-to-face communication and the development of a collective identity is needed to counteract these processes.

There may be problems if the roles are imposed undemocratically: Moreno (1953, cited in Bass 1980) noted "formal ... groupings which are superimposed upon informal, spontaneous groupings by some authority are a chronic source of conflict". Also, groups may perceive a difference between formal and informal roles. Wood (1989) describes a case study of a group which believed that adherence to formal group structures would inhibit creativity. For example, the group agreed to work as equals rather than in any hierarchical arrangement, refused to designate a chairperson, and were determined to reach decisions through consensus. The group failed to achieve their task after fifteen months. The lack of clearly defined roles meant that no one person had responsibility for focusing the group's attention. Furthermore the group tended to avoid conflict and critical discussion, preferring to suppress their anxieties about progress in the name of politeness. Although it is not clear how much this was due to the lack of role assignment, Wood concludes that failure to use task-holding mechanisms "increases the likelihood that a task group will evolve into an informal group that fails to complete the task" (p. 445).

Chapter 8 offers another view of the assignment of roles in collaborative groups. For a discussion of the role of leader, see Assertion Q, p. 37.

1.2.2 Causes of Conflict

The assertions in this section are concerned with particular causes of conflict. We do not attempt an exhaustive coverage of the many potential sources of conflict. Such attempts may be found elsewhere. For example, Deutsch (1973) lists the following issues involved in conflicts:

- Control over resources
- Preferences and nuisances, where the tastes or activities of one party impinge upon another
- Values, where there is a claim that a value or set of values should dominate
- Beliefs, when there is a dispute over facts, information, reality, etc.
- The nature of the relationship between the parties

Robbins (1989) groups the conditions under which conflicts arise as:

- Communicational, including insufficient exchange of information, noise, and the semantic differences that arise from selective perception and difference of background
- Structural, which includes the goal compatibility of members of the group, jurisdictional clarity, and leadership style
- Personal factors, including individual value systems and personality characteristics

F Conflicts arise from misunderstandings as opposed to ill will

While the lists above help to characterize conflict, they do not offer any hint about how to detect and differentiate the different types. Part of the problem is that the causes of a conflict are not necessarily reflected in its manifestation. Deutsch (1969), for example, makes a distinction between manifest and underlying conflict. Raven and Kruglanski (1970) relate this distinction to personal and impersonal conflict, in that the manifest conflict may appear to be impersonal, such as children quarrelling over a toy, while the underlying conflict may be personal, in that the children might be using the toy as an excuse to quarrel because they really do not like one another. Deutsch terms these displaced or "pseudo"-conflicts.

However, such a simple relation between manifest and impersonal conflict is unlikely. Both personalized (or "affective") and depersonalized (or "substantive") conflicts can be observed to occur in group interactions (Putnam and Poole 1987), and some studies have compared the occurrence of the two. Intuitively, one might expect a highly cohesive task-focused group to have little ill will, hence little affective conflict. In fact Pace's (1990) findings indicate that this might not be so. High consensus groups (i.e. effective decision making groups) differed from other groups not so much in the amount of conflict, but in the group's ability to differentiate personalized and depersonalized conflict. In particular, such groups are better able to identify and understand positive (cooperative) conflicts, and can use them to clarify the issues prior to forming a common perspective (Folger and Poole 1984)

While negative, personalized conflict can be regarded as ill will, depersonalized (substantive) conflict does not necessarily equate to misunderstanding. In this context, misunderstanding could refer strictly to miscommunication (see Assertion D, p. 19), or it could include problems arising from differences of interpretation of a situation, and cognitive dissonance. If we define misunderstanding as referring to problems of communication, this excludes the "real" substantive conflicts, over which there is no miscommunication, and no personalized clash. These might concern the substance of the task, and the meta-task, i.e. how to go about the task, including how the group is organized and the relationship between the members.

Social judgement theory examines exactly this type of conflict (Brehmer and Hammond 1977). The focus of this area is differences in cognitive views of a problem, and in particular differences of policy. This is in sharp contrast to much research on conflict which concentrates on motivation and conflict of interest. The cognitive differences are observed in the exercise of individual judgement on tasks with uncertain information. Experiments in social judgement theory are deliberately set up to exclude affective elements, so that the cognitive process of making judgements can be studied. Findings suggest that there is no significant reduction in the amount of conflict when affective factors are excluded. Also, conflict persists because people give up their judgement policies too rapidly, in the process of seeking new policies which resolve the conflict. This premature abandonment then causes them to appear inconsistent. Such conflicts are hard to resolve because participants lack the necessary insights into their own policies (Brehmer 1976).

G *Technological mediation introduces conflicts*

The use of technology to support group interactions seems to affect the behaviour of the group, and there is much anecdotal evidence concerning the quirks of facilities such as e-mail. Disciplined empirical studies are harder to come by. As Kiesler et al. (1984) point out, research on the impact of computer technologies tends to concentrate on cost and technical facilities, neglecting the social-psychological aspects. While the psychology of individual users has received much attention in the human–computer interaction (HCI) literature (for example, see Norman and Draper 1986), social aspects have not, because they pose methodological problems. The changes that introduction of a technology cause in an organization are difficult to re-create experimentally, and field studies do not usually provide the comparative data needed. With the current interest in CSCW, recent research has sought ways of studying the social aspects; subsequent chapters of this book present some of this work.

Some limited studies have been conducted. For example, Sainfort et al. (1990) conducted a study of group decision making, comparing use of videotape, the use of a computerized decision support system (DSS) and a control group with neither technology. In subsequent questioning, groups with access to the two technologies perceived greater progress in reaching a resolution, and rated that resolution significantly higher than did the control group. Also, the group using the DSS generated more alternative solutions to the problem than those using videotape. However, it is not clear how much of this effect can be traced to the appropriateness of the technology to the problems tackled. Clegg (1988) points out that many problems with the introduction of new technology can be put down to the inappropriateness of the technology chosen.

One area of technology that has been studied from a social-psychological viewpoint is the use of CMC. It has been widely reported that the anonymity afforded by electronic communication leads to, among other things, a reduction of normal restraints on behaviour. This effect is believed to be a result of de-individuation (Jessup et al. 1990; Lea and Spears 1991), which we discuss under Assertion H.

H *Anonymity and physical separation contribute to conflict*

Use of CMC, such as e-mail, does more than just speed up the flow of information. It may change the pattern of communication, the distribution of information and the nature of interactions between people (Sproull and Kiesler 1986). In particular, CMC provides the possibility for anonymous engagement in group activities, and it is this anonymity that has been the focus of many studies and much speculation. Note, however, that CMC does not have to be anonymous.

By varying the amount of communication available, Crott et al. (1980) discovered that there is an increased tendency for more aggressive and less cooperative behaviour when communication channels are restricted, and in particular, when there is no voice component. Their study compared the behaviour of pairs of students in a bargaining game in which one partici-pant has much greater payoff possibilities than the other; however, the participants could only discover this through communication. Of particular interest in this study was the observation that audio communication reduced the use of bluffs and other high-risk/aggressive behaviour modes, but did not significantly equalize the participants' payoffs.

Jessup et al. (1990) conducted a laboratory experiment to compare the use of group decision support systems (GDSS) in which comments were identified by name with those in which all contributions are anonymous. They concluded that "GDSS anonymity serves to detach an individual from his or her comments and from others" and they "suspect that this leads to a reduction in normal restraints on behaviour". Although their experiment could not tell them why GDSS anonymity had this effect, their suspicion was that it was a de-individuation effect; in other words, an effect of the loss of a sense of individuality among participants. However, they also discovered that the size of the room in which the subjects were situated had a much greater impact on de-individuation than any changes to the software.

De-individuation arises when cues necessary to distinguish different people are missing. Kiesler et al. (1984) point out that CMC fails to provide "individuating details about people that might be embodied in their dress, location, demeanour, and expressiveness". They list the following aspects of CMC that provide the conditions for de-individuation: time and information processing pressures, absence of regulating feedback, dramaturgical weakness, lack of status and position cues, social anonymity and the lack of a mature etiquette. They investigated these empirically using groups of three given a choice-dilemma problem. Groups using CMC took longer to reach consensus, participated more equally, showed greater choice shift and were less inhibited. Three possible explanations are offered for these findings: (i) absence of feedback between speaker and listener delaying consensus formation and leading to frustration; (ii) less influence and control by a dominant person; and (iii) depersonalization causing group members to be more impulsive and more assertive. The experiments were not detailed enough to support any one of these explanations and doubt was expressed about any generalization of the results.

Sproull and Kiesler (1986) showed that e-mail reduces social context cues, and hence people behave irresponsibly more often and focus on themselves rather than others in salutations and closings. However, they did not compare this behaviour specifically with other modes of communication such as memos, telephone and face-to-face. Despite this, their conclusions about the utility of e-mail are positive, in that although e-mail clearly changes organizations, many of the changes are for the better, including increased social communication, uninhibited behaviour allowing new ideas to flow, and the reduction of geographic, temporal, departmental and status barriers.

Lea and Spears (1991) criticize the explanations for changes in behaviour put forward by Kiesler's group, including the absence of social cues, breakdown of social constraint through de-individuation, and the exposure to a greater pool of arguments leading to polarization. In particular, the weakening of social norms through de-individuation is questioned. An alternative view of de-individuation is put forward which emphasizes the role of the social context. In this view, de-individuation associated with immersion in a group enhances the salience of the group, and hence strengthens norms, while if the group identity is not already salient, then de-individuation only serves to strengthen one's sense of individuality, and so weaken group norms. This was investigated empirically by situating each subject in a separate room to create de-individuation, and in the same room for individuation, while varying group immersion by altering the wording of the initial instructions and the headers of the messages. As predicted, the results showed that subjects in de-individuating conditions, where the group identity was strong, were significantly more polarized in the direction of the group norm. This polarization was not associated with uninhibited behaviour.

1.2.3 Utility of Conflict

From our discussions so far, it should be clear that conflict is not necessarily dysfunctional. The assertions in this section consider how conflict can be productive. The idea of productive conflict is not new; Dahrendorf (1959) puts it this way:

> May we perhaps go so far as to say that conflict is a condition necessary for life to be possible at all? I would suggest, in any case, that all that is creativity, innovation, and development in the life of the individual, his group, and his society is due, in no small extent, to the operation of conflicts between group and group, individual and individual, emotion and emotion within one individual. This fundamental fact alone seems to me to justify the value judgement that conflict is essentially "good" and "desirable" (p. 208).

I Conflict can be productive

Deutsch (1969) suggests that most of the literature has concentrated on the destructive effects of conflict and has failed to deal adequately with cases where conflict has productive consequences. In his view, its very pervasiveness is indicative of a number of positive functions: "it prevents stagnation, it stimulates interest and curiosity, it is the medium through which problems can be aired and solutions arrived at; it is the root of personal and social change" (p. 19). In addition, it can be a useful and enjoyable way of stretching oneself to limits, and it can help to establish group and individual identities. He suggests that conflict can lead to "arousal of the optimal level of motivation" (p. 21) to solve problems and move beyond the status quo. Necessary circumstances for such action rest on a non-threatening and non-pressurized environment and confidence in one's capacities to deal with the situation. Indeed, he stresses the importance of cognitive resources for dealing with conflicts creatively.

Thomas (1976) also refers to ways in which the literature on conflict tended to concentrate on its elimination or avoidance, but suggests that there is growing recognition that interpersonal and intergroup conflict often serve useful functions. He itemizes a number of these, based on his review of the literature. First, conflict can serve to maintain optimal levels of stimulation in conditions of boredom and low tension, where people may welcome divergent opinions, competition, and, at times, overt hostility. Second, like Deutsch, he also suggests that the confrontation of divergent views can produce new perspectives and more comprehensive views, leading to superior decisions. Supporting this view, he cites Hall's studies of group decision making (1971), in which he concludes that "conflict, effectively managed, is a necessary precondition for creativity" (p. 88). Third, aggressive behaviour is not necessarily irrational or destructive in conflict situations and "the aggressive pursuit of apparently conflicting goals by two parties may well lead to constructive outcomes" (p. 892). Two parties actively seeking to improve their own lot may succeed in forging a new set of conditions which is of mutual benefit and may constitute progress. Viewed from this perspective, the suppression of conflict may impede progress and help maintain the status quo.

Further, he suggests that conflict can foster cohesiveness and stability within a group where there is intergroup hostility. Power struggles can help to determine the balance of power and the group can then be organized consistent with this balance, which will give a more stable structure.

The recognition of these positive attributes of conflict has led to a more balanced view which acknowledges that there are aspects of conflict that can be both destructive and productive. Rather than a consideration of its elimination and avoidance, the emphasis has shifted to the effective *management* of conflict (Robbins 1989). In research on group work in software development, Pasch (1991) suggests that argumentative dialogue (in which concepts or models are suggested, challenged, possibly refuted, and met by counter proposals) is necessary to the creative process of design. Indeed, he comments that "vehement situations are considered as normal" (p. 559) but a framework of consensus on such things as working practices, roles and acceptable behaviour is a prerequisite.

It seems that conflict can be productive. It may be that some conflicts that are more concerned with the power struggles, personal antagonisms and competition between groups may be more negative than positive. However, conflict concerned with ideas and issues has a positive effect on the resulting decision and should not be suppressed. The utility of issue-related conflict is discussed more fully under Assertion J, concerning "group-think" (p. 28). The utility of issue-related conflict may depend on whether people take a positive attitude towards it. We discuss attitudes to conflict under Assertion V (p. 43).

Supporting the notion that the synthesis or exploration of divergent views can lead to superior decisions is a body of educational research, influenced by Piagetian theories, which suggests that conflict is necessary to generate learning and that articulation of differing perspectives can lead to re-evaluation. The work of the Genevan school (Doise et al. 1975; Mugny and Doise 1978) suggests that cognitive development arises out of cognitive conflict between individuals, whether at different levels of cognitive development or simply with different viewpoints, and this causes cognitive restructuring (see Chapter 4). Perret-Clermont (1980, pp. 195–196) states that "for a task to have educational value, it is not sufficient for it merely to engage children in joint activity; there must also be confrontation between different points of view". Glachan and Light (1982, p. 258) suggest that merely perceiving a conflicting viewpoint is insufficient to induce learning. Their research leads them to infer that "interaction between inferior strategies can lead to superior strategies or, in other words, two wrongs can make a right". They suggest that it is the disruption of established inefficient strategies that can lead to the perception of better strategies. This work is based on children's cognition, but it is perhaps not too fanciful to suggest that some similar processes are at work when adults engage in conflict that is based on conflicting opinions and views.

J Actively eliciting conflicting viewpoints can reduce group-think

The "group-think" phenomenon was presented by Janis (1972) as one possible contributing factor in his analysis of various poor US foreign policy decisions, including the Bay of Pigs fiasco. Conditions for group-think include (i) that the group should be highly cohesive, (ii) that there is a preference for a leader's voice and (iii) that there is insulation from experts. In group-think there is a sense of invulnerability where the risks of making a poor decision are ignored, past decisions are rationalized and not critically reappraised, and information and expert opinion which might conflict with the consensus is not sought. Loyal group members are expected not to dissent from the consensus view and are sanctioned if they do. There is self-censorship by individuals and also the emergence of "mindguards" who try to protect members of the group from information and opinion which might cause them to doubt the consensus. The members of the group thus maintain high cohesion, certainty of their correctness and an illusion of unanimity by artificially suppressing their critical faculties. Moorhead et al. (1991) describe a particularly disastrous instance of group-think in the decision to launch the space shuttle *Challenger* (see Assertion M, p. 31).

Janis (1972) recommends that various structural measures be taken to guard against group-think, such as encouraging the group to air doubts, having impartial leaders, forming subgroups within the group, having discussions with people from outside the group, and having a "devil's advocate". Gero (1985) argues that all of these can be interpreted as ways to "positively sanction conflict as desirable and necessary" (p. 491). She found that, in general, group members have anti-disagreement norms if they are expecting to participate in a consensual process. This could give rise to a self-fulfilling prophecy where disagreement is suppressed and group-think develops. Though consensus is desirable at the end of a decision making session, it is counter-productive to try to reach consensus from the start as alternatives will not be properly considered and the quality of the decision will suffer. The premature self-reinforcing consensus associated with group-think might be contrasted with "vigilant appraisal" where, in an atmosphere of trusting personal relationships, there is healthy suspicion of one another's ideas, explicit discussion of the issues, acknowledgement of the risks of a decision and the possibility of reversals of judgement.

There are problems with encouraging conflict, however. Priem and Price (1991) found that people expect less harmony where the decision making process uses devil's advocacy or dialectical inquiry than they do in consensus decision making. They expect to have less confidence in the result (unlike group-think where the participants display certainty that they are right) and there may consequently be less enthusiasm for implementation of the resulting decision.

It seems that a healthy balance, where participants feel free to voice their disagreements about the issues under discussion in a cooperative atmosphere, is most likely to steer between the problems of group tension and the danger of group-think.

1.2.4 Development of Conflict

K *Conflict has to be resolved for parties to continue to work together*

Much effort is devoted to resolution of conflicts, in the belief that they hamper the ability of people to work together. This is clearly appropriate if the conflict is dysfunctional for the group. However, it is possible that some resolutions are more dysfunctional than the original conflict. For example, from an external perspective, a standoff in a power struggle may be preferable to the defeat of either party. Furthermore, we have shown (in Assertion I, p. 26) that conflict can be productive. Hence, the question then arises as to whether conflicts hamper the ability of parties to work together, and where they do not, whether resolution is desirable.

Smith and Berg (1987) point out that to talk about "working through" or resolving conflict is misleading, because conflicts are part of the nature of a group. To emphasize the point, they identify seven fundamental paradoxes of groups, covering identity, disclosure, trust, individuality, authority, regression and creativity. For example, the first paradox is that people think about their identity in terms of the variety of groups to which they belong, and they think about a group identity in terms of the different individuals which comprise it. The paradox of trust is that for members to trust a group, the group must trust its members; hence, individuals wish to know whether the group will accept and trust them before they trust the group. The point made is that any group embodies a number of contradictions, so that groups have to accept them as part of their nature, rather than seeking to resolve the conflicts that arise from them. Smith and Berg suggest that simply recognizing and coming to terms with these conflicts is sufficient.

On the other hand, Baxter (1982) warns that if avoidance is frequently used for coping with conflict, then the end result may be a "super-conflict" of stockpiled issues. By saving up unresolved conflicts, it becomes harder to reconcile the parties involved (see assertion R, p. 38, on entrenched positions). Baxter noted a pattern of conflict avoidance, or "fight-flight" in the groups she studied, and uses this to explain her observation of a marked increase of information-giving during conflict resolutions in later stages of the group activity. Specifically, members of the group were explicitly summarizing the implications of particular resolutions, in order to link them with previous unresolved conflicts. In this way the stockpile of unresolved issues is reduced.

L Conflicts follow a set pattern

Although many theoretical treatments of conflict present a series of stages of individual conflict episodes, the empirical basis of many of these models is unclear. In most cases they simply offer frameworks for investigation of conflict rather than descriptive (or even prescriptive) models. For example, Pondy (1967) treats conflict as a series of episodes (see Fig. 1.5), with each episode including the following stages: latent conflict (conditions), perceived conflict (cognition), felt conflict (affect), manifest conflict (behaviour) and conflict aftermath (conditions). This pattern, which distinguishes latent tensions from perception of conflict and subsequent action, is also adopted in similar models by other authors (e.g. Robbins 1974; Thomas 1976). However, the stages are vague, and reflect an emphasis on the role of perception, and a suggestion that conflict must be perceived before it is felt, and felt before it is acted on. The latter point is not so much a testable hypothesis as a definitional issue.

Studies of negotiation offer more detailed analyses, being more concerned with prescriptive models. For example, Gulliver (1979) presents two models of the negotiation process: a cyclic model and a developmental model. The cyclic model shows how behaviour and information from each party affects the other, and the developmental model describes a number of phases, including search for arena, agenda definition, exploring the field, narrowing the differences, preliminaries to final bargaining, final bargaining, ritualization of outcome and execution of outcome. These models are supported by a number of apt examples that come from empirical observation, but these do no more that illustrate the plausibility of the models as

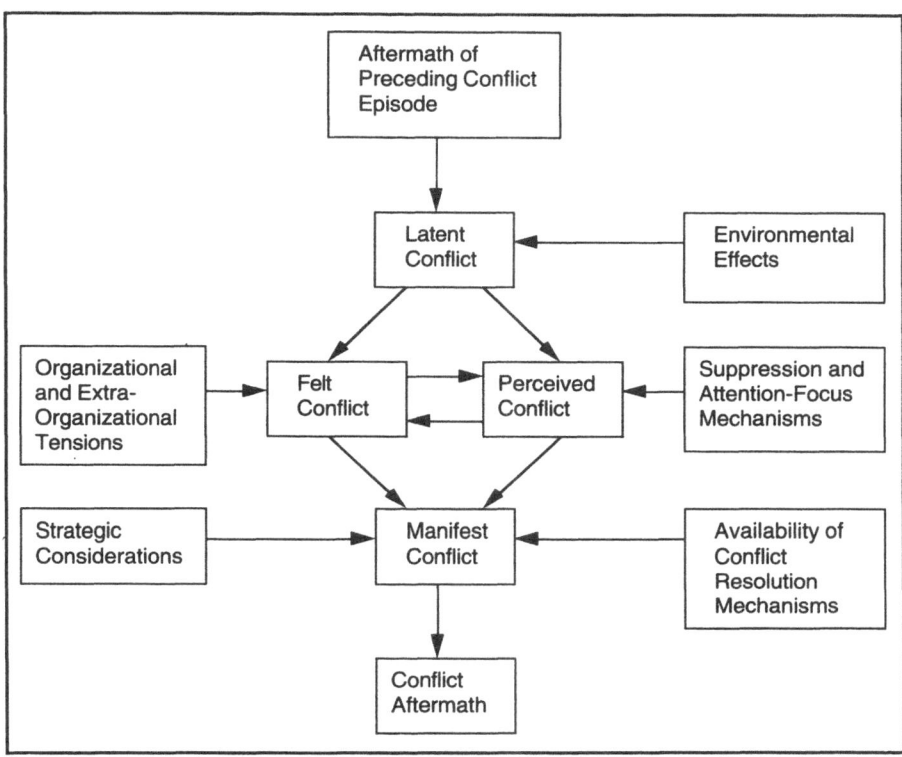

Fig. 1.5. The dynamics of a conflict episode, adapted from Pondy (1967).

theoretical frameworks. Effectively, the models are generalized ideals, and are not intended to be rigidly applied to particular empirical cases. Also, the models are intended for formal negotiation, rather than conflict resolution in general, and hence their applicability may not be very wide.

M *Styles of handling conflict vary with pressures of time*

Many studies of group behaviour have ignored temporal aspects, other than recognition that a group may develop through a series of phases as time progresses (see Assertion C, p. 16). In recognition of this, McGrath (1991) puts forward a theory of group activities that explicitly recognizes that any action not only takes its meaning from the context, but also from its timing: if an action is regarded as conflictful at one point, it might not be seen so at a later time. The theory suggests there are three generic temporal problems: temporal ambiguity, in that it is not clear when events will occur or recur; conflicts between temporal requirements; and scarcity of temporal resources. These are handled by the group through scheduling, synchronization and time allocation, and by individuals by making temporal commitments, negotiating event sequences and regulating task interaction. The mismatch between these group and individual responses leads to problems of establishing and enforcing deadlines, coordinating dynamic team-work, and resolving demand-capability mismatches.

McGrath goes on to point out that time is basically "lumpy" in that neither periods of time nor bundles of activity can be efficiently subdivided without limit, and periods of time are not always interchangeable for particular activities. Pressures of time strongly affect the rate at which work is done, in a process known as *entrainment*. This refers to the synchronization, or loose coupling, of the phase and periodicity of two or more activities. Typically, groups that are given shorter times to do a task work faster, while those given more time work slower. Through entrainment, these rates persist: a group will continue to work at the same rate on subsequent tasks, even if the allotted time is varied. Kelly et al. (1990) discovered that this general result does not necessarily hold if groups encounter difficulties with the task. They explain the anomalies by considering capacity and capability. If the group feels the problems are to do with capacity – where steady progress was made, but time ran out – then they will work faster in subsequent trials. On the other hand, if the group feels the problem is one of capability – progress slows because the problem needs deeper thought or is beyond the ability of the group – then they will work at a slower rate on subsequent trials, in order to try and produce better quality solutions.

Although Kelly et al. do not refer explicitly to conflict, the results are clearly relevant. Perception of a capacity problem implies that the group perceives the quality of their solutions to be adequate – they will work faster and ignore doubts and conflicts. If the group perceives a capability problem they will take more time, and pay more attention to task-related conflicts. Note that although this result strictly applies only to entrainment – how pressures on an initial task affect rates on subsequent similar tasks – there is a more general result. Group members are more likely to ignore conflicts when deadlines approach if they feel adequate to the task. For example, Moorhead et al. (1991), in their analysis of the decisions made leading to the launch of the ill-fated *Challenger* space shuttle, suggest that a limited time frame leads to pressure to agree. Group leaders then push forward a particular point of view rather than directing group activities towards critical appraisal. This leads to an atmosphere of group-think (see Assertion J, p. 28).

N *Size of a group affects the occurrence and resolution of conflict*

In a lengthy presentation of a framework for studying teamwork, Bass (1980) points out that the effects of the size of a group are hard to isolate from many other factors. However, he points out that in larger groups the patterns of interactions are vastly more complex, and this has a number of implications. The first of these is that in large groups cliques are likely to form, both because of communication barriers and where there are differences of opinion. In particular, minority views often lead to cliques that are then likely to conflict with and compete with the rest of the group.

Bales and Borgatta (1955) observed groups ranging in size from two to seven members, and demonstrated a number of trends that illustrate two factors: larger groups mean less talking time per person and each person has to maintain more relationships. Bass cites a study by Gibb (1954), which investigated a public relations problem given to a variety of groups of sizes up to 96 members. The groups spent 30 minutes listing suggested solutions and 30 minutes evaluating them. In the larger groups there was a larger percentage of team members who reported that they had ideas they did not express, and a larger percentage of members who never talked directly. Members who failed to interact felt more threatened in the larger groups: they felt their ideas might be misinterpreted, they felt it was easier to let someone else speak, or another group member proposed their idea before they had formulated it. The results of these two studies are broadly comparable, even though they investigated substantially different ranges of group size.

If members of a larger group are unable to contribute as much, or are suppressing their contributions, then the level of disagreement should decrease. Bales and Borgatta substantiated this, but note that the observer had more to observe with the larger groups, and may have missed signs of tension. However, this does not explain away all their results, and they put forward two further explanations. First, in larger groups, the roles required by the task may be allocated over a larger number of persons, increasing the chance that each role will be performed by someone without much difficulty. The second reason is that larger groups offer more anonymity for people who are more likely to conflict when forced into greater involvement.

The conclusion must be that occurrence of conflict increases in smaller groups, and that this is at least in part because each member is more fully engaged in the task. However, this does not imply that the conflict is destructive. Adding members to a group does not necessarily increase the resources of the group, due to the increased complexity in communication patterns (Brooks 1975). Also, extra members may be redundant. However, Bales and Borgatta warn that for small groups, it may matter more whether the group has an odd or an even number of members, as even-numbered groups can spend longer in deadlocked situations.

O *(The course of) conflict is culturally sensitive*

That different cultures have different attitudes to conflict is self-evident. There are many books on conducting commercial negotiations (e.g. Scott 1988) which present lists of "dos and don'ts" when negotiating or bargaining in different parts of the world. Such tips reflect the fact that different cultures display conflict in different ways, and expect different behaviours when resolving conflicts. However, it is not so self-evident to what extent culture affects perceptions of conflict, treatment of conflict when it arises, and even ideals for what constitutes a good solution to a conflict. These issues become particularly important when considering the prospect of global networks, in which communication barriers between cultures are removed.

Many studies have compared conflict and conflict handling in particular national cultures, and discovered variations. For example, Corsaro and Rizzo (1990) compared disputes among American and Italian children using conversation analysis, and discovered that peer disputes, and especially the discussions surrounding them, play a more significant role among Italian children. While disputes among the American children were relatively straightforward, the Italian children embellished their arguments, and seemed to consider participating in the dispute more important than any resolution. In keeping with the ethno-methodological approach, these differences were not hypothesized beforehand; but emerged from analysis of the data.

A more common approach involves identifying cultural traits and examining how these affect conflict. For example, Leung (1987) examined the cultural dimensions identified by Hofstede (1980), and showed that *individualist* and *collectivist* societies had marked differences in their preferences for mechanisms for conflict resolution: in individualist societies (e.g. the US) there is a preference for adjudicatory procedures, in which an independent judge makes the final decision, while in collectivist societies (e.g. China) the preference is for bargaining and mediation. In explaining this result, Leung identified reduction of animosity as a key factor, and offers two explanations: the preference for bargaining and mediation could be a result of a stronger desire for animosity reduction, or it could be that both societies desire animosity reduction to the same extent, but differ in how they expect this to be achieved. A subsequent study (Leung et al. 1990) looked at "cultural femininity", where "feminine" cultures emphasize cooperation, friendliness and sympathy for the weak, while "masculine" cultures value achievement, recognition and challenge. Dutch and Canadian subjects were used as examples of "feminine" and "masculine" cultures, respectively. This study supported the hypothesis that both cultures would desire animosity reduction, but would differ in how they expected this to be achieved. The Canadian subjects preferred confrontational methods as more likely to both grant them more process control and reduce animosity, while the Dutch subjects preferred compromise for the same reasons. Note that although the traits are referred to as "masculinity" and "femininity", they have little to do with gender, and the above study found no significant variation with the sex of the subjects. (See Assertion W for a discussion of gender and conflict, p. 46).

Kozan (1989) points out that commonly cited cultural dimensions, such as the empirically derived dimensions of Hofstede (1980), do not explain all the differences. In a comparison of the conflict management styles of Jordanian, Turkish and US managers, Kozan expected to find many similarities between the two middle-eastern cultures, and much contrast with the US. In fact there were many differences between all three, and although particular features of the cultures studied could be found to explain the results, these features are not reflected in the generalized cultural dimensions.

The mix of cultures within a group also makes a difference. While the studies described above examine separate cultures, Zamarripa and Krueger (1983) compare mono-cultural groups with intercultural ones, in particular looking at leadership norms. Their key finding was that mixed cultural groups initially had a varied set of norms, while mono-cultural groups had very similar initial norms, especially where the members of the group were from the same social class. Furthermore, the variance of norms within each group only changed slightly over the group's existence. In other words, the implicit norms of members of the intercultural groups did not converge significantly, even though some negotiation of norms was taking place.

Two conclusions may be drawn: preferences for handling conflict do vary significantly between cultures, and cultural differences in a group complicate the negotiation of group norms, which in turn degrades task performance. However, broad cultural traits provide relatively poor predictors of preference. At first sight it might seem that these conclusions imply that many of the studies of conflict described throughout this chapter are of limited value, as they draw on a fairly narrow mix of cultures. However, as Leung et al. (1990) point out, the differences are quantitative rather than qualitative, and the different cultures have much in common in terms of their rationale for preferring one resolution method over another. For example, in Leung's later study, both cultures clearly preferred harmony-enhancing methods over confrontational ones; the difference lay in the degree of this preference.

P Personality has little effect on the development of conflict

There is a popular belief that people's personalities strongly affect the way they handle conflict, yet the psychology literature suggests the opposite, that personality does not have a great effect. For instance, although Putnam and Poole (1987) include "actor attributes" as one of four major variables in conflict situations (see Section 1.1.2.2), they subsume gender, beliefs, skills, and cognitive styles, as well as personality, within this category. In their survey, they conclude that personality traits have very little to do with the style of conflict strategy. This is consistent with other authors, who suggest that although the participants in conflicts attribute a lot to personality, this is in fact a fallacy (e.g. see Blake and Mouton 1962).

Terhune (1970) takes a closer look at this question. He notes that sociological studies tend to discount personality as less interesting than situational factors. There are also methodological problems: personality characteristics appear to affect behaviour in some situations but not in others. Terhune cites many game theoretic studies of personality and conflict, and shows that the conclusions are remarkably equivocal, with the effects that have been discovered in some studies not replicated in others. There are also problems with measuring personality and assembling sufficient numbers of subjects with particular personality traits.

A later game theoretic study, that of Hermann and Kogan (1977), supports Terhune's suggestion that personality may have its greatest effect on the initial behaviour of participants. The participant's approach to negotiation is determined, in the absence of other constraints, by his or her personality. Their study showed that traits such as self-esteem and cognitive complexity affect whether a person expects to cooperate or compete, and also affect a person's expectation of what the opponent will do. Once a negotiation is underway, the personality of the other person is far more important, in that the course of a negotiation will depend on how each participant reacts to the other. Hermann and Kogan identify two types of personality characteristic as important: interpersonal style (e.g. tendency to conciliate, suspiciousness, etc.), and decision style (e.g. cognitive complexity, dogmatism and risk-avoidance).

In contrast to the task game theoretic studies, Sternberg and Soriano (1984) conducted a psychological study of responses to stories presenting conflict situations. The stories covered conflict at personal, organizational and international levels, and for each, subjects were offered a choice of specific resolutions, covering modes such as physical action, wait-and-see, third-party intervention, and so on. The study showed that subjects had preferred modes of resolution which applied across different situations. Furthermore, the preferences were related both to perceptual styles and personality. Personality traits such as needs for deference, autonomy, dominance and change were shown to be mildly predictive of resolution preferences, and in particular whether a subject was likely to choose an intensification or a mitigation style. Similarly, Jones and White (1985) found empirical support for linkages between personality characteristics (affiliation, deference and aggression) and preferences for different modes of conflict resolution (smoothing, forcing and confrontation), where the preferences were associated with actual behaviours.

In conclusion, it seems that although many researchers have dismissed the role of personality in deciding the course of conflicts, there is some evidence that some personality traits are correlated with some attitudes towards conflict (see also Assertion V, p. 43). However, in many cases the effect of personality is overshadowed by situational and perceptual factors, and one of the reasons why some studies have found correlations is that they manage to minimize these other variables. Part of the problem with both game theoretic and psychological studies of personality and conflict is that they tend to isolate the subjects from their everyday situations. Hence it is not clear whether any effects (or non-effects) of personality in these studies apply outside the abstracted situations examined in the studies.

1.2.5 Management and Resolution of Conflict

Q A strong leader is needed to resolve conflict

The issue of leadership in small group behaviour is a complex one, and can affect conflict in a number of ways. The selection of a leader might itself lead to conflict. Bass (1980) considers the possibility of two or more group members having equal leadership potential. If the person chosen as leader has both the highest esteem and status then little conflict is likely, but if this is not the case, and different members have potential to be the most influential, then conflict may arise if they do not share the same approaches to the group's problems. Shaw and Harkey (1976) tested this empirically, by setting up congruent and incongruent groups. In the congruent groups, the status of the leader was assigned to the member high in self-reported initiative and social boldness. In the incongruent group, such a person was assigned the status of a follower. As expected, congruent groups were more effective in accomplishing the group task. The one effect on interaction processes was the tendency of the leaders of incongruent groups to interrupt discussions more frequently than did leaders of congruent groups. If the chosen leader does not behave as a leader should, then group tension increases.

So the appropriateness of a choice of leader, and the subsequent performance of an explicitly chosen leader may affect the occurrence of conflict. To establish whether a strong leader is an asset in conflict resolution, however, requires an examination of the nature of leadership. Homans (1950) presents the thesis that a leader gives the group what its members want. Dyson et al. (1976) found in their empirical studies that this was "not entirely substantiated" (p. 125) because some leaders get from groups what they want as opposed to the other way round. They also found that leaders are likely to have attitudes similar to the other group members, and hence it is difficult to say much about the effect of the leadership.

Gemmill (1989) questions the assumption that such a role as leadership exists in the general sense. In an earlier paper (Gemmill 1986), he examines the history of the concept of leadership, arguing that a process of reification has elevated an ambiguous expression to the status of a leader role which determines the effectiveness of a group and the satisfaction of its members: "It is assumed by researchers and practitioners that because there is a word (leadership), there must be an entity to be studied. Nothing, of course, could be further from the truth, as it is a matter of personal preference and value judgement as to what empirical referents are connected to the label 'leader role' or 'leadership'" (p. 41). He argues that the role of leader is a projection of feelings by the group members created to avoid confronting their own lack of control. The displacement of positive feelings, such as confidence and skill, serve to support the idea of the superiority of the leader, and the displacement of negative feelings, such as uncertainty and aggression, serve to support the notion of the leader having the ultimate responsibility for developments in the group and its members.

Central to this process is that it is an unconscious protection against disturbing the perceived status quo: an individual can continue believing in the reassuring idea of responsible and knowledgeable leaders who determine the courses of groups and their work. Because this preserves the social order, it is experienced as reassuring for both those assigned leadership and those assigned following roles. However, as it restricts the expression of the full potential of (all) the individuals concerned, this ultimately reduces group effectiveness. In Gemmill and Kraus (1988) and Gemmill (1989) this thesis is developed further to explore the more general process of creating roles, including various scapegoats, in groups. This and other roles are a product of, and serve to deflect, feelings which the participants have but do not accept in themselves. The result is to stifle creativity in the group.

This literature does not address the question of resolution of conflict as such, but does deny the call for a strong leader as it questions the validity of creating a "leader" role. In more formal groupings, such as those studied in organizational behaviour, the existence of leadership is taken for granted. In this case, the question is more to do with how a given leader should lead, as opposed to whether leadership *per se* is useful. The issue of strong leadership could be interpreted as one of autocratic versus democratic decision making. Again, a general answer concerning the effectiveness of either of these styles is not apparent, as the effectiveness of any particular style of leadership depends on the situation (Howell et al. 1986). Clearly, an autocratic leader may appear to help resolve conflicts, but might really be causing them to be suppressed, while a democratic leader might simply prolong the conflict.

The above implies that evidence that strong leadership is a prerequisite for conflict resolution is equivocal. The effectiveness of any particular leadership style, or indeed whether a leader is needed at all, depends on the particular conflict. When designing group activities (e.g. for CSCW systems), one must be careful about the assumptions about leadership that become embedded in the design.

R *Conflicts are unlikely to be resolved if participants argue from entrenched positions*

If participants become entrenched this makes exploration of the middle ground difficult. This may occur where participants have opposing basic beliefs, values or principles which they believe must be mutually exclusive. If this sort of polarization occurs participants may be unwilling to attempt to understand one another's positions. This sort of conflict has been termed "competitive conflict" (Pace 1990) and is characterized by defensiveness, hostility and escalation. Pace contrasts this with "cooperative conflict" which is "positive, supportive and peace-keeping in nature".

One of the major problems identified with polarization is that the resulting entrenchment stifles creativity (Fisher and Ury 1981). Authors such as de Bono (1985) put great emphasis on the role of creativity, and suggest that the best way to resolve a conflict is to reformulate the problem. However, creativity is hard to study experimentally, although it is possible to find case studies. For example, Hare and Naveh (1985) describe the role of creativity in the Camp David Summit of 1978. At the beginning of the summit meeting the participants were far apart on many of the issues, but through a creative process of reformulating problems and altering the composition of the group, a successful outcome (i.e. a peace treaty) was arrived at. Several important steps were taken to foster creativity, including reorganizing the groups when it became apparent that face-to-face talks between the leaders were not working, and introducing a draft treaty prepared earlier to divert attention away from the sticking points. This treaty went through 23 drafts as it bounced back and forth between participants, but most importantly it remained a focus for a problem solving process.

These considerations would tend to suggest that the advice of Fisher and Ury (1981) to detach the originators from their viewpoints is sound. On the other hand we could argue that ideas need champions. This is especially the case for more radical ideas. Moscovici and Zavalloni (1969) observed that the most extremist or the most committed individuals made greater efforts to persuade the group members that their response was the right one and that the group should accept it. They usually succeeded, and as a result the consensus was in their favour. Consequently, the common decision was far more extreme than the average of the individual choices before the discussion. If these people had not argued strenuously in favour of their own position, then it is unlikely they would have achieved the same outcome.

In conclusion, it seems likely that separating people from their positions will foster creativity, and hence may lead to a quicker or better resolution of conflict. However, it is by no means certain that this is always desirable, let alone always possible. de Bono (1985), for example, argues that such a separation is not possible, and that a third party needs to be introduced to design a resolution (see Assertion U, p. 42). Also, such an approach may lead to the problems associated with anonymity and depersonalization discussed under Assertion H (see p. 24). What may be more important is the effect of the resolution process on the participants. A confrontational process may be very costly, while a collaborative problem solving process is likely to be mutually rewarding (Deutsch 1973). Detaching people from positions may be one way to achieve the latter.

S *Articulating conflict helps in its resolution*

There is little doubt that a group which talks about a task will perform significantly better than one which does not. A recent study by Elias et al. (1989) confirmed that a session of task-focused self-disclosure between group activities had a significant positive effect on group cohesiveness, commitment to task and productivity. There is also evidence that conflicts that are not articulated may accumulate to produce breakdowns in group interaction (Baxter 1982).

These observations have led to an interest in techniques for making conflicts explicit. An example of a CSCW system which assumes this goal is Argnoter (Stefik et al. 1987; see Section 1.3). Lane et al. (1982) note that matters such as who will make decisions may be decided at a covert level or at an explicit level, and if they are made covertly then they are open to different interpretations by group members. On the other hand, making things explicit should enhance understanding and focus the group members on the same set of issues. Hence they studied the effects of intervention in a group to persuade them to strive for acceptance – generating a group solution they could all accept. By varying the instructions, the experimenters made acceptance an explicit group goal, which increased the quality of the group decision, increased the individual acceptance of the group decision, and produced a persistent increase in quality of subsequent individual responses. On the other hand, asking a group to strive for quality actually decreased both the group's decision quality and the individual member acceptance of the group decision. The explanation offered is that making acceptance an explicit group goal turns it into a norm, and creates a more favourable climate for offering and discussing ideas.

We could even go so far as to say that conflict cannot be resolved unless it is expressed. Pace (1990) uses the term "differentiation" to refer to the group process of identifying and understanding the parameters of a conflict. This involves making the conflict explicit, recognizing the issues involved, and having individual views acknowledged by the other members of a group. Pace identifies four aspects of conflict that are salient for differentiation: (i) the strength of the disagreement; (ii) the level to which the disagreement is personalized (embedded in interpersonal relationships, emotions and personalities, as opposed to being more purely concerned with task-focused issues and ideas); (iii) the competitiveness of the dispute (see the distinction between cooperative and competitive conflict in Assertion R, p. 38); and (iv) centrality (how important the issue is for the disagreeing member and the group – this will influence how willing they are to compromise). Pace found that differentiation of depersonalized conflict was very important for group consensus and cohesion. On the other hand, the results suggest that a thorough differentiation does not ensure that consensus will be reached, and that for personalized, competitive conflicts, a prolonged differentiation process can damage personal relations in the group.

This last point leads us to express a note of caution. If articulation of conflict is used as a prelude to resolution, then conflicts that should not or cannot be resolved perhaps should not be articulated. For some conflicts, suppression may be a sensible approach if it avoids a senseless confrontation: we discuss this point further under Assertion K, p. 29. Furthermore, too much concentration on conflict may overemphasize its importance. Price (1989) studied the effects of messages concentrating on conflict between groups (as opposed to within groups), and concluded that such messages encourage people to think in terms of their group membership, thus reinforcing stereotypical images and increasing polarization.

T People can be trained to handle conflict in a constructive way

Many of the assertions in this chapter describe factors which affect whether conflict will occur, and how it will be resolved. Given at least an initial understanding of these issues, it seems likely that training has a role in conflict resolution. Deutsch (1969) points out that conflicts may be constructive or destructive, depending on, among other things, the frame of mind of the participants. He asserts that a mutual willingness to resolve the conflict in a cooperative way will lead to a constructive conflict. The question then becomes: in what ways can training help?

In Assertion S (p. 40) we argued that articulation of conflict was a necessary precondition to resolution. If this is the case, then training people to articulate perceived conflicts should be helpful. Hence communication skills are important: the way in which the conflict is communicated may determine its utility in the group process. A useful distinction here is between "regulated" communication, where information is shared and issues debated, and "unregulated" communication, where participants attempt to injure or eliminate other parties through verbal abuse and hostile behaviour. In a study of groups engaged in problem solving using either regulated or unregulated modes of communication, Pood (1980) showed that more effective decisions were reached where a regulated mode was used. If the resolution process is to remain constructive, then the articulation of it needs to be regulated.

Related to the articulation of conflict is awareness of group processes. Gemmill (1989) argues that covert roles arise from pressures for group members to find outlets for unexpressed and inexpressible feelings by assigning them to certain individuals in the group: scapegoats. The more group members are aware of the scapegoating process, the more accurately group members will perceive themselves and each other, and the greater their capacity to resolve interpersonal conflicts constructively within the group. This implies that it is possible to train people, through awareness, to become better at interacting in group situations.

Another way in which training may help is to provide group members with specific strategies for dealing with conflicts. Deutsch (1973) reports on studies of strategies used in games, and found that strategies like "turn-the-other-cheek" fail, whereas non-punitive but reward-giving strategies tend to work best. They encourage an opponent to reciprocate, and hence cooperate rather than compete. There is a large body of work in game theory (e.g. see Axelrod 1984) and in negotiation (e.g. see Gulliver 1979) devoted to the development of successful strategies. However, it is not always clear that strategies that work in abstract games and formal negotiations are useful in the complex reality of group interaction.

Finally, previous experience plays a role. Although it has been shown that both individuals and groups will improve performance on repetition of particular tasks (Axelrod 1984), it is not so clear that experience of one type of conflict can help with others. Thompson (1990) examined this question using various negotiation tasks, and showed that people were able to apply some negotiation skills learnt in one task to different situations. However, not all skills transferred in this way, and in particular, experience did not appear to improve the subjects' skill at finding compatible interests between participants.

We have argued that training in articulation of conflict, regulated communication, awareness of covert roles and group processes, and use of specific strategies may all help to produce constructive resolution behaviour. Elsewhere in this chapter we discuss the use of particular conflict management techniques, such as "consensus", "a strong leader", "third-party intervention", and so on. However, none of these techniques by themselves offers a universal panacea, and training needs to include both a range of techniques and an awareness of their limitations.

U *Difficult conflicts need a third party to introduce a resolution*

This assertion is made by de Bono (1985), who claims that the introduction of a third party is necessary because the participants become "bogged down by tradition, training and complacency, in the argument mode of thinking", and "simply cannot carry out certain thinking operations because these would not be consistent with their position in the conflict". However, he argues the case rather strongly: are third parties really necessary?

It is clear that third parties can play a useful role. Deutsch (1969) points out that interested third parties often provide the attitudes, strength and resources that are crucial determinants of whether participants in a conflict will favour a cooperative or a competitive approach. Two roles of third parties are introduced: the encouragement of cooperative resolution, especially by powerful and prestigious third parties, and the provision of problem solving resources. One particular type of third-party intervention is the group facilitator (Viller 1991), who coordinates the discussions of the group to ensure that each member is participating fully.

While not providing an answer to the question of the need for a third party to resolve conflicts, Deutsch (1969) and Viller (1991), point to useful roles that are performed by third parties. By implication, the deliberate introduction of a third party into a conflict or a potential conflict may well help in its resolution. However, there appears to be no reason to believe that this will always be the case. The key point may be under what conditions the intercession of a third party is likely to be most beneficial.

One area in which a third party appears to be necessary is resource conflicts. Edney and Bell (1984) investigate the conflict inherent in the consumption of scarce resources: in particular, they investigate the "tragedy of the commons", in which common resources are over-consumed when all members of a community have equally free access to them. Through a series of game-like studies they discovered that artificially tying the individual's outcome to the rest of the group is good for the group, preserving the commons, and promoting perception of cooperation. However, they go on to consider the practicalities of applying this result, and in particular the political difficulties, in which such an action may be seen to reduce individual freedom where it is imposed by a superordinate authority.

V Different people prefer different approaches for tackling conflict

There are clearly many different ways in which conflicts may be tackled, some of which we have discussed in the preceding assertions. Furthermore, there are many different types of conflict, and many different ways in which conflict may manifest itself. Studies such as Sternberg and Soriano (1984) show that people are predisposed to handle conflicts in particular ways; the interesting question, therefore, is whether individual preferences or predispositions can be generalized to produce a model of responses to conflict. Such a model might then be used as a basis for principled study of the factors that affect preferences.

A number of different models have been proposed with which to classify responses to conflict. For intergroup conflicts, Blake et al. (1964) identify three possible assumptions that might determine strategy for conflict management. These are:

1. Disagreement is inevitable and permanent.

2. Conflict can be avoided since interdependence between groups is unnecessary.

3. Agreement and maintaining interdependence is possible.

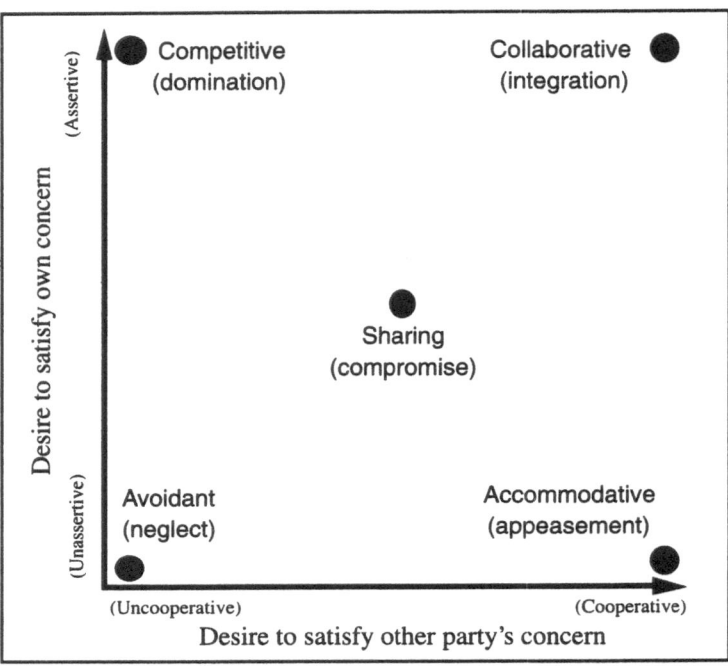

Fig. 1.6. Behavioural modes of tackling conflict with (in brackets) the outcome sought in each mode. Adapted from Thomas (1976).

Clearly, the assumption made will determine the mechanism chosen for managing the conflict. For example, the first assumption implies that the points of view of the conflicting parties are mutually exclusive, and some means of selecting a winner is needed, whether through struggle, third-party decision or fate. The second assertion implies that some form of withdrawal or indifference is needed, while the third would lead to a search for an integration or compromise.

Another commonly used model offers five different orientations that an individual might have to conflict, based on a two-dimensional space of possibilities. The two dimensions are assertiveness (or desire to satisfy one's own concern) and cooperation (or desire to satisfy the other party's concern). The resulting space offers five interesting conjunctions, as shown in Fig. 1.6. Note that these refer merely to a single party's orientation, which may change upon interaction with other parties to the conflict. Thomas (1976) describes, for each orientation, the conditions under which it is likely to be useful:

1. Competitive – one participant seeks to dominate the process, without regard for the others. A competitive mode may be useful for quick decisive action, or where unpopular actions are perceived as necessary for important issues.

2. Collaborative – participants seek to understand their differences and achieve a mutually beneficial solution. This may be appropriate where participants' insights and commitment are important and need to be merged rather than compromised.

3. Avoidant – the conflict is recognized to exist but is suppressed by one or more parties, or handled by withdrawal. It may be useful where an issue is unimportant, where the potential disruption would outweigh the benefits of resolution, or where information gathering is most important.

4. Accommodative – a party becomes self-sacrificing to appease another, and places the interests of the other above their own. It may be useful when issues are far more important to one party than another, where one party is losing and needs to minimize loss, or where there is a desire to build harmony and gain social credits.

5. Sharing – each party makes some concessions in order to reach a compromise. This is most appropriate where temporary settlements or expedient solutions are needed, especially under time pressure, or where goals are directly opposed.

Thomas argues that each of these five modes is appropriate in some circumstances, and hence individuals should use situational factors to choose an appropriate response. The more aware people are of the possibilities, the more likely a suitable mode will be used.

Although this model has been widely used to develop instruments for measuring conflict style, it is not without its critics. Volkema and Bergmann (1989) raise two concerns: first, the model does not cover demonstrative responses that often occur in interpersonal conflict, such as revenge, regression and various forms of aggression; and second, instruments developed from it tend to focus on abstract, generalized principles, and so are more indicative of intended rather than actual behaviour. They investigated these concerns by asking subjects which of a large number of specific responses they have used, might use and would never use. Cluster analyses revealed a group of emotive responses as well as groups of confrontational and withdrawal responses. Daves and Holland (1989) point out that the model assumes the perspective of the person whose style is examined, and that the "other party" might view actions very differently. Factor analysis of self and subordinate ratings revealed that a three-dimensional space might be more appropriate, with the dimensions: openness, distribution and control.

A completely different model is offered by Druckman et al. (1977), who compare the interplay of values and interests in resolution of conflicts, and identify two perspectives that have driven empirical research. The first is that participants balance interests against their values, with the empirical question being to find out which are assigned greater weight. The second perspective is that values and interests interact, each deriving from and influencing the other, with the empirical question being how the relationship between the two affects the intensity of a conflict. From their investigations, they conclude that the relative importance of the two varies with context; so, for example, interests were far more important than ideology in a prison services dispute, while the reverse was true in a population policy negotiation.

There are of course many factors affecting the preference, which we discuss elsewhere: culture (see Assertion O, p. 33), gender (see Assertion W), personality (see Assertion P, p. 35), size of the group (see Assertion N, p. 32), effect of time pressures (see Assertion M, p. 31), technological mediation (see Assertion G, p. 23) and the structure of the group (see Assertions D, E and Q, pp. 19–22 and 37). Finally, Assertion Y (p. 50) describes variations in individuals' perceptions of outcomes.

W *Styles of handling conflict vary with gender*

In a section of his paper dealing with conditions that influence the course of conflict resolution, Deutsch (1969) mentions, *en passant*, that "the strategy and tactics associated with competitive struggle may seem more manly or intriguing than those associated with cooperation" (p. 28). This assertion is not empirically based, but reflects a general assumption that women favour a more collaborative approach to conflict resolution than men. Given the widespread belief that there are gender differences operating in the management of conflict, the literature is marked by its failure to address this issue. Here we survey some of the studies that have given more than just a passing comment on the issue.

Putnam and Poole (1987) briefly review the literature on the effects of gender differences on choice of conflict behaviour. They cite Jamieson and Thomas' (1974) findings that men tend to use "forcing" resolution styles, while women favoured "compromizing" ones (cf. Fig. 1.6). Other studies, though, conclude that there is no difference in the choice of conflict resolution style. Renwick (1977), for instance, examined the impact of sex differences on the management of interpersonal conflict in the work environment, but found that the sex of a supervisor was unrelated to female subordinates' perceptions of conflict management, and no differences were observed between methods adopted by either male or female subordinates to deal with disagreement.

Mabry (1985) comments that neither the specific question of male and female participation in groups, or the issue of gender-mix as a factor in small group composition, has received adequate attention. He cites Nemeth et al. (1976) as failing to find significant differences between male and female members of simulated jury deliberation groups on the frequency of positive or negative social-emotional acts, or the frequency of questions asking for task-orientated statements. Other studies (Aries 1976; Ellis and McAllister 1980; Strodtbeck and Mann 1956), by contrast, report findings which support the traditional sex-role conceptions of male and female behaviour.

It seems that the preconceptions of traditional sex-roles have a significant effect. For example, Bartos (1970) discovered that negotiators tend to be tough against women, and, furthermore, gender of the other party was the *only* "first impression" factor that correlated significantly with toughness across all the experiments. The conclusion is that in American society, women are *expected* to play submissive roles. Piliavin and Martin (1978) found that these traditional sex-role expectations about participation and domination were more valid for same-sex groups than for mixed-sex groups. They suggest that group members tend to adapt to what they perceive to be the expectations of other group members, according to traditional sex-roles. This adaptation hypothesis is also supported by Eskilson and Wiley (1976), who found that both men and women exhibit more leader-like behaviours in same-sex groups, as opposed to mixed-sex groups, although the proportion of men and women in group composition was a significant variable.

Mabry (1985) argues that these studies do not take adequate account of the effect of task characteristics. Accordingly, Mabry investigated the combination of effects by varying both group gender compositions and the task requirements under which they were working. Results for the 44 groups studied show that both these factors have some influence. Gender differences were found in respect to some variables (female or mainly female groups displayed less disagreement but more tension than other groups, for example), though differences generally varied more with task structure than with gender. Structured tasks produced more dominance behaviours generally, but all-male groups responded more aggressively to such situations than did other gender composition and task structure combinations, but "the presence of one or two women in these groups apparently suppressed the incidence of dominance behaviour" (p. 92). There was no evidence of gender difference on task-related communicative acts. This seems to question the broadness of our assertion: according to Mabry's research, it is a combination of gender and task structure which affects behaviour, and he concludes that small group interaction is not substantively affected by the gender composition of groups.

Given the centrality of communication in both the generation and resolution of conflict, examination of differences in the ways men and women use language may be enlightening. Tannen's (1991) thesis is that because adults learn their ways of speaking as children growing up in mainly separate social worlds of same-sex peers, then "conversation between women and men is cross-cultural communication" (p. 47) and "each group interprets the other's ways of talking in terms of its own" (p. 244). Broadly speaking, women use language to create connections and intimacy, whereas men use language to promote and identify status and independence. She suggests that women are more at ease with speaking in small groups of known individuals (rapport talk) and that men are more confident with public speaking (report talk).

In the light of this thesis, Tannen explores the belief that males are competitive and prone to seek conflict, whereas females seek cooperation and affiliation. She suggests that this is over-simplistic, because conflict can be a means of creating involvement with others and can provide a kind of bonding for men. Her view is that gender-based language differences largely account for different attitudes to conflict, as men tend towards a more antagonistic style of disputation. Women are inclined to misinterpret and be puzzled by the adversarial nature of men's ways of speaking and miss the ritual nature of friendly aggression. But women's "enactment of community can be ritualized just as easily as the enactment of combat" (p. 150). This appearance of community among women can mask power struggles and profound differences in points of view, and hence "men can be as confused by women's verbal rituals as women are by men's" (p. 151).

It is difficult to draw coherent conclusions from all these studies. The studies that found no gender difference in conflict style seem to be contradicted by those that identify gender composition of groups as significant in determining group behaviour. We have covered two key factors: the effect of preconceptions of traditional sex-roles, and the differences in communication styles between men and women. This is an important and complex topic, and we have done little more than raise the issue as one that requires consideration. We would also suggest that the design and use of CSCW systems are not necessarily gender-neutral.

1.2.6 Results of Conflict

X *There is a positive relationship between levels of participation and satisfaction*

This assertion is commonly held in the software engineering community, and used as an argument for involvement of users in the development process. Wastell explores issues of user involvement further in Chapter 2; here we concentrate on the issue of participation in conflict resolutions in small group interaction. Thomas (1976) found that satisfaction of group members increases if they feel able to articulate conflicts without fear of disrupting the group, while Gibb (1954) found that members tend to be less satisfied in larger groups. Clearly, both these factors influence levels of participation, and it may be that it is the level of participation that determines member satisfaction.

Hagen and Burch (1985) studied participation directly, and found, perhaps unsurprisingly, that participation by all group members resulted in higher satisfaction. A more interesting observation is that perception of conflict and tense or anxious emotional tone lowered satisfaction, but that this effect is reduced in later stages of group development once the group develops a bond.

However, the relationship between participation and satisfaction is not as simple as it may appear. First, it is not clear exactly what satisfaction is. Pood (1980) distinguishes two types of satisfaction: satisfaction with the interactions of the group (social satisfaction) and satisfaction with the resolution (decision satisfaction). Although conflict management techniques have a positive effect on social satisfaction, decision satisfaction does not increase through the realization and management of conflict. Pood postulates that this is because the conflict is never really resolved as far as each individual is concerned, a point we discuss further under Assertion K, p. 29.

In addition, there are other factors which affect satisfaction independently of participation levels. Wall and Nolan (1987) concentrate on perceived inequity, showing that inequity is negatively related to satisfaction with the group and positively related to the amount of perceived conflict, especially affective conflict, within the group. In another study they showed that inequity can be reduced, and hence satisfaction increased, using integrative conflict management techniques (Wall et al. 1987). However, they did not directly study any relationship between participation and inequity.

Kimberly (1987) addresses another source of satisfaction in small group decisions: division of labour. Members of a group seek to integrate the distribution of task skills and the division of labour in a group. Places in the division of labour are referred to as positions. For a member of a group, if the person's skill is too high for his/her position, the position is not sufficiently demanding and boredom results. This reduces rewards based on performance. If the skill is too low for the position, the part of rewards based on position incumbency is high, but the person cannot perform adequately in the position, so the reward based on performance is low. Both types of mismatch produce dissatisfaction.

Finally, Falk (1981) discusses the use of unanimity in group decision making. The results of his study of role-playing groups using majority rule, unanimity or no decision rule, challenge the notion of the superiority of unanimity rule over majority. In fact, the type of decision rule which best promotes participation of all group members and attainment of high quality solutions depends on initial distribution of power. While unanimity strengthens and maintains equality in groups where there is already an equal distribution of power, majority rule has greater potential for equalizing power distribution in unequal power groups. Greater equality in distribution of power among group members facilitates group discussion, leading to higher quality solutions and greater satisfaction.

It seems that although a relationship between participation and group member satisfaction is evident, there are many other factors that mitigate satisfaction. Furthermore, participation itself does not guarantee successful resolution, and insistence on unanimity in group decision making may be counter-productive in groups with unequal power distributions. Additionally, DeStephen and Hirokawa (1988) question the use of informal democratic discussion groups as a basis for conclusions about members' feelings of agreement and satisfaction, pointing out that immediately after a decision exercise, group discussion will act as a group reinforcement.

Y *The "loser" in a conflict will try to save face, and the "victor" may help the "loser" do this*

When negotiating resolution of a conflict the issue of loss of face may be as important to the participants, if not more so, than the substantive issues. A fear of loss of face may lead participants to avoid a resolution, and even to escalate the conflict. Hence, when negotiating a resolution, it may be important to build face-saving elements into any agreement, to make a compromise or capitulation more palatable. This might be achieved by trivializing the subject of the conflict, spuriously claiming that no concessions have been made, or stressing the importance of agreement itself. Our assertion claims that these face-saving measures are cooperatively negotiated.

There is clear evidence that face-saving occurs, and that people are willing to help others save face. Sermat (1964) demonstrated the presence of the face-saving motive, using the prisoner's dilemma, played against an unconditionally uncooperative opponent. Players who believed their opponent was absent exploited the situation more often than players who thought their opponent was being informed of the outcome of each game. Evidence that the need to save face sometimes becomes more important than resolution comes from studies of international relations. Swingle (1970) cites the Cuban missile crisis as a prime example. An escalation of the crisis by President Kennedy was deemed necessary, as the threat to the reputation of the presidency and the country were perceived as far more pertinent than the military threat. Offers from Khrushchev to negotiate over mutual withdrawal of missiles from Cuba and Turkey were spurned by Kennedy, even though he had already ordered removal of the missiles in Turkey several months before.

An interesting question concerns the source of the motive to save face. Brown (1977) offers two fundamental explanations. First, there is a paradox in the necessity of yielding to achieve agreement, and the strategic value of not yielding, so as to increase one's outcome. This leads to a problem for negotiators of offering a concession without appearing to weaken their bargaining position. An appearance of strength is needed because of uncertainty about the other party's intentions, while the cost of not reaching agreement may be high. The second explanation is that it is a result of social norms that place a positive value on shows of strength, and a negative value on weakness and deference.

Brown goes on to survey work on face maintenance, distinguishing between *face-saving*, which is anticipatory and preventative, and *face-*

restoration, which is reparative of damage already done. The distinction is useful because they affect the conflict resolution process in different ways. Face-saving manifests itself in verbal behaviour in the use of disclaimers, hedges and vagueness, which soften the negative effect of statements. It also leads to various overt behaviours, usually designed to keep weakness hidden, including, on a large scale, deployment of resources and staging demonstrations as displays of strength, and, on a smaller scale, procrastinating, introducing irrelevancies, and preoccupation with procedural issues. Face-restoration manifests itself in threats of future resistance, and coded retraction or modification of (or reduction of commitment to) previous statements now seen as damaging.

A number of other situational factors affect face-maintenance. For example, anonymity should reduce the need to save face. Swingle (1970) discusses a number of game theoretic studies that support this suggestion, in the case where subjects are led to believe they will never meet their opponent. Also, whether the opponent or other parties have knowledge of the cost of various face-saving measures affects their deployment. Note that in this case the face-saving might not be reduced In Brown's (1968) study, the participants found other ways of retaliating, outside the rules of the games, in order to restore face.

To return to the assertion, it seems that many studies of face-maintenance have concentrated on situations where the motive originates from the opponent, because of a need to maintain a strong bargaining position, or simply because of not wishing to have the opponent declare victory. In this case, cooperation to avoid face loss is out of the question, and escalation of the conflict might be the only course of action. If the motive originates from other audiences, then it is plausible that the participants might cooperate to include face-saving measures. This may depend on how much they can conceal from these audiences, and how much they know about each other. There are too few studies of cooperative face-maintenance to draw any firm conclusions.

Z *Groups use sanctions to enforce resolution decisions*

The effect of possible sanctions on decision making is well known. Gross et al. (1958) showed that people perceive expectations of themselves from other relevant parties, and behave accordingly. However, there are likely to be many competing expectations, and the choice of behaviour depends on the legitimacy of each set of expectations and the likely sanctions that might be applied for nonconformity to those expectations.

One type of sanction is rejection from the group, which is frequently applied to members who deviate from group norms. Katz (1982) investigated the factors that lead to rejection from the group, and discovered that rejection is greater for a deviant who has not conformed previously than for one who has. He also investigated the link between status and rejection, but could find no support for his hypothesis that rejection is greater for a high-status deviant than a low-status deviant, where status is defined in terms of competence at a task, perceived acceptance, aptitude for unfamiliar tasks, and social ability, as well as location in a business hierarchy. This latter hypothesis derives from Wahrman (1977), who suggests that the higher a person's status in a group the stronger the expectation that that person will conform to group norms. The results of Katz's work indicate that previous conformity is more important than status in determining whether a deviant will be rejected.

Wahrman (1977) also discusses the differences between individual responses to deviance and the sanctions that the group applies, pointing out that group members tend to react to nonconformity by negotiating an interpretation of the meaning of the behaviour. Hence, group applications of sanctions cannot be predicted by examining the reactions of the members in isolation. In fact, his study showed that group discussion is used to demonstrate commitment to the group norms publicly, so that subsequent punishment can be more lenient, and group cohesion and loyalty can be maintained.

1.3 CSCW Systems

In the previous section we have examined some of the folklore surrounding conflict in group interactions, in the light of empirical studies described in the literature. We will now attempt to set the design of some established CSCW systems in the context of that literature. To some extent, we have inferred the attitudes of the designers of these systems towards the significance, development, management and utility of conflict among their systems' users.

The CSCW systems discussed are categorized according to their function (with respect to conflict). It should be noted that the categorization is not claimed to be complete, or the categories to be disjoint – others have adopted different classifications, and even assigned different categories to systems discussed below (for example, see Ellis et al. 1991; Wilson 1991a).

1.3.1 Computer-Mediated Communication Systems

All groupware involves computer-mediation of communication in some form. For the purpose of this review, we regard a system as belonging to the CMC camp if the emphasis of its support for communication rests with:

* The quality and type of information shared, e.g. real-time video, asynchronous text, contextual information

- How collaborators may control those information channels, e.g. issues of privacy, awareness of other collaborators, and selection of audience

- The effects of the medium on the communication, e.g. eye gaze behaviour in a video conferencing system, object reference through an audio communication system, speed of transport and de-individuation

CMC systems as such do not mediate conflict. However, their design can and does influence the occurrence and course of conflict among the collaborators who use them for communication.

The systems discussed are grouped according to the principal medium of communication. It is reasonable to assume that those designers who have chosen the higher bandwidth communication channels have done so in an attempt to improve the quality of the communication, so reducing the likelihood of misunderstandings arising (see Assertion F, p. 22), to support team building, thus reducing conflict by building group cohesion (see Assertion B, p. 15) and reducing anonymity (see Assertion H, p. 24), and possibly to allow users a little more scope in choosing a conflict management strategy when conflict does arise.

1.3.1.1 Textual Communication

The most basic and most widely used medium for computer-supported communication is text. The following discussion illustrates the two main types of textual communication: e-mail and synchronous conferencing. Individual systems differ very little, so there is little point in mentioning more than one or two examples of each type.

E-mail By far the most widely used asynchronous, text-based CMC system is e-mail. As a communication system, e-mail has a number of advantages:

- Message delivery is fast compared to postal mail and even to the telephone, as there is no need for both parties to the exchange to be available simultaneously (Ehrlich 1987)

- Some contextual information is included in the message. The header of the message contains the message's sender, audience, subject, date of creation and possibly a reference to a previous message in an ongoing conversation. All of this helps the recipient of the message better interpret the message's content

- Messages are not ephemeral. Once received, they can be reread, archived or forwarded to other individuals

Unfortunately for its users, e-mail is also a rich source of conflict. Sproull and Kiesler (1991) have reported the de-individuating effects of the electronic isolation of composers of e-mail messages from their audiences, a process that can cause users to "flame" one another, i.e. to over-react to each other's messages, causing a rapid escalation in expressed hostility. This phenomenon is discussed further under Assertions G and H (see pp. 23–26).

Another problem associated with the use of e-mail lies with the ease with which users can "delegate" work to others – the "requesters"/"performers" imbalance (Mackay 1988). The tasks off-loaded are often information requests, where the task of retrieval becomes trivial for the sender of the message, but at the expense of the receiver. Further, the combination of the sense of distance from one's actions and the lack of status cues in e-mail messages means that established organizational norms may be disregarded in this new task management strategy (Sproull and Kiesler 1991). In other words, e-mail may undermine the established roles of individuals within a group or organization, which adds further complications to the notion that clearly defined roles reduce conflict (Assertion E, p. 21).

For an analysis of these problems for a specific e-mail system, see Pliskin (1989), who relates experiences of BITNET mail, and in particular the effects of the medium on group work.

Text conferencing   Text conferencing systems are the synchronous counterparts to e-mail systems – they support the passing of text messages between users and differ from e-mail only in that all users are expected to be simultaneously using the system. Nearly every CSCW system with a shared object and the ability to represent text can be used as a text conferencing system. We will focus on those systems that are specifically intended to support conversations between users, rather than those which users may adapt to that purpose.

McCarthy et. al. (1991) report on a series of experiments to determine the facility with which users of a text-based, synchronous communication system can establish a shared understanding or common ground. They found that common ground was particularly difficult to achieve in pure message passing systems because the medium does not possess some of the characteristics suggested by Clark and Brennan (1991) as necessary for minimum cost grounding, significantly "co-presence", "visibility" and "audibility". Miles et al. (1992) go on to explore some ways in which text-based conferencing could be extended to support at least some aspects of the "co-presence" and "visibility" aspects of face-to-face communication. Other researchers have foregone text as the sole medium for communication, and started experimenting with higher bandwidths.

1.3.1.2 Audio Communication

In the past few years, there has been a quite marked increase in the number of computer systems that make use of audio input/output, and this seems to be particularly true of CSCW systems. While some of this increase can be attributed to the technology becoming cheap and available (i.e. free, in some form, with many types of computer workstations), it is more likely that it represents a general move away from pure text-based communication.

Computer-mediated audio communication is not necessarily a replacement for textual communication: many systems, such as Quilt (Leland et al. 1988), offer both text and audio facilities. Chalfonte et al. (1991) report that collaborators prefer to use voice and text communication for different level issues in their collaboration, voice being preferred for the higher level concerns. Further, messages sent through the audio channel are inherently less "reviewable" than their textual counterparts (Clark and Brennan 1991).

Wang's Digital Voice Exchange (DVX)   Ehrlich (1987) discusses the use of a voice messaging system, DVX, in various organizational contexts. DVX allows users to send messages to one another for subsequent reviewing and processing. Messages contain header information (such as the sender's identity), can be annotated and forwarded by the recipient, and can be sent to groups of people via distribution lists.

Comparing DVX to "pink slip" paper telephone messages, the system it replaced, she finds that DVX messages share many of the advantages of text-based e-mail systems, but with the added benefit of the message medium; since the sender's voice is accurately recorded, all the verbal cues are preserved in the message, helping the recipient better understand the context in which the message was composed.

Audio Windows   Cohen and Ludwig (1991) describe Audio Windows, their prototype audio output/gesture input system. Audio Windows combines digital signal processing with a spatial sound presentation system to control the apparent location of audio sources in the user's environment.

The application of Audio Windows to synchronous computer conferencing is described. Consistent, manipulable spatial positioning of conference participants lets the user subconsciously identify the source of contributions to the conversation, creating a feeling of co-presence through the generation of an "aural image" of the collaborators. This addresses some of the problems of conflicts generated by feelings of physical separation (Assertion H, p. 24).

1.3.1.3 Video Communication

One step further up the ladder of communicative bandwidth lie video communication systems. Although a number of such systems exist, they tend to be restricted to expensive machines with access to high speed local area networks, due to the volume of data which has to be transmitted and processed to maintain a video channel. Like other media, there is a synchronous/asynchronous distinction in video communication, the latter being commonly referred to as video mail. Video mail can be regarded as an extension of voice mail. The systems discussed below support real-time video conferencing.

Rank Xerox EuroPARC   EuroPARC, at Cambridge, UK, has been equipped with a multi-media infrastructure, which allows users to establish audio/visual communication with others throughout the labs, controlled from their workstations. Heath and Luff (1991) report the results of an extended period of naturalistic observation of the system in use. They found that users of the video communication facility act as if they were physically co-present with their co-participants. For example, users were observed attempting to echo the postures of their colleagues, a technique used to indicate likemindedness. Unfortunately, many of the non-verbal cues deployed in face-to-face communication – such as gestures, body movements and gaze behaviour – are apparently not noticed by listeners, disconcerting the speakers and degrading the quality of the communication.

This reinforces the suggestion in Assertion D (p. 19) that effective communication matters more than communication bandwidth. While video mediation does introduce significantly better awareness of the status and disposition of one's partners in a conversation, the increase in communicative power does not seem to be commensurate with the increase in telecommunications bandwidth required over an audio connection.

CRUISER   CRUISER is a computer-mediated audio/visual communication tool in use at Bellcore's New Jersey laboratories (Root 1988). The system interconnects individuals' offices, which are sufficiently physically separate to make it inconvenient for the users to meet with any frequency. CRUISER differs from the majority of other CMC systems in that it is designed for social, rather than task-orientated, interaction. Root emphasizes the importance of group cohesion (Assertion B, p. 15), citing research which attributes the effectiveness of an organization to the quality of the social interactions between its members.

1.3.2 Information Sharing Tools

Information sharing tools are intended to help individuals in groups communicate with one another, and as such can be thought of as CMC systems. However, whereas the emphasis in CMC is on the transport of information, information sharing tools concentrate on the ways in which the meaning of the information can be more effectively communicated, and on the function of each message in the continuing dialogue between users. Hence, such systems have been designed to reduce the amount of misunderstanding caused by differing interpretations of messages, as suggested in Assertion F, p. 22.

Information Lens Information Lens (Malone et al. 1987) works with an asynchronous message passing system, such as e-mail, providing tools to filter messages based on the structural information that has been associated with them. The addition of this structural information serves to clarify each message's content. User controlled selection of messages tackles two additional sources of conflict within e-mail, namely, the effects of sending too much and of sending too little mail to an individual (see Assertion D, p. 19). The former, the lack of selectivity, will overwhelm the recipient, causing resentment; the latter, for important messages, inappropriately places the non-recipient in the outgroup, casting doubt on the sender's motives. Both are addressed by allowing the sender to better express the content of the message and its intended readership, and the receiver to better select which messages to read.

NLS/AUGMENT NLS/AUGMENT (Engelbart 1984), the first implemented hypertext system, has many facets that support collaboration. With respect to the creation of a shared artefact (a shared document, a shared understanding), the AUGMENT Mail system is of particular note. This supports collaborators sending structured documents to one another, in particular documents containing "citations", NLS/AUGMENT's hypertext link facility. Citations refer to globally accessible information (e.g. contributions "published" in NLS/AUGMENT's electronic journals), and the cited material is immediately available from the document being viewed.

Heavy use of the citation facility allows collaborators to situate their communications much more firmly in the context in which they are to be understood, presumably reducing misunderstanding (Assertion F, p. 22).

The Coordinator The Coordinator (Winograd 1988) is an integrated office automation or "workgroup productivity" tool, which clarifies and structures communication through its "conversation manager". This module is based on a speech act model of organizational conversations, with the illocutionary force of each message being made explicit, and constrained by the conversational context of the message.

A number of assumptions about conflict underpin the design of the Coordinator. The assumption pervasive to information sharing tools, that conflict is caused by (interpretative–symbolic) misunderstandings (Assertion F, p. 22), is evident in Flores' belief that a deeper understanding of the commitments involved in conversation enhances people's ability to communicate effectively (Winograd and Flores 1986). Moreover, the language/action perspective assumes that conflict is inevitable (Assertion A, p. 13), and its subsequent treatment of conflict is based on the articulation of conflict aiding its resolution (Assertion S, p. 40), and possibly the belief that conflict itself is productive (Assertion I, p. 26).

However, the theoretical underpinnings of the Coordinator themselves may be the cause of conflict. Dietz and Widdershoven (1991) compare Austin and Searle's speech act theory with Habermas' theory of communicative action. They conclude that the former is seriously flawed because its disregard for the orientation of collaborators makes it impossible for the Coordinator to distinguish between genuine cooperation and that inspired by the desire to avoid sanctions. Cosmos (Bowers and Churcher 1988) is a structured message system based on Habermas' theory. Aside from its claimed more stable theoretical basis, Cosmos's designers treat conflict in the same way as Flores and Winograd.

Amsterdam Conversation Environment (ACE)   ACE (Dykstra and Carasik 1991) is described as a semi-structured application to support group interaction in face-to-face meetings. "Semi-structured" indicates that it is built with the intention of extension and development by its users. Instead of imposing a rigid structure on the conversation, the designers of ACE concentrate on facilitating the construction of new concepts and behaviour.

1.3.3 Concept Development Tools

Concept development tools recognize conflict as a central component of group work, and in particular the development (or design) of concepts. The design process is regarded as "a dialectic between goals and possibilities" (Stefik et al. 1987), with the goals and possibilities mutually inspiring one another as the concept is refined. This is clearly related to Assertion I (p. 26), that substantive conflict can be productive.

It is possible for individuals to apply this technique, but it is most effective when used by groups. In group use, these systems can be thought of as information sharing tools. However, the distinction made here represents the different emphases and attitudes towards conflict.

Cognoter   Cognoter (Stefik et al. 1987), a tool in Xerox PARC's "Colab", is a group outliner, providing support for brainstorming, organizing and ultimately evaluating ideas. Participants do not normally prepare for Cognoter – the purpose of the tool is to help the members of the group air and discuss their ideas in a highly interactive environment. Individual ideas are generated in private workstations, and once complete are posted to a shared "liveboard", where other users may then inspect and develop them. The simultaneity of note generation and the isolation in which the notes are generated free the group members from the effects of "evaluation apprehension" (discussed in Section 1.3.5), and encourage more (conflicting) viewpoints to be expressed (Assertion J, p. 28).

Interestingly, in a later review of Cognoter's user acceptance, Tatar et al. (1991) found that the private generation of notes disconcerted some users and frustrated others. This is the flipside of the effect of Assertion J: although users were being encouraged to compose notes containing conflicting viewpoints, the restriction on the "visibility" of their status and actions (Clark and Brennan 1991) was a source of conflict to the rest of the group. On balance, Tatar et al. decided that the conflict was too disruptive, and designed a new version of Cognoter, called Cnoter, which provided shared, rather than private, editing facilities, and enforced a much more rigid "what you see is what I see" (WYSIWIS) paradigm on the liveboard and individuals' workstation screens.

Issue-Based Information System (IBIS)   The concept of an issue-based information system was developed by Kunz and Rittel (1970) with the purpose of developing a tool to support the coordination and planning of political decision processes. The original model of rhetoric has been widely adapted and used to represent design argumentation (e.g. Conklin and Begeman 1988; Goodlet 1988; MacLean et al. 1989; McCall 1989; Rein and Ellis 1991). All of these tools aim to support groups developing shared designs by providing a gross model of design deliberation to which all contributions to the design must conform. The model imposes structural ("rhetorical") constraints on where and in what manner classes of contributions may be added to the design.

The whole IBIS paradigm is focused on the elicitation of alternative viewpoints ("positions"), a process which is clearly based on the assumption that eliciting conflict is productive (Assertions I and J, pp. 26–29), and that the expression of the conflict in an objective form aids in its resolution (Assertion S, p. 40). In addition, since the shared data object, the design artefact, is a hypertext of semantically labelled nodes and links, additional information is associated with each piece of text in the network. This information can assist in the process of reconstructing the context in which the text was generated (see Assertion F, p. 22).

Distributed NoteCards   Trigg et al. (1986) describe the development of Distributed NoteCards, an extension of the Xerox PARC NoteCards hypertext system, intended to support collaborative development of hypertexts. They focus on the need for collaborators to make themselves "mutually intelligible", concluding that collaborators do this by communicating at two meta-levels, "annotative" and "procedural", over and above their substantive interchange.

It is assumed that collaborators have other communication channels available to them to support their procedural and annotative discussions, since Distributed NoteCards provides none. Even with external communication facilities, it would be difficult to use Distributed NoteCards effectively, because of the problems of establishing common ground, which also applied to text-based CMC systems (see Section 1.3.1).

1.3.4 Group Decision Support Systems

Group decision support systems (GDSSs) support their users in making one or more choices from a set of proposals. The original proposals normally form part of the task specification, and are constructed before the decision making process starts. However, once support is added for the proposals to be augmented during the decision making process, as ideas arise, then the distinction between GDSSs and concept development tools becomes marginal.

Argnoter   Argnoter is one of the components of Xerox PARC's "Colab", intended to support "proposal meetings", where the purpose of the meeting is to select the best proposal from a number of competing, and possibly unexpressed, alternatives. Argnoter (Stefik et al. 1987) directly addresses the major sources of conflict in proposal meetings, namely "owned positions" (personal attachment to a proposal; Assertion R, p. 38), "unstated assumptions" and "unstated criteria" (Assertion F, p. 22).

1.3.5 Computer Supported Meeting Environments

A fairly recent development in CSCW has been the construction of custom-designed meeting rooms, packed with groupware intended to support a range of professional meetings requirements, such as group decision making, brainstorming and so on. As such, computer-supported meeting environments (CSMEs) as a field overlaps (most notably) with group decision support systems and concept development tools. CSMEs are similar to GDSSs and concept development tools since they are designed with the same general attitude to conflict: that if it is there, it should be brought out, represented and discussed (see Assertion S, p. 40).

Arizona GroupSystems   The University of Arizona has developed what is commercially the most popular CSME, the GroupSystems environment (Valacich et al. 1991). The main theoretical foundation for GroupSystems is the concept of process losses and gains. The central aim of the environment's design is to "reduce or eliminate" the process losses, which are caused by dysfunctions of the group interaction.

For the purposes of this review, the most important process losses addressed are (i) "evaluation apprehension", where group members hesitate to contribute, fearing negative comments from other members, and (ii) "incomplete analysis", where group members fail to use available information to challenge assumptions held by other members. Tackling these losses involves encouraging group members to express conflicting views (Assertion J, p. 28).

One other process loss which GroupSystems' designers want to reduce bears mentioning: "socializing", which is described as "dysfunctional non-task related behaviour"! While they concede that some group socializing is necessary, their attitude contrasts sharply with, for example, that of Dykstra and Carasik (1991), the designers of ACE.

Finally, an integral component of GroupSystems is the facilitator, who controls the environment, and, in particular, governs access to the shared workspace. Experience of using GroupSystems (Mantei 1991), however, reveals that the facilitator is not an arbitrator (Assertion U, p. 42), but instead is a perpetual source of conflict! This may be due to problems of leadership (see Assertion Q, p. 33).

Electronic Data Systems' Capture Lab   Mantei (1988) presents the design concepts of Electronic Data Systems' "Capture Lab". A significant feature is the attention paid to ensuring that participants feel that they are in the immediate presence of their counterparts, thus addressing the effects of de-individuation (Assertion H, p. 24).

One type of meeting supported by the Capture Lab has a "designated scribe", an individual positioned between the CSME and the other meeting participants. Mantei observed that the other participants would get frustrated if a large amount of information had to be communicated to the scribe. If each party could express their ideas directly (therefore reducing the amount of interpersonal, direct communication), rather than having to go through a scribe, then the opportunity for conflict would be reduced (Assertion D, p. 19).

As for Arizona's GroupSystems, it is asserted that the group should be organized so as to minimize non-task related conflict, presumably by minimizing non-task related interaction.

CAVECAT   The two CSMEs above are intended for use in specially designed meeting rooms, supporting face-to-face meetings. CAVECAT (Mantei et al. 1991) supports distributed meetings, where participants use desktop video conferencing from their own offices to collaborate. However, CAVECAT's impact on users is similar to that of the synchronous CSMEs. One difference is the perception of co-presence. Since CAVECAT's users were not physically co-present, the reduction of participants' sense of separation became a design issue (cf. Assertion H, p. 24). Unfortunately, use of the system where some of the users shared an office made it difficult to achieve uniform perceptions of co-presence, especially since the quality of the network audio connection was quite poor.

A related issue is the participants' perception of social distance: without physically changing position, a participant could be made to appear remote or overly close, simply by altering the video image size on the monitor. Normal social control mechanisms could not be deployed to re-negotiate the social space, since the perception of distance was not shared between the parties.

1.3.6 Collaborative Writing Tools

One of the most popular application domains for CSCW is the support of collaborative writing (Sharples 1992), presumably since this is an activity relevant to all researchers and designers. In spite of its popularity, none of the systems currently available supports the scope and complexity of collaborative writing, as Wilson (1991b) and Leland et al. (1988) note.

Writing complex, expository documents is a design task, and therefore systems in this section will bear resemblance to the "concept development tools" of Section 1.3.3, though the designers of the latter are more immediately concerned with the elicitation of conflict. The systems here also have similarities to those for "information sharing" (Section 1.3.2).

The emphasis of much of the work in supporting collaborative writing has been on the manipulation and representation of the shared document, rather than on the communicative aspects of the task (Leland et al. 1988), and within the support of communication, conflict appears to have been overlooked.

ShrEdit   ShrEdit, a "shared editor", is the University of Michigan's attempt to provide computer support for simultaneous, multi-user editing of a shared document (CSMIL 1991). Olson and Olson (1991) and Olson et al. (1990) established the theoretical framework for shared editing, combining the results of observational studies with analyses of existing group editors. Focusing on the cognitive aspects of collaborative activities, they concluded that a suitable architecture to support collaboration involves:

- A shared workspace, containing a single information object (e.g. a document)
- No constraint on the size and complexity of the shared object (unlike, say, a whiteboard)
- Easy editing of the shared object (again unlike a whiteboard)
- Both shared and private views of the object
- The ability to construct a variety of useful views of the object

With the exception of the last item, the design of ShrEdit rests upon this architecture.

Note, however, that there is no mention of a mechanism for users to communicate with one another. Hence, ShrEdit has neither a conferencing facility nor the ability to include "meta-level" text, i.e. text which is not intended to form part of the substance of the document. Olson et al. (1990) expect that other channels of communication will be available to the users, and it is clear that users of ShrEdit are intended to rely on communication around, rather than through, the tool.

The design of ShrEdit is not influenced by the desire to recognize, elicit or manage conflict. In face-to-face use, it is expected that the normal social control protocols will deal with these aspects of collaboration. Indeed, ShrEdit has few mechanism to prevent non-productive changes to the text, which may result from ongoing conflict among its users: the designers rely on the pressure of the social presence of the other users to prevent such destructive behaviour.

PREP PREP is a "work in progress" editor (Neuwirth et al. 1990), with the focus on support of the social and cognitive aspects of co-authoring and commenting. In particular, PREP supports the annotation of draft documents, allowing each new commentor to add comments, keeping them distinct from the existing text and comments, while maintaining the relationship between each comment and the fragment of the original document annotated. PREP only supports loosely-coupled collaboration, which in this context means that there is no support for shared or simultaneous editing of the draft document. In fact the only document writing strategy available in PREP is draft passing.

PREP users are given roles when they start to edit a draft document. Currently, they can be either a "co-author" (i.e. with permission to edit the base document), or "commenter" (with only sufficient privilege to annotate the base document). These roles seem scarcely more than a gloss on the access privileges for the base document, but they can be seen as an attempt to address Assertion E (p. 21), that defined roles reduce conflict.

Co-authors of the document may communicate with one another through the plan of the document – which is very much like a special set of annotations on the document content. The purpose of the plan is to allow co-authors to communicate their intentions for specific sections of the document, in the hope that revisions to the text will maintain this purpose, or at least not change it accidentally. Clarifying the purpose of the text may well avoid conflict over subsequent re-interpretations (Assertion F, p. 22).

GroupWriter Malcolm, the designer of GroupWriter, treats support for collaborative writing as document version management (Malcolm 1991). Indeed, from a user perspective, there is scant difference between using GroupWriter in a writing group and using it alone: the changes made by other authors might as well have been made by oneself earlier.

The tool is designed to support asynchronous collaboration. Although it is possible for more than one user to be editing the document at one time, the changes made by each will not be immediately visible to the others. Communication facilities are provided, but only in the form of anchored annotations. As a communications mechanism, these annotations are weak as GroupWriter does not record the name of each annotation's creator: thus it is not possible to reply to a comment, other than by attaching another note to the text.

Malcolm asserts that the lack of group organization facilities in GroupWriter allows writing groups to choose their own organization. However, the lack of such facilities in the tool, by restricting the flow of meta-level information between co-authors, is likely to lead to tensions and misunderstandings in the group, both sources of conflict (Assertion D, p. 19).

GROVE   GROVE (Ellis et al. 1990, 1991) is a real-time group editor for the production of shared outlines. Each user of GROVE has the power to configure their workstation to provide any combination of private, (subgroup) shared, and public views of the outline. Each group (i.e. shared or public) window indicates which of the other group members also have access to that window, so that each user is aware of the form of the other group members' participation.

GROVE also supports a number of locking strategies on the shared document, but the designers' preferred mode is one where GROVE performs no locking whatsoever. This is only possible because of the very sophisticated groupware concurrency mechanism employed, which transforms editing operations before application to the shared document on the basis of a state vector transmitted by the user's GROVE process along with the edit operation, and on a log of operations already applied to the document. This mechanism is necessary, for example, to prevent corruption of the shared document when two users simultaneous attempt to fix a typo by deleting a character – only the first operation is applied, the second being transformed to the null operation.

This anarchic editing mode was chosen to encourage users to develop social protocols to mediate their interactions. The effectiveness of this strategy depends on users communicating their intentions to each other before commencing an edit operation. This communication, of course, need not be verbal. The fact that the incidence of destructive behaviour abated after some use of the system supports a relationship of conflict to the development of the group (Assertion C, p. 16).

Finally, GROVE does not support explicit communication between users, and therefore distributed sessions are supplemented with other communication channels, such as audio over speaker phones. As for text-based CMC, this interferes with deictic communication and hinders the establishment of common ground in the conversation.

Quilt   In contrast to the majority of collaborative writing tools, Quilt focuses on communication, annotation and the social aspects of collaboration (Leland et al. 1988). This has important results:

- Message passing is fully integrated. Messages can be sent by users to named others, on a user's behalf, by the system, when a predicate on the system's representation of the document becomes true, and by the system from the task definition (e.g. when a deadline is approaching). The messages themselves, though sent by e-mail, can be anchored in the text of the document

- Typed annotations are the central elements in the representation of the document. Indeed, the text of the document is merely a set of "base document" annotations, linked to show the flow of the text

- The role of each group member is precisely defined in terms the tool can use. Each user is assigned a role (e.g. "reader", "commenter"), and the document a "collaboration style", which defines, for all action and annotation type pairs, what a user in that role can do

Quilt goes to some length to help users attain a shared understanding of their text: public comments, anchored to an obscure part of the text, can help convey the function of that piece of the text in the document, anchoring and voice format "revision suggestion" annotations help clarify the focus, nature and extent of such a revision, while "major change notification" e-mail messages allow the authors a chance to tell their cohort the significance of the change (see Assertions F and D, pp. 22 and 19).

However, Quilt does not support synchronous working, which the designers consider a deficiency. Without a synchronous mode, it is very likely that the collaborative group will use other means to execute those parts of the task which benefit most from "quick associations from group members" (Olson et al. 1990). It is quite likely that latent conflicts will surface during these face-to-face meetings, to be resolved using social protocols, rather than being expressed and managed through Quilt. Without such coordinating meetings, Quilt is likely to suffer from the pathological consequences of technological mediation and the effects of de-individuation (see Assertions G and H, pp. 23–26).

Aside from its support for annotations, Quilt's other pillar is its sensitivity to "collaboration styles" and the designated role of each user. Assertion E (p. 21) suggests that this is beneficial, but some doubts remain. Groups are not static, and members may re-negotiate their roles. Changing role in Quilt, even only briefly, is necessarily not easy. The inability to contribute is at least likely to cause dissatisfaction (Assertion X, p. 48), and seems to reveal a distrust in promotive interdependence. Secondly, Quilt is neutral to choice of permissions associated with each role in each "collaboration style". It would be possible, therefore, for a role to have so few permitted actions that a group member given that role may cease to participate

(Assertions K and X, pp. 29 and 48), or be denied the opportunity to dissent (running against Assertions I, J and S, pp. 26–29 and 40).

Contexts   Delisle and Schwartz (1987) describe Contexts, an extension of the Neptune hypertext system that can be used for collaborative writing. Contexts extends Neptune by providing private views of the shared hypertext database. Only one user may edit a context at a time, and the effects of the editing are not propagated to the shared document until the user explicitly merges the private context back into the master context. It is possible for contexts to overlap, but this is not recommended as Contexts will only detect that the merge operation cannot proceed automatically, and pass control back to the user to determine how the private and modified master contexts should be combined.

   Since the contexts are completely private, there is no opportunity for subgroups to form, and users are not provided with any information as to the activities and/or progress made by their collaborators. Among other things, these facets of Contexts will undermine group cohesion, leading to more general conflict between group members (Assertion B, p. 15).

   This effect is exacerbated by the lack of support for communication between authors. From the absence of attention to conflict issues, it is easy to conclude that Contexts was developed to explore the technical possibilities of extending Neptune, rather than the interpersonal issues of producing shared hypertexts.

1.3.7 Shared Workspace Systems

The CSCW systems above have all been custom-designed to support collaborating groups of users. There is, however, another approach to providing computer support for group working: the shared workspace. Shared workspace systems commonly multiplex the input and output between a group of users, each with a terminal or workstation, with a single application running somewhere on a common network. For these systems, the wider groupware issues devolve to issues concerning the multiplexing of input – free-for-all, or managed using a suitable "floor control" strategy – and for each user, the presentation of information about the other group members using the system.

SharedX   Garfinkel et al. (1989) introduce a workspace sharing system called SharedX. This is an extension to the X Window System (Scheifler et al. 1990) which allows groups of users to direct input to a shared X client, and view the output from it on their own workstations. As a tool in itself, collaboration is inhibited by the lack of information on the presence and activities of other users.

Timbuktu Timbuktu (Farallon 1988) provides many of the features of SharedX for networks of Macintosh computers. Awareness of presence is slightly improved because Timbuktu provides status indicators in the corner of the screen. Unfortunately, for most Macintosh installations, it is impractical to use Timbuktu for groups of more than two users, as the performance degradation is intrusive.

1.4 Conclusions

This chapter has reviewed a wide range of literature on conflict, relevant to CSCW. We have argued CSCW systems must build on a thorough understanding of collaborative work if they are to provide appropriate support for group work. Collaborative work is rarely conflict-free, due to the nature of social interaction (see Assertion A, p. 13). Hence, examination of conflict is needed to develop an understanding of how collaboration breaks down, and how collaborative workers deal with conflict, in order to continue to work together.

The survey was presented as a series of assertions about conflict, representing common beliefs and assumptions. In many cases the evidence for an assertion is equivocal. Some suffer definitional problems, while some present methodological problems for empirical investigation. Many of the assertions describe individual factors which affect the occurrence and development of conflicts, but which are hard or impossible to isolate in any naturalistic study. If any single conclusion is to be drawn it is that conflict is a complex, pervasive phenomenon.

Such a survey is necessarily ambitious, and we have had to restrict the scope in some ways. For example, we have intentionally restricted ourselves to empirical studies, although we have introduced theoretical work where it offers insight in interpreting the empirical data. Also, because the survey is aimed at a CSCW audience, we have concentrated exclusively on task-focused groups, deliberately ignoring other types of group.

At the beginning of the chapter, we suggested that work from areas such as psychology and the social sciences might not be directly applicable to CSCW, as it might not tackle the questions that concern designers of CSCW systems. Furthermore, although our survey should contribute to a general understanding of the nature of conflict, and hence the nature of collaborative work, it might still seem somewhat peripheral to CSCW systems design. However, we maintain that conflict should be a central concern in CSCW. The last section of the survey demonstrates that existing CSCW systems often make simplistic assumptions about conflict, and in many cases these assumptions can be seen to cause problems in the use of the systems. At the very least, we hope to have persuaded designers of CSCW systems to question their assumptions carefully.

In fact, we believe we have done more than that. The survey has identified a number of important factors that need to be taken into account, many of which require further study in the context of CSCW. For instance, group development and group cohesion are both factors which have been largely ignored in CSCW, but which strongly affect how collaborative activities are organized, and how a group perceives and reacts to conflict. Similarly, factors such as size of the group, pressures of time, culture and cultural mix, gender and personality each play a role to some extent.

The expression and management of conflict is an integral part of group behaviour. If CSCW is to become anything other than an enabling technology, this aspect of group interaction must be recognized and addressed.

Chapter 2

The Social Dynamics of Systems Development: Conflict, Change and Organizational Politics

D.G. Wastell

This chapter is about the system design process. More explicitly, it is about the process of developing computer-based artefacts "supporting" work in human organizations, primarily business organizations. It does not deal specifically with systems for supporting cooperative work; indeed all the case studies and theory that are discussed have been taken from the domain of information systems (IS) research. The querulous reader might wonder about the relevance of IS research to computer supported cooperative work (CSCW). Behind this demurring, I suspect, lurks the question, unresolved in CSCW, of whether CSCW systems are (or ought to be) fundamentally different from traditional systems. If they are, then it is more than likely that their design will evoke new issues and the relevance of conventional knowledge will need to be qualified, perhaps profoundly.

CSCW systems supporting non-routine professional tasks (e.g. collaborative writing) would indeed seem to be qualitatively different from traditional information systems. Other CSCW systems, however, seem less radically different (e.g. procedural automation, work-flow systems). Perhaps systems supporting routine work are not CSCW? Yes they are, I assert; no they are not, you retort. In this chapter I finesse the identity question. Let me simply say that whatever CSCW systems are – whether they are radically new or "old wine in new bottles" – we know relatively little about their design and development in organizational settings. We do, in contrast, know a lot about the development of information systems in organizations. Moreover, the sorts of issues (e.g. user involvement, user resistance) that have been researched in that field would seem to be relevant to the design and implementation of CSCW systems. Indeed they are broadly relevant to any systems work, whether the development of a computer artefact is involved or not (e.g. the new system might be a new set of office procedures or a new organizational design).

2.1 Social Factors in Design: Factor Research

What sort of an activity is system design? Is it the rational—technical process depicted in the textbooks on system development, in which design, the prerogative of the data processing professional, proceeds in a smooth, linear way from definitive specification to implementation? Or is it, as Lyytinen (1988) avers, "a pluralistic, ambiguous, conflict-laden process"? Systems often fail, in the sense that performance falls significantly short of expectations. Some projects, indeed, are not completed at all. Others reach implementation but are rejected as unusable. Others become institutionalized despite their poor quality. Why should it be so difficult to bring systems projects to a successful conclusion? Why are new systems so often met by resistance and rejection? These are key issues in IS research.

The dominant paradigm in IS research is the positivist paradigm, referred to by Markus and Robey (1988) as the factor research model. We know this paradigm rather well in psychology; it dominates many areas of social, cognitive, and occupational psychology, and other subdisciplines. The essence of the factor model is the development of causal models relating independent variables (e.g. user participation) and outcome variables (e.g. user satisfaction). The factor model makes some strong epistemological claims, principally that valid knowledge can be achieved through the use of the objective methods of the natural sciences: careful operationalization of constructs, quantitative measurement by detached investigators, hypothetico-deductive theory-testing logic. We will now look at the factor model at work in IS research.

Although conventional design methodologies (e.g. structured methodologies such as SSADM, Downs et al. 1988) pay scant attention to the social dynamics of development work, design is manifestly a social process, i.e. people do it, and social factors are widely acknowledged to play a role (possibly even a decisive one). Hence prescriptions for "end-user involvement", "top management support" etc. are often offered as therapies for improving the prospects of developing systems that are both internally and externally valid. In the factor research literature, user involvement is a heavily researched issue. Is user involvement "the key to successful implementation", as Olson and Ives (1981) put it? Let us examine some factor research.

As an example of the genre, let us consider Olson and Ives' much-quoted study. In the best positivist manner, Olson and Ives carefully articulate their hypotheses and operationalize their variables. The main hypothesis was, of course, that user involvement predisposes system projects to a greater chance of success. Olson and Ives' study is distinctive for their careful attention to the concept of user involvement; it is a very good example of well-conducted factor research. Participation was measured for each stage in the life cycle (requirements capture, screen design etc.) using a five-point Likert scale ranging from "The DP [data processing] department takes full responsibility for this" to "We [i.e. the users] take full responsibility for this". System satisfaction was measured as the gap between the users' perceived needs for information and the quality of the information delivered by the system. Mailshots were sent to 110 IS managers and 40 companies responded, of whom 23 agreed to participate.

Turning to the results of the study, of the twelve measures of user involvement only one showed a significant correlation with system success. The degree of user involvement in "signing-off" the project correlated 0.33 with system satisfaction! No other variables showed a smidgen of statistical significance.

This result is typical of factor studies on user involvement. Ives and Olson (1984) and Tait and Vessey (1988) have reviewed the factor literature, finding, in general, very low correlations with success and in the bulk of studies, no tangible relationship at all. What may be concluded from this research? That user involvement is not important!? Surely not. Why then the persistent negative findings?

Perhaps methodological defects are the problem. Of course, the methodology of individual studies can be criticized. Many factor studies are less sophisticated than that of Olson and Ives. Often user involvement is tackled very coarsely; different sorts of involvement are often crudely bundled together. But, in many ways, what is most remarkable about the corpus of factor research is not so much its substantive results, but to find the positivist paradigm being used at all! Do factor researchers seriously expect to find simple cause—effect laws relating independent variables (user involvement) to dependent variables (system acceptance)? One is reminded of Dr Johnson's comment about dogs walking on their hind legs. Or more aptly, of the Academy of Lagado in *Gulliver's Travels*.

Factor research is the dominant IS paradigm. Yet such research has produced very little knowledge of palpable benefit to the IS field. "Our attempts to apply modern scientific method to the study of information systems in organizations is not producing the steady flow of results we had expected", observes Boland, the iconoclast, in a restrained turn of phrase (Boland 1989). The correlations obtained in factor studies explain trivially little variance. In terms of real explanation (i.e. why certain outcomes occurred, not just what happened), they are even more otiose. No advice for serious practitioners can derive from studies seeking general laws at this level of abstraction. Moreover, the theories under test are often naive to the point of vacuity; rigour is more than a question of method! Design is a social process, yes. But surely the social dynamics of design are too complex and protean to be reduced to simple cause—effect laws?

2.2 The Dynamics of Design: Process Research

Dissatisfied with the factor model, a number of IS researchers (Hirschheim et al. 1987; Tait and Vessey 1988) have called for more process research, that is, longitudinal qualitative case studies of systems projects. Qualitative field research is hard work and the number of process studies is still regrettably small. The process research of a number of leading IS figures – Newman, Robey, Markus and others – will be discussed below. Although not dealt with here, the reader should also be aware of Kling's seminal case studies and theorizing in this area (see, for example, Kling and Iacono 1984).

In essence, process research differs from the factor paradigm by its incorporation of the historical (diachronic) dimension: systems development is seen as an unfolding flow of events in which one stage leads accountably to the next. Newman and Noble (1990), with reference to the process of user involvement, state that by "observing the interaction between users and designers over time, it is possible to clarify many aspects of user involvement. One can see, for example, how the nature of user involvement differs at each stage of the process, and how what has occurred in the preceding stage affects the next one". Process models are in essence "stories" which fill the interstices between antecedents and outcomes.

What do the process theorists have to say about system development? Again, we will dissect a specimen of the genus, namely Markus's much-quoted study of user resistance at the pseudonymous Golden Triangle Corporation (GTC) (Markus 1983).

Markus divides theories of resistance into two main groups depending on the latent assumptions implied by the theories about the nature of organizations. Modern organizational theorists (Huczynski and Buchanan 1991) typically distinguish two main perspectives on the nature of organizations. The perspective "chosen" will decisively affect one's understanding and evaluation of manifestations of conflict, such as user resistance. In the traditional managerial literature, organizations are portrayed as unitary cooperative structures ("happy families", machines, organisms – choose your metaphor), free from conflict (normatively). Of course, conflicts do arise but these are seen as exceptional, originating from misunderstandings, confusions, personality clashes and personality defects (e.g. bloody-mindedness). The egregious rhetoric of "teams" is the hallmark of this view: "any business must build a true team and weld individual efforts into a common effort. ... Their efforts must all pull in the same direction, without friction" (Drucker 1968).

In contrast to the unitary view, the pluralist (political) view sees conflict (and therefore user resistance) as a natural, even healthy, phenomenon. Many points of view and interests exist in organizations. Different individuals and groups (formal and informal) compete to increase their power and rewards. Conflict reflects the ineluctable collision of selfish interests; the job of managers is to sustain satisfactory compromises that allow different stakeholders to pursue their aspirations within a workable collaborative framework. Conflict can be beneficial: it is certainly functional. A peaceful society of Houyhnhnms may become complacent and inflexible; a degree of conflict keeps groups self-critical and creative. Huczynski and Buchanan

(1991) cite Coser's (1956) observation that "conflict, rather than being disruptive and dissociating, may indeed be a means of balancing and hence maintaining a society as a going concern. A flexible society benefits from conflict because such behaviour, by helping to create and modify norms, assists its continuation under changed conditions".

Thus Markus classifies theories of resistance into those which are consistent with the "harmony" view of organizations ("the rational theory of management") and those which adopt a political, pluralistic perspective. In the former category are those theories which attribute resistance to "factors internal to individuals/groups" (people-centred theories: people resist change, analytical thinkers accept systems etc.) and those which attribute resistance to deficiencies in the technical design of the system (system-centred theories: poor ergonomics, user unfriendliness etc.). Resistance is seen in both cases as a pathological state; user participation (either to "obtain commitment" or to produce a better design) is offered as a remedy by both.

Subscribing to the political theory of organizations leads to a different view of resistance. Put crudely, new systems perturb the political status quo. They are valuable resources ("information is power") and as such become the object of territorial struggles. Those groups/cliques that perceive themselves to be beneficiaries of the new system will welcome it; those that stand to lose will resist. System success is therefore a relative phenomenon. Participation, clearly, cannot be a cure-all; like the system itself, it will inevitably become caught up in the political cut-and-thrust.

The introduction of a new information system at GTC provided Markus with a naturally-occurring quasi-experiment to evaluate the different theories of resistance. GTC had a divisional structure, with separate management accounting systems for each operating division. The new system (the FIS) replaced the divisional systems with a single central corporate database. In terms of winners and losers, the new system clearly benefited corporate managers, giving them direct access to raw operational data. Markus quotes a corporate accountant: "Howard [the corporate controller] felt that the divisions were doing things behind his back, and that he needed a better way of ferreting out how the knaves were doing in the trenches. A large part of the reason for FIS was to provide this information".

While the corporate accountants were "delighted" with FIS, divisional staff apparently hated it and resisted it bitterly over a period of several years: they rubbished its data, said it was useless to them, continued to run their old accounting systems, wrote angry memos, launched a task force with the public aim of eliminating FIS, and so on. Neither the people-centred nor system-centred theories of resistance could adequately explain the chronic problems at GTC; the causes were clearly political in origin. Put simply, the divisional accountants were to lose control over financial data for their divisions; they stood to lose and so resisted.

2.3 Process Studies of User Involvement

In contrast to the factor studies, the view of design that emerges from process studies such as GTC, is, to repeat Lyytinen's excellent phrase, that of a social (not technical) process that is "pluralistic, ambiguous and conflict-laden". User resistance is a manifestation of conflict in systems development. It can take many forms: sabotage, non-use, rubbishing the system, etc. It is tempting to use a disease metaphor when discussing user resistance, to speak of "symptoms of resistance". But this implies a pejorative view of resistance, as an aberrant pathological state. Is it not more realistic to see conflict as endemic to design, as the normal to-be-expected state of affairs? Let us consider again the issue of user involvement.

Newman and Noble (1990) abstract two main classes of process model for user involvement: the learning model and the conflict model. The learning model is consistent with the unitary theory of organizations and represents the conventional (normative) wisdom about user participation, embodied in, speaking very broadly, human relations/sociotechnical theory (Mumford 1983). User involvement works because designers and users learn more about each other's domain; they cooperate to produce a joint resolution to a common problem. The learning model views systems development as "cognitive, bounded and technical", i.e. the rational solving of a well-defined problem. Of course, the learning model (the Houyhnhnm model?) is blind to the existence of conflicting goals and interests.

Perhaps the assumption of harmony is relevant in some situations, but clearly not for all. Markus' study at GTC is one example. Newman and Noble provide another. They describe the vicissitudes of a project to introduce a new admissions system into a North American university, "Middleton" State University (MSU). The new system was designed by an external firm. Initially, participation was negligible; users were "consulted" in the traditional way, i.e. their requirements were "extracted" (an unfortunate, dental-sounding, phrase much used by systems people; "elicited" and "capture" are not much better; "expropriated" would at least be more honest). As the project progressed, users began to play more of a part. They learned more about systems work and about the system being designed. But this did not lead to their welcoming the new system. They opposed it, and their opposition became more and more determined. When the system was finally delivered, it was uncompromisingly rejected, ostensibly on the grounds that it would make work more not less difficult. User involvement did not produce peace, goodwill and a successful system. The conflict grew more hostile, with both sides taking more entrenched, dogmatic positions: users insisted on changes, designers insisted on keeping to their original design. One user commented:

> We were very defensive, because we felt they were trying to have us fit the system and we wanted to have the system fit us. But it really didn't start out in

an adversarial kind of way. We were convinced that they weren't after our best interests and they were convinced we weren't after theirs.

Rapidly, the situation escalated into a "win–lose situation": reasonable attempts at persuasion and negotiation broke down, threats were made ("We resist the change ... we don't want to give", "Look you have no choice ... the old system will be turned off"), until eventually the user manager appealed to senior management, who intervened, forcing the designers to give way.

User involvement is clearly not a panacea, and simple learning models do not adequately handle the complex psycho-social dynamics of systems projects, except perhaps in simple, straightforward situations. Robey (with various coworkers), over a series of articles, has attempted to develop a formal conflict model for user involvement in system development, based on theories of organizational conflict and group dynamics (Robey and Farrow 1982; Robey et al. 1989). Conflict is defined in Robey et al. (1989) as "the interference by one individual or group in the attempts by another individual or group to achieve a goal". Systems projects are particularly prone to conflict because they are complex, often under-resourced and subject to acute time pressure. And we could add, they are frequently prestigious initiatives, often perceived as fundamentally challenging the balance of power (Markus 1983).

Based on earlier field work, Robey et al. (1989) put forward a conflict model relating participation, influence, conflict and conflict resolution, which they subject to empirical evaluation in a real-world study of the introduction of a new information system in an insurance company. The conflict model put to the test is shown in Fig. 2.1. The model shows

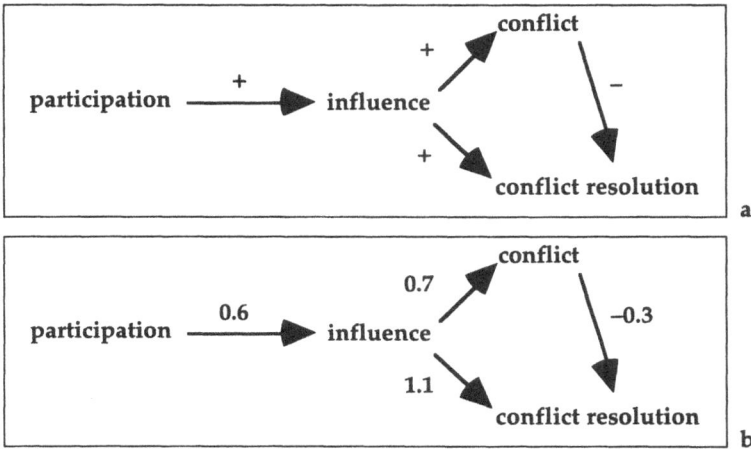

Fig. 2.1. **a** General form of Robey et al.'s (1989) conflict model. Path coefficients derived for a typical meeting (the last of the series) are shown in **b**.

influence (the degree to which individuals perceive themselves to be influential, operationalized through questionnaire items such as "How successful were you in asserting your opinion?") to be the pivotal variable. Greater influence (the model claims) produces more (perceived) conflict. But it also affords more potential for resolving conflict. Interestingly, participation is not directly related to conflict in the model. It is a precondition for influence but influence is the decisive factor.

The field-work for the research was carried out over a two-year period during the attempted introduction of a new system (AINS) for processing automobile policies in an insurance company known by the pseudonym "Northeast". The rigour of the methodology of Robey et al. (1989) is impressive. Their major constructs were carefully operationalized; scales with 3/4 Likert items were developed to measure each construct. Reliability of scales was evaluated. So too was content validity – rather ingeniously, by looking at patterns of group speech. As well as questionnaires, data was collected from interviews, archives, observations of meetings, tape recordings and critical incident files. A narrative account of the project was reported in an influential article by Franz and Robey (1984).

Questionnaire data relating to the conflict model was collected at eight meetings (design group and steering group meetings) over the course of the project; most of these meetings were also tape recorded. Initial meetings apparently focused on requirements and project methodology. Although senior management wished to see the user department lead the project, the data processing (DP) department successfully took the initiative in the early days, insisting on a traditional analyst-led approach, first enhancing the old system before designing the new. After a struggle, users reasserted their control. But the DP people by no means gave up and the story of the project is dominated by this tug-of-war between the users and the DP staff. At one design meeting, for instance, DP attempted to regain the initiative by producing a one-hundred-page manual prescribing a set of standardized procedures for system development. Apparently, the users were unimpressed, disregarding the document completely. Eventually, the users' victory was completed with the total abandonment of the approach favoured by DP (i.e. enhance the old system first).

But trouble lay ahead. Robey et al. comment ominously: "the user department's victory in the struggle for project control left the DP group feeling resentful, and they remained minimally cooperative for the duration of the project". Robey et al. note that at one meeting only two per cent of "speech acts" came from DP people – a sure sign of trouble! Further meetings proceeded, on the surface rather constructively (lots of vigorous discussion, declining conflict, increasing agreement about system requirements), but with the DP group making little active input. At the "sign off" meeting one year into the project, dissension unexpectedly broke out among the users: the claims department, for example, insisted that their requirements had not been understood properly. After a short delay, functional specifications were formally handed over to DP for implementation. After this point, progress on AINS began to be seriously impeded. There were further arguments over the implementation plan, which DP saw as their responsibility. These were eventually resolved. Further problems blew up now that DP had regained some control. A senior programmer changed some screen formats without any consultation; the users appealed against these changes and the programmer resigned shortly afterwards. Other technical staff started to leave. The claims department resurrected some of their previous grouses. The DP manager refused to meet users because "they always wanted to change froze specs". DP staff became demoralized and pessimistic about ever completing the project. Eventually, after a year of implementation, the system was subjected to a complete redesign. There, at the point of failure, the narrative of Robey et al. finishes.

The story of AINS provides another convincing demonstration of the complex socio-political dynamics of information system development (ISD). The primary conflict was between the users and the designers, but other conflicts were manifest too (e.g. the carping from the claims department). But it is more than another case study. A formal, quantitative model of group processes in ISD was under empirical test. How did it fare? What insights were gained?

By and large the conflict model did very well. Questionnaires completed after the eight meetings were analysed using path analysis. For all the meetings analysed, path diagrams confirmed the expected pattern shown in Fig. 2.1. Path coefficients were generally significant throughout and in the right direction: an example is shown in the lower half of the figure. More sophisticated models were tested by the authors (e.g. direct links between participation and conflict) but only the pruned-down model consistently fitted the evidence.

2.4 Design as Social Action: The Issue of Success

While Robey's work gives some insight into the dynamics of system development and is impressive for its methodological rigour, the conflict model by no means provides a general understanding of the nature of the development process. In particular, the relationship between developmental dynamics and outcome (success or failure) is not addressed.

Hirschheim et al. (1987) have proposed a process model of ISD which provides a general model of system development from a social perspective and which deals centrally with the issue of outcome. Hirschheim et al. dub the traditional way of developing systems the *technical perspective*. Development work is seen as fundamentally non-polemical. It proceeds in a smooth, linear progression from requirements to specification, design and implementation (the waterfall model). More sophisticated variants of this basic model acknowledge behavioural consequences and incorporate "human factors" measures, but the general philosophy of design is essentially mechanical–technical, based on an underlying engineering metaphor. In contrast, Hirschheim et al. adumbrate a *social action perspective*. From this viewpoint, system development "consists of interlocked sequences of purposive performances by different actors to achieve meaningful responses from each other. Systems development is a series of episodes, where each episode involves interaction between the analyst and the user. ... The unfolding sequence of social actions ... determine the outcome of any system development project. A project fails or succeeds by the accumulated quality of these episodes".

From the social action perspective, the quality of social interaction is the key to system success, not technological quality. But what does this mean? For Hirschheim et al. (1987), design is seen as a discourse. The quality of this discourse is decisive: mutual understanding leading to consensus is the key to effective design work. Habermas's theory of communication (see Wastell and Cronin 1988) is helpful in tying down this nebulous idea. Habermas distinguishes two categories of discourse: dialogue "oriented to understanding" and strategic dialogue, in which one party attempts to manipulate the other. Successful design depends on the former. Achieving such understanding requires conditions of "ideal speech" (Habermas) which we may understand as "free and fair debate", the free exchange of knowledge and ideas, an openness to critical discussion even of the most fundamental paradigmatic axioms. Distorted communication (strategic communication) reflects a falling away from this ideal. Hirschheim et al. (1987) cite a range of typical manipulative stratagems common in "the discourse of system development": the withholding of pertinent information, spurious claims of expertise, immunizing certain values or policies from criticism, blocking questions by procedural manoeuvres, one side arranging to have better research done to support its argument, appeals to authority to support a point of view. A droll example of strategic communication is the "walk through" (to validate specifications) which becomes the "walk over".

Hirschheim et al. (1987) present a number of examples taken from interviews with analysts and users illustrating defective communication and political manipulation. The authors' rhetorical technique is to present a series of fragments of conversations and to persuade the reader of the power of their analysis by showing their exegetical tools in action. For example, an analyst working on the implementation of a materials management system is quoted as saying:

> They were so difficult to deal with. Their manager really does not understand anything about this sort of thing. He can't see any advantages in it, but his manager can. There is a marvellous conflict trying to get through ...
>   You have got to have a lot of weight to fling about, unfortunately in these cases. You can't just force them on the users. Obviously it has to be done by

agreement but when you run into these problems you have got to be able to rely on somebody to clear the path.

The authors' interpret this as:

> Because of differences in the KNOWLEDGE between the analyst and the user, the latter attaches a different kind of MEANING to the proposed project: the analyst sees its value, the user does not. The difference in knowledge leads to CONFLICT. In response to this, the analyst tries to marshal LEGITIMATE POWER by appealing to higher authority. The basis is SELF-INTEREST. The analyst clearly sees CONSENSUS FORMATION as preferable; only if it fails does he wish "somebody to clear the path". (original capitals)

From further examples of the same stamp, the authors conclude: "the interpretation of this evidence has made it clear that systems success is not primarily a technical issue ... that politics and technical design are inseparable. One might say that system development in practice is politics". Such very strong claims for the social action perspective provide a cogent and challenging antidote to the conventional engineering metaphor of design. Their model of the design process is normative as well as descriptive. The emphasis on communication and consensus is laudable, although, one feels, a little idealistic.

2.5 Models of Change: Punctuated Equilibrium

Human organizations are not static entities: they are open systems, changing through time, adapting, in the conventional wisdom, to changing circumstances or perishing if they fail to respond. Designers might like to see design as a closed system but it is not; circumstances always change, nothing rests in its original state.

How should the flux of human activity be understood? Gersick (1991) poses the question: "how do individuals, groups, organizations evolve over time?" Darwin's theory of evolution (she claims) is our tacit model of change, of incremental, cumulative adaptation. This is the view of change implicit in the learning model of system development; it underpins "new" approaches to design such as prototyping. Indeed, the metaphor is directly expressed when we refer to design, as we commonly do, as an evolutionary process, although how much of the metaphor we intend to apply is arguable (I certainly suspect that random mutation and natural selection are not what prototypers have in mind).

Within biology, Darwinian gradualism is under challenge and a different view of evolution is emerging as "punctuated equilibrium" (Gersick 1991). In this view, lineages do not change slowly but are essentially static; new species arise abruptly, through sudden revolutionary "punctuations" of rapid change. Gersick believes this model of change to be a very general one. In her own work, she applies it to the study of group processes and group development (Gersick 1988, 1989). In a series of field studies of teams engaged on project work, Gersick (1988) consistently observed the following spontaneous triphasic structure, despite wide differences in project substance and time-scales (some projects lasted days, others months). First, groups adopted some distinctive approach which they stayed with through "a period of inertia", that lasted until about half-way through the allotted span of the project. Then a transition occurred: "a concentrated burst of activity [in which] groups dropped old patterns, re-engaged with outside supervisors, adopted new perspectives on their work, and made dramatic progress". This new paradigm carried the groups through a second inertial period before a final burst of activity brought the project to completion. This same pattern of inertial movement and radical change was observed in a subsequent series of laboratory studies (Gersick 1989), which also confirmed the importance of the mid-point as the trigger for change.

How may this phasic pattern be explained? Gersick (1991) introduces the idea of "deep structure" to characterize the equilibrium periods. Deep structure refers to a group's deepest ontological, epistemological and methodological assumptions: its *weltanschauung* or world view. Gersick defines deep structure as the group's "basic organization, chosen goals and activity patterns". While groups (human systems in general) may make minor adjustments to changing circumstances, deep structure has a strong tendency to persist, even if it is no longer effective. There are many reasons why this should be. A paradigm is a hermeneutic schema; it limits what can be seen and interprets the world consistently with its continuing existence. There are also motivational barriers to change: a paradigm provides ontological security, change causes fear and anxiety. Moreover, the paradigm is retained because it does actually work; it provides the means to pursue goals and get things done.

Paradigms persist. But ultimately the writing on the wall is read and a crisis occurs. The arrival of a newcomer (e.g. an outside consultant, a new manager) and the passing of a temporal milestone (the mid-point: "time to move") are two possible triggers described by Gersick. Revolutionary periods are traumatic times (e.g. mid-life crises): "the sheer urgency and discomfort of being without a functioning structure lend intensity to the search for new solutions". The resolution of the crisis is often a sudden moment of illumination; Gersick speaks of the "dawning of insight during transitions", of "things falling into place". "There is a moment that can be directly observed in project groups when a system in transition turns from confusion towards clarity. The system pivots on the insight around which a new deep structure will crystallize".

Is punctuated equilibrium a good way of describing the social dynamics of system development? Does the image of stasis and sudden change more realistically reflect the life cycle of systems development than the conventional metaphor of incremental learning and evolutionary change? Robey and Newman apparently think so. Building on their previous work,

Newman and Robey (1991) propound a view of systems development based on punctuated equilibrium. They depict ISD as "a sequence of events classified as either encounters or episodes". Episodes are periods of stability; encounters are transitional periods which mark the beginning and end of episodes, i.e. where a fundamental restructuring of the status quo takes place.

Newman and Robey are principally concerned with changing patterns of analyst–user relationships during systems projects, continuing the interests of both researchers in the dynamics of user involvement. As a first approximation, they distinguish four types of user–analyst relationship: analyst-led development, user-led development, joint development and equivocation. In term of user involvement, episodes in ISD may thus be classified into one of these categories, depending on the mode of relationship which dominates. The first three social modes reflect equilibrium states "where parties have agreed on project leadership responsibilities". By the principle of behavioural inertia, Newman and Robey expect to see such stable patterns, once established, as tending to persist, reinforcing and recursively reproducing themselves, until some critical event (encounter) occurs, calling the status quo into question. Such encounters provide the occasions for change: "encounters are thus necessary, but not sufficient, events for changing the relationship between analysts and users". The fourth type of episode is equivocation: "equivocation occurs when either party adopts an uncommitted, wait-and-see stance. Equivocation postpones the endorsement of an established relationship. ... During episodes of equivocation, both analysts and users have opportunities to influence the course of events that follow ... [such episodes] are the most susceptible to intervention by interested parties outside of the analyst–user relationship. For example, top management may intervene by supporting users who want to assume project leadership".

In Newman and Robey's theory, ISD is portrayed as a social process, a sequence of episodes (periods where a given social mode prevails) punctuated by encounters, where the social mode is susceptible to change. In this process, the first encounter is of special significance, as the initial social trajectory of the project is determined here. A previously successful user–analyst mode (i.e. a mode that has led to successful project outcomes in the past) is likely to be established if such experience exists. In general, methodological proposals are made during encounters. Such proposals may be accepted, leading to conflict-free episodes where the proposed mode prevails by mutual consent. They may be rejected, ushering in a period of conflict. Or perhaps the response will be delay and hedging, leading to an episode of equivocation. Two further points before considering the evidence: although Newman and Robey are concerned with outcome (i.e. the social mode of the last episode), they are not concerned with success; nor do they claim any predictive power for their model (e.g. of when encounters will occur): their theory is purely descriptive.

What, then, is the evidence that systems development is a saltatory process of aperiodically punctuated equilibrium? Newman and Robey bring forward two case studies to support their theory. The first is Newman's case study of the university admissions systems at MSU which was described briefly in Section 2.3. Newman and Robey distinguish four main episodes demarcated by five encounters. As there was little system experience amongst MSU's users, the claims (in the initial encounter) for a traditional analyst-led approach were accepted with reservations by the users, ushering in an initial episode of equivocation. The signing off of specifications provided a natural opportunity to restructure the project, but control in the end remained with the analysts, and a second period of equivocation ensued in which the first version of the system was built by the analysts with some user involvement. Then the third significant encounter – the turning point of the project – occurred. At hand-over, the users absolutely rejected the system, claiming that it was unworkable. An episode of conflict then ensued, an escalating power struggle brought to head (the final encounter) by the intervention, as we have seen, of the user manager. The outcome of the project was the establishment of a user-dominant pattern (although one wonders how stable this status quo would be: we saw in Robey's study of the Northeast insurance company that the DP department never gave up their struggle for control).

2.6 A Dialectical View of the Design Process

Case studies of real design projects undermine the conventional assumptions of systems development, of clarity, cooperation, consensus, incremental development and so on. Design is revealed not as a smooth, linear process moving from a clear beginning to a clear end (in both senses of end). Instead, a darker view of development work emerges, of a complex process fundamentally characterized by conflict and ambiguity, by contradictions and crises, by flux and transformation. Design, in short, emerges as a dialectic.

At the core of the dialectical *weltanschauung* is the idea of bipolarity, of contradiction, that all phenomena ineluctably produce their opposites. From the dialectical perspective, the study of opposites and contradictions is central to the study of all social activity. All social phenomena (including systems development) involve a balance of contradictions; indeed, this tension lies at the heart of all change. All movement evokes a counter-movement; everything, as it comes into being, "produces" its own negation and is transformed by that negation. This idea has, of course, a long pedigree. Taoism depicts and understands the world as a continuous flux, the interplay of the opposite but complementary principles of Yin and Yang, of a continuous cycle of coming and going, of everything in the process of becoming something else. And of course the idea of the dialectic in western philosophy is associated with Marx, the contradiction between the interests of capital-owners and workers being the primary dynamic of capitalism, providing its laws of motion, as it were.

Marx inherited the idea of the dialectic from Hegel, while rejecting much of Hegel's idealism. What, concretely, is meant by "dialectic"? The master–slave relationship is the example usually cited from Hegel. The following account is adapted from Singer (1980):

> Suppose we have two independent people. Each sees the other as a rival, a limit to his own power. This situation is unstable and a struggle ensues, in which one conquers and enslaves the other. The master–slave relationship is not stable either. Although it seems that the master is everything, the slave nothing, it is the slave who works. By his work, his competence and mastery of the world develops, while the master becomes effete and dependent on the slave. The ultimate outcome must therefore be the liberation of the slave, and the overcoming of the initial conflict.

How well this dialectic of power fits the politics of systems development, especially the user–analyst relationship. Rewriting the master–slave dialectic with analysts in the part of masters and users as slaves results in a perfect description of events at MSU: a period of instability, of analysts taking the whip hand, of users fighting back, gaining skills and eventually wresting control. Here we have the three phases of the Hegelian dialectic: the initial movement (the thesis), the resistance to it (the antithesis), and the transformation of the initial movement and the emergence of the new order (the synthesis).

The idea of the dialectic as the central governing principle of change is the key precept of activity theory, which has been applied, primarily by Scandinavian researchers, to the study of organizational behaviour and development. In some recent papers, its application to systems design has been discussed (Bødker 1990; Kuutti 1990), although this work is currently at a rather speculative stage.

Conflict in systems design is not just political, although antagonistic political interests may constitute the primary dialectic. Within system development, there are many nested contradictions, pairs of dialectical oppositions that shape the large-scale and small-scale detail of its unfolding development. Bødker lists a number of conflicts (contradictions) on different dimensions (e.g. cognitive, economic) and at different levels. Conflicts between the outlook of designers and users is one source of contradictions. Differing views of the role of design techniques can be another source of conflict; Bødker gives the data flow diagram as an example: a tool for specification versus a group communication medium. An important dialectic springs from the contradiction between the designer's idealized view of work, as a specifiable closed system, and the real nature of work, as contingent and ever-changing, as problem-solving not rule-following (Gasser 1986; White and Wastell 1991). The contradiction between design and use is a key one: "the artifacts that we work with are under constant reconstruction, due to conflicts in the way they are applied. ... The future will always shape itself differently from predicted. ... We ought to think of design as redesign, not as a one-shot process" (Bødker 1990).

2.7 The Two Sides of User Involvement

I have argued that systems development is a complex social phenomenon. Conflict and uncertainty are endemic; the search for simple prescriptions, so-called laws, is naive and fatuous. For a final perspective on the design process, I will turn to psychoanalytic theory, which offers a further outlook on the dynamics of systems development as a social process. Two case studies of participative design will be considered as user involvement has emerged as the leitmotif of this chapter. The studies will be presented in greater detail than those described hitherto, as they constitute a significant pair of parables that have not been published before. Both projects involved the development of bibliographic databases at two American universities using participative design. The studies were carried out consecutively and involved the same systems analyst. Yet the outcomes were as different as chalk and cheese.

The descriptions of the two projects are based on recent interviews with the analyst, conducted by myself. The first case study involved the installation of an on-line catalogue for a large research library, at, let us call it, Yang university. A key task was the design of the user interface (screen layouts, dialogue structures etc.). This task clearly required careful attention to user needs, and a participative approach was therefore followed. A design group was convened, consisting of the systems analyst and ten librarians. The group first met in 1983. They continued to meet twice a week, progressing the design through a series of prototypes. It was apparent that the design group, after a hesitant start, worked in a diligent, focused and effective way. The exercise was by no means a primrose path; the design work was arduous and frustrating. However, the librarians recognized that their involvement was crucial. The analyst comments:

> They [the librarians] felt extremely threatened by the development before it started because they felt it would make their jobs much more difficult. What they feared was that they were going to get two groups of questions [from library users], problems related to the card catalogue and problems relating to using the database system and that if they weren't part of the design process front and centre, they would be overwhelmed with user problems
>
> The process took a very, very long time, because ... it was hard for them to understand that they could design a system on their own and it took a while for them to understand they had the power to do it. They weren't designers, their jobs were primarily elsewhere. The biggest problem was that because people weren't used to making decisions, it took a very long time before they would commit themselves. That was the first thing. The second was that the design phase was very attenuated because they didn't think like designers did. Typically

they would say they didn't know what they wanted. The only way you could do it was to mock up a screen and show it to them and they decide from that.

The people themselves were getting very frustrated with lack of development. You get tired of just being in the same room as people and working on a project for so long and working at a snail's pace. You tend to get very very frustrated.

Despite the frustration and aggravations, the design group stuck at its task, and produced a system after two years' work. They manifestly enjoyed the freedom and control that the project gave them and in the end became strongly attached to the system:

Right before the end when all the pieces started coming together you see it coming alive, then, of course, everybody got emotional about it ... they started to cry. They were very attached to it. In fact they became so emotionally attached to it that they asked me to put a record into the user interface so that if you pushed a key the names of all the designers would appear on the screen ... like the way people sign Rolls Royces

There was quite an esprit de corps at the end. There was no moaning about it ... they were really happy about it. And the best thing about it was that the limitations of the system were limitations that they understood. They really understood why the system wasn't doing certain things ... they really knew the lineage of those problems.

The design process itself gave them a chance to think. It gave them a chance to design a system, something they could control. When I look at it now, they had these responsibilities that they didn't have before and the control. Librarians, as you can imagine, are never given responsibility, they have the worst of all possible jobs ... lots of responsibilities and no authority. And this was the first time they were able to play that out. And they really flowered.

The analyst described the second case study as "the underside of participative design". Again, an on-line catalogue was required. This time the catalogue was to computerize an index for a large collection of pieces of art in a history of art department at "Yin" university. The project was sponsored by the then director of the index. The analyst worked for the university computer centre (UCC) and was on secondment to the project. A user group comprising the index's five indexers was formed and met regularly (twice a week). Again, I will let the analyst tell the story:

Instead of my coming in there and doing it myself, I wanted to work with the indexers to sort out how it would work and what the options would be. I thought that that would be the best way of working because I felt that, as at Yang, if everybody worked together, they could feel sort of at one with the system.

What actually happened was ... they didn't really want to sit down and discuss how the system was going to function because they didn't really see it as part of their job. They wanted something given to them but they were never clear about what they wanted and the more I tried to get them involved in it, the more obstreperous, the angrier they became. A lot of people had worked on this index for 30 years. ... Every so often they would say to me, "you're not an art historian, you don't understand". And they said that to me right at the very beginning, and so I thought that the only way to get legitimacy was to say, "Well, fine, I'm not. I'm just a facilitator, you guys are the art historians and I could help you a lot, why not work together to do this?"

It was the absolute opposite of Yang. It took me a long time, about two months, to realize what was going on. I was walking around in a fool's paradise, going to the meetings thinking, "this is great, building up this system, working together ...". After a while I thought I was going to a Japanese funeral, rather than to a meeting. It was very formal. It was terrible.

The sponsor left towards the end of the first year and the original project was abandoned shortly afterwards. Unlike the first study, the users completely failed to respond to the design process. Subsequently, they appeared to accept happily a system imposed on them by the new director:

What happened though was she [the original director of the index] left and they brought in another person and he just came in there and he said, "This is what were going to do. We're closing this file ... this is what the fields are going to be, and this is what we're doing and we're doing it". And he did it on his own and he contracted with the vendor. It took him a couple of years to do but he did it. And they accepted it and they were happy with it. At the time I thought they didn't want a system, but when the new person came and said this is what you're doing, shut up and do it, they did it. That really shocked me. I thought that human nature was such that if you give people a choice, if you allow people to control their work environment, they would leap at that, and that the more professional training they had had, the more independence and autonomy they would want. It never dawned on me that there are people in the world who don't want any autonomy.

2.8 The Psychoanalytic Perspective

The back-to-back case studies provide an intriguing interpretive challenge. In the Yang case, we have the pattern to be expected from champions of participation, of user involvement producing a successful outcome. The Yin case shows the exact opposite: resistance to participation, acceptance of an imposed system. How may these findings be understood? Here we digress into psychoanalytic theory.

The conventional view of human conduct pictures it in purely conscious, logical terms. A quite different view of human nature is presented by psychoanalytic theory, which portrays behaviour and conscious mental life as the surface expression of a complex interplay between unconscious drives and the constraints of social norms. Anxiety, not reason, plays a fundamental role in shaping behavioural dynamics, of individuals and indeed of groups. Menzies-Lyth (1988) writes:

In developing a structure, culture and mode of functioning, an organization is influenced by a number of interacting factors: crucial among these are the primary task, the technologies available for performing the task, the needs of members for social satisfaction and, above all, the task of dealing with anxiety. ... the influence of primary task and technology is often exaggerated.

This is indeed a radical and provocative outlook. In Menzies-Lyth's view, group structures and processes do not, at bottom, reflect rational purposes but are shaped by the "struggle against anxiety", i.e. that many aspects of group organization and group dynamics need to be seen first and foremost as an elaborate system of social defences, erected to contain anxiety. Their apparent rationality is an epiphenomenon, a rationalization. These defences develop over time "as a result of collusive interaction and agreement, often unconscious". Hirschhorn (1988), in a similar vein, interprets many routines and procedures of organizational life as "rituals" set up as defence mechanisms against the anxieties of decision-making, face-to-face contact, and so on.

Hirschhorn (1988) develops a broad analysis of organizational life based on psychoanalytic principles. Menzies-Lyth's concept of the social defence is central to his analysis. By using social defences, people and work groups retreat from roles, responsibilities and tasks and their sense of reality becomes distorted. Hirschhorn makes much use of the concept of the psychological boundary. Boundaries are interfaces which separate the inner, controllable world of the group from the outer world of risks, uncertainty and challenges. The rational view of boundary is that of an objective frontier. Hirschhorn goes further. He argues that when people feel at risk, they set up psychological boundaries to create womb-like areas of security. Set up to contain anxiety, these psychological boundaries often violate "pragmatic boundaries" based on tasks and real exigencies.

Hirschhorn describes several vivid case studies showing the social defences at work. He draws on Bion's psychodynamic studies of work groups (Bion 1961). Faced with some task, groups may respond positively, deploying their energies effectively to carry out the task and remaining "in touch with reality". Alternatively, faced with a difficult situation, they may direct their energies inward, engaging in behaviours which ameliorate the group's anxieties but which inhibit effective action. Bion distinguished several such maladaptive group modes. In the *dependency mode*, group members proclaim individual helplessness in coping with the external situation and seek out a leader who will protect them. In the *fight/flight mode*, the group projects its fears onto an enemy of some kind, deploying its energies in a spurious battle against this persecutory foe, while again withdrawing from the real task. The third mode is the *pairing mode*, a group culture characterized by the Messianic fantasy that a new leader will emerge to solve the group's problems. These defences have in common an anxiety-reducing function; they are maladaptive in the sense that they paralyse the group's ability to work effectively.

Hirschhorn also makes use of the psychoanalytical (Kleinian) idea of the "transitional object". Such objects are important in the development of independence and responsibility in childhood. The child's teddy bear is the textbook example of such an object: it helps the child separate from his mother by serving as a surrogate-mother while the child's self-confidence develops. Hirschhorn argues that transitional objects are important for adults too. Methodologies, change-agents can all function as transitional objects, supporting the individual in times of stress and anxiety, while new competencies develop. Ultimately, the transitional object serves its useful purpose and, like a crutch, may be discarded. In practice, however, blockage often occurs and a dependence on the transitional object develops. Methodology, for instance, becomes a fetish, a procedure used with pathological rigidity, avoiding the risks of real engagement with people and problems. Morgan (1986) uses the transitional object idea to explain resistance to change: "just as a child may rely on his doll or teddy bear, managers and workers may rely on equivalent phenomena [e. g. traditional skills and methods] for their sense of identity ... this explains why there is so much resistance to change in organizations".

2.9 Interpretation of the Case Studies: The Psychodynamics of Design

Systems development is a stressful enterprise; it involves change and uncertainty. Theoreticians of ISD, even those of a psycho-social persuasion (e.g. Robey), surprisingly neglect the role of emotions in systems development work, yet we may expect emotional factors to play an influential, possibly decisive, role. In this section I argue that many of the practices and phenomena of ISD can be revealingly illuminated from a psychoanalytic perspective, in which anxiety, not reason, is the central dynamic principle. Formal design methodologies, for instance, can be seen as social defences to contain the anxiety and risk of design. The desire to simplify by breaking activities down into component parts, at the heart of systems analysis, can be seen as a means of making the complex simple and thereby creating a reassuring (but illusory) sense of control. Let us look at the case studies from a psychoanalytic perspective.

It should first be said that a treatment of systems development from a stress-anxiety perspective can of course be attempted from a non-psychoanalytic standpoint. Occupational stress is a major area of occupational/ organizational psychology and the subject of much empirical research in the positivist tradition. For a review of the area, see Sloan and Cooper (1987). The occupational stress perspective sees stressors (e.g. role change) as aetiological agents which cause negative outcomes (absenteeism, resistance etc.), the basic relationship being moderated by such factors as personality and control. Certainly, systems development involves organizational change and many conventional stress factors can readily be identified: changes to jobs, new responsibilities, loss of status, careers jeopardized. Examples may easily be identified in the case studies. The phenomenon of resistance can be dealt with within this framework. Why are systems resisted? Because people are fearful of the unknown; they resist any change; under stress they become defensive and antagonistic.

The occupational stress perspective is positivist, and, again, we find positivism associated with simple, mechanistic laws. What does this perspective tell us with reference to systems development? That systems development is often stressful, and that these stresses can be diagnosed and quantified. This knowledge might help to predict the likelihood of stress-related illness as a result of systems development (one suspects the correlations would be trivially small), but as far as the internal dynamics of individual projects are concerned, the conventional stress perspective has little to say. Why did the cataloguers at Yin resist the panacea of participation? Why did they accept the imposed system? Let us return to the psychodynamic perspective.

The psychoanalytic perspective provides a much richer interpretive scheme, in which the notions of social defences and transitional objects seem genuinely helpful in understanding events. From this perspective, the contrast between Yin and Yang presents a striking illustration of the different ways in which work groups can respond to challenges. Both the librarians (Yang) and the indexers (Yin) were involved in the design of a new system and it is obvious that in both cases this was a new and stressful experience. Here, the similarity ends. The librarians responded to the challenge, worked effectively together, overcame frustrations and built a successful system. The indexers, on the other hand, turned their energies inwards. They needed a system, but they refused to have anything to do with its design. Their response suggests Bion's fight/flight mode of abnormal functioning: they withdrew from their real task and made the facilitator, who was there to help them, into their persecutor. In terms of psychological boundaries, they drew a tight, protective boundary around themselves. This barrier excluded the analyst and served to insulate the group from a reality they preferred not to face.

Transitional phenomena are also manifest in the two case studies. The rather excessive attachment of the librarians to the system they designed is one suggestive example; interestingly, many of them resigned when "their" system was replaced in a subsequent management reorganization. The devotion of the indexers to their traditional methods is another. Perhaps also the failure of the analyst in the Yin case reflects a reluctance on his part to "let go" of a method used successfully in the past, a failure to search out a different way of working with the second group. For the analyst, the "teddy bear" of participative design was too comforting to relinquish.

2.10 Conclusions

The world view of positivist science, the stance of the factor researcher in IS research, is one of simple unilateral cause–effect laws: user involvement, top management support, and so on – such factors are envisaged as standing in causal relationship to system success. Relationships may be direct or factors may interact; intervening variables and context may also play a modulating role. Nonetheless, a simple, easily graspable view of social reality is offered. Social phenomena (like system development) may be understood in terms of a tractable number of static, mechanical, social laws. The reality of systems design is, however, not an easily graspable reality, not a rectilinear sequence of cause and effect. There is a causal logic, not of simple lines, but of circularity and mutual, reciprocating influences, of movement, resistance, transcendence: a dialectical reality.

The view of systems development presented in most textbooks is a caricature. Design is not a discrete technical activity guided by instrumental rationality, nor is design amenable to investigation by the methods of natural science. Simple prescriptions such as "top management support" or the pious call for user involvement grotesquely over-simplify the difficult and exacting realities of actual systems work. Systems development is a complex, protean, social phenomenon; conflict is endemic, even functional. Careful qualitative research and process theories are required; simple causal models and panaceas should be eschewed. It is fatuous to speak of predicting outcomes, as positivists do, although understanding why things turn out as they do is a practical and worthwhile aspiration.

I have described systems development as protean advisedly. Attempt to grasp it and it changes its character, rather like language: "we murder to dissect". What we may be sure of is that no single account or process theory will do to apprehend "it". Several perspectives have been presented here. These perspectives are, of course, not mutually exclusive; they are simply different places to stand. Different viewpoints bring different features into view, obscure or re-illuminate old ones. What may be said in one language cannot be said in another. The psychodynamic perspective, for instance, brings to bear a rich language and symbolism for interpreting some aspects of the social dynamics of project groups; it does not exclude, but complements, other points of view. Pluralism applies to science too!

What I aimed for in this chapter was not to present a definitive body of knowledge but, to paraphrase Wittgenstein's famous prefatory remarks to the *Philosophical Investigations*, "to travel over a field of thought criss-cross in several directions making a number of sketches in the course of these journeyings". This essay has presented a sample of recent work on the social dynamics of systems development. Some features recur in our journeyings across this field. Flux and reflux, that is one theme, the metaphor of the tide. Mutability, the "whirling wheel of change" another. A world peopled by Yahoos, another image. Circles not lines; the triadic figure of the dialectic, another motif. The field is inchoate. Some of the work I have presented seems crude and makeshift; "merely" descriptive and *post hoc*, so-what-ish. Nonetheless the theories described are among the best on offer in a relatively small and new research field; it is fair to say the theories reflect work-in-progress, not definitive positions. I hope the reader has enjoyed the trip.

Chapter *3*

Cooperation Without Consensus in Scientific Problem Solving: Dynamics of Closure in Open Systems

S.L. Star

This chapter presents a theoretical model for scientific problem solving as a successful example of cooperative work without consensus. The dynamics of the open systems nature of scientific communities are examined, particularly with respect to problems of closure and adaptability. One particular mechanism, that of boundary objects, is examined in detail. These are objects which are held in common across different parts of a scientific community, but which are adapted to customized use. A typology of such objects is presented.

3.1 Introduction

Scientific problem solving is both a good example of routinely successful cooperative work, and a testbed for a number of distributed computer-supported cooperative work (CSCW) systems designed to support such cooperation. This chapter begins with a theoretical examination of scientific communities as open systems, and looks at some of the larger-scale dynamics involved in achieving local closure in open systems. It then moves to a discussion of boundary objects and some implications for CSCW.

3.2 Science, Work and Problem Solving

Scientific theories begin with situations: a charity hospital with a mandate, its desperate clients having seizures on the doorstep; antivivisectionists lobbying for an end to those same doctors' experiments; a war that results in coded messages, and the attempt to decode them, and so on . Theories are responses to the contingencies of these situations – courses of action articulated with yet more courses of action. The theories that scientists form about nature are the actions that both meet specific contingencies and frame future solutions. As George Herbert Mead defined the term "situation", it is an organization of perspectives which "stratifies nature": "These stratifications are not only there in nature but they are the only forms of nature that are there" (1964, p. 315).

A scientific perspective participates in many such forms. For most of us, this is an unfamiliar way to think about nature or perception. Perspectives are not ways to "approach" a nature that is already there; rather, the intersection of perspectives stratifies nature and makes it meaningful. Perspectives in this sense are not limited to human beings, although human beings have some unique reflexive capacities. Nor are perspectives only traditionally "cognitive" events, but rather refer to practice, experience and position. In this sense, a theory is inseparable from a situation – from its origins, practice and consequences. That is, scientific theories are work, not disembodied ideas.

Examining the creation of scientific theories as a form of cooperative work means understanding the ways in which they are made, not born, regardless of how we would evaluate their truth status. That is, people do not unearth facts, but, rather, assemble, array, propose and defend them from their situations. One important aspect of this process for scientists is managing the constant uncertainty and complexity that work-places present (Star 1985; 1989a); another, overlapping, one, is understanding the deep pluralism that is part of scientific work, in the form of different viewpoints, situations, contingencies and lines of work.

Scientific change and stability deeply concern sociologists, historians and philosophers of science. Kuhn (1970) has accounted for scientific change via the action of anomalies as catalysts. According to him, anomalies pile up and form the base for a quantum leap into the next paradigm. Some sociologists of science have recently (amid a great deal of controversy) used the concept of "interests" to explain how scientists come to adhere to one theory or another; and changes in those interests to explain why they switch allegiance. In order to understand how this works, we first need to analyse the collective nature of scientific action.

3.3 Work is Collective: The *Sui Generis* Nature of Organizations

Scientific work is collective in nature. The situations which create scientific theories are not single experiments, laboratories or moments in individual biographies. The stratification of perspectives occurs as a result of numerous interactions and power relationships (see Latour 1987). These collective going concerns have personnel, clients and financial support. They may be well- or ill-organized, old or new, imply a firm mandate for action or none at all (Hughes 1971, pp. 52–64). Thus, to understand truth and scientific theories, we need to understand how collectives work, and how joint action in the course of science is undertaken. To the philosophical sense of truth, then, we add robustness in the organizational sense, and for our purposes they need not be separated. Robust findings are collections of actions which, taken singly, may not hold up as valid or reliable, but which collectively describe or manipulate the world well enough for a number of purposes. The robustness of a finding or approach is not affected by changing single elements; it is composed of interdependent parts. Robust theories in this sense have historical continuity, and enough political allies to guarantee their survival.

This means the cooperative nature of scientific problem solving is not just about a set of elegant formulae which fit together consistently and completely to encompass the world. Rather, robustness is found in clumps of workable imperfect techniques, partial sightings, somewhat successful experiments, and local *ad hoc* alterations to idealized descriptions. The philosopher Arthur F. Bentley gave this kind of robustness the delightful label of "clotted references" (Bentley 1926).

The emphasis here is on the terms "hold up", "collectively" and "well enough" in the preceding paragraphs. Each of these terms is problematic for even a small and relatively cohesive group of investigators. Truth, viewed pragmatically, means shared consequences. Scientific theories cannot be understood completely from any single vantage point – there is a fundamental epistemological democracy that is useful from the point of view of both CSCW and social theory.

3.4 Scientific Theories are Open Systems

The understanding of scientific practice has benefited from fine- grained sociological analysis of the construction of scientific facts, the flow of information and "inscriptions" in the laboratory and in scientific journals (Latour and Woolgar 1979; Law 1987; Lynch 1991; Star 1990). Another rich source of analysis comes from computer science. For several years I collaborated with a group of artificial intelligence researchers – Carl Hewitt and the Message Passing Semantics Group – at Massachusetts Institute of Technology's (MIT) artificial intelligence laboratory, on a project to use problem solving in the scientific community as a source of metaphors for models in artificial intelligence.

Hewitt (1985) has described several characteristics of modern real-world information systems, which he calls "open systems". His analysis of open system characteristics can usefully be applied to the scientific community (Hewitt and DeJong 1984) and to work-places in general (Bowker and Star 1991; Gerson and Star 1986; Hewitt 1985; 1986). Hewitt's use of the term "open systems" stands in contrast to information systems based purely on logic or maths, which assume a closed world, logical consistency and centralized control. By contrast, he argues that real-world information systems are continuously evolving and decentralized. They require negotiation between distributed parts in order to function, and as a result contain arm's length relationships between components. The internal consistency of an open system cannot be assured, due to its very character as open and evolving.

Information comes into an open system asynchronously – one site may find out long before another about a new piece of information. The information in an open system is also heterogeneous, that is, different locales have different knowledge sources, viewpoints and means of accomplishing tasks based on local contingencies. Scientific work-places are open systems in Hewitt's sense of the term, and it is a useful term because it reminds us of the decentralized, evolving nature of information. In the scientific work-place, new information is continually being added to the situation in an asynchronous fashion. That is, there is no central "broadcasting" station giving out information simultaneously to scientists. Rather, information is carried piecemeal from site to site, with lags of days, months or years.

Scientific work is decentralized in this way, as is most routine work in organizations. Thus, there is no guarantee that the same information reaches participants at any time, or that people are working in the same way toward common goals. People's definitions of their situations are fluid and differ sharply by location; the boundaries of a locality are also permeable and fluid. Scientific work is deeply heterogeneous: different viewpoints are constantly being adduced and reconciled. Information from different sources, with different ways of structuring data and different access to data, is continually being added.

3.5 Plasticity and Coherence: The Paradox of Open Systems

Within what may sound like near chaos, scientists manage to produce robust findings: they are able to create smooth-working procedures and descriptions of nature that hold up well enough in various situations. Their ability to do so was what originally fascinated Hewitt about the scientific community. In the absence of a central authority or standardized protocol, how is robustness achieved? The answer in human systems is complex: they create theories which are *both* plastic and coherent, through a *collective* process of action. Herein lie some very useful lessons for CSCW.

Any scientific theory can thus be described in two ways: the set of actions that meets those local contingencies that constantly buffet investigators, or the set of actions that preserves continuity of information in spite of local contingencies. These are the joint problems of plasticity and coherence, both of which are required for theories to be robust. Plasticity here means the ability of the theory to adapt to different local circumstances, to meet the heterogeneity of the local requirements of the system. Coherence means the capacity of the theory to incorporate many local circumstances and still retain a recognizable identity. Scientific truth as actually created is not a point-by- point elegant logical creation. Rather, in the words of Levins (1966): "our truth is the intersection of independent lies". (This is not a lie in the sense of mendacity, but rather, a local (weak) truth.)

Understanding how scientific theories are formed as the intersection of independent lies can be difficult. It is easier to list or name factors that somehow add up to a school of thought or down to a fact. But the dynamics of theories are more than just a hydra-headed list of factors. Rather, there are ways in which actions of various sorts are coordinated in scientific work that are interesting for their dynamics and modelling properties, especially for CSCW. Section 3.6 discusses some of the dynamics of coherence and plasticity in open problem solving systems.

3.6 The Dynamics of Coherence in Open Systems: The Clotting of Ideas and Practice

Successful scientific theories exhibit a certain amount of inertia, an important basis for coherence. Inertia, in physics, is defined by the statement that a "body in motion stays in motion unless acted upon by some outside force". Successful scientific theories reflect commitments to work practices that are not easily changed. This does not occur as the result of some self-propelling quality of ideas, but rather as the consequence of commitments to training programmes, technologies, standards and vocabularies. Such multiple and overlapping "side bets" are difficult to disentangle or dismantle (Becker 1960).

Furthermore, alliances and conflicts between researchers make revision of theories increasingly difficult over time (Strauss 1978). As increasing numbers of researchers develop a theory's ramifications and adopt them in different kinds of work sites, the theory rapidly becomes complexly rooted. Commitments, for example, to a particular size of cage entail further commitments to a certain size of experimental animal; in turn, the animal's rhythms may dictate a conventional time frame for experiments (see Becker 1982, for a discussion of this phenomenon in the art world).

For scientific change to occur, the payoff for abandoning the theory and its entailed conventions must be higher than the payoff for keeping it. There is an asymmetry involved here, since future research payoff is always uncertain, and what one has in the present, while it may not be perfect, is at least known and tried.

This inertia is implicated in the local versus general applicability of results. Anomalies or difficulties are often perceived as more local than the impact of potential results. This means that there is an asymmetry between perceived problems with a potentially high payoff solution and perceived advantages for the solution. A problem in achieving clear results is often seen as local to a laboratory; potential payoff for solution from that same laboratory, however, would be seen as impacting the entire line of work.

Theories do not develop in single sites, but diffusely and often rapidly. This incurs another important open systems dynamic: momentum, a process which contributes to the plasticity of findings. Momentum in this sense stems not from an intrinsic quality of the ideas at stake, but rather from the social organization of work. There may be many reasons for rapid diffuse growth, including the way in which results from multiple sites are reported by scientists. They are often simplified, and reported in a fashion that deletes many of the work contingencies involved in doing the research (Star 1983). That is, when reports of results are made, qualifications and difficulties have often been jettisoned (Latour and Woolgar 1979). Various types of band- wagons are another source of momentum; they may form around popular notions or techniques (Fujimura 1988), funnelling funding in particular directions or transforming problems into popular terms.

The learning curve holds in science as elsewhere. Thus, by the time difficulties and problems with a theory emerge, inertia has already set in and many conventions adopted. There is a honeymoon period in which aspects of a theory or technology may be tried out before flaws in it are taken seriously, but during which equipment and experimental animals are purchased, clinical training proceeds, and results are published.

Hierarchies of credibility (Becker 1967) form rapidly, and good results reported by prominent investigators at the top of one line of work are picked up and used as valid by others in other lines of work. Thus, when Nobel prize-winning physicists want to comment on developments in neurobiology, their word is taken more readily than that of a junior researcher in neurobiology – and the theory endorsed by the physicist gathers momentum across work sites.

Theories do not appear in their entirety in any one site or situation – this is their distributed nature, as discussed above. While some parts of a theory will often be explicitly developed in one site, a full elaboration of it can only be found on an aggregate level. Theories include tacit local knowledge developed differently in scattered sites. They also reflect widespread assumptions about nature: "that's only nature" or "of course, that's just the way the world is put together" (Garfinkel 1967). All these conditions preclude comprehensive description from any one point. Temporal factors are also important for incompleteness. Theories are constantly in motion, often very rapid motion. Thus, simply keeping up with developments as perspectives are forming is impossible. No one has an "overview" because events are happening too rapidly – one can not stop the world to describe it in its entirety. Furthermore, updates are made asynchronously to different parts of the scientific community, reflecting the lack of a centralized "update" mechanism or simultaneous broadcast facility.

Pluralism, in the form of different viewpoints, also makes theories incomplete at any one point. All participants in the development of a theory have different (albeit often only slightly different) versions of what is happening. Recall Levins' definition of robustness as "the intersection of independent lies". The aggregate view that emerges from a perspective cannot be robustly represented by any individual viewpoint, since there is never complete agreement about phenomena.

Reification is another important contributor to open systems dynamics. As results are generated and made robust by multiplying commitments (especially institutional, technological and sentimental), the origins of these abstract results in the process of work are forgotten (see Restivo 1983 for a discussion of this process in the ideologies of "pure" mathematics). The abstractions generated within perspectives are made concrete, and the facts made unproblematic (Dewey 1920). As Mead described in his essay "Scientific method and the individual thinker" (1917): "Their actuality as events is lost in the necessity of their occurrence as expressions of the law".

Wimsatt (1986) discusses another source of reification: the occurrence of what he calls "frozen accidents", unplanned events that happen early in the development of an organism or organization. These events precipitate commitments to ways of working or standard operating procedures that in many cases are awkward or clumsy (Gasser 1986). Like their analogues in embryological development, these events ramify throughout the system, becoming entwined in all its various aspects. Thus, changing or eradicating their effects at points later in the developmental trajectory is nearly impossible, if only because the expense of doing so is so much greater than living with the effects of the frozen accident.

A similar situation is found in the use of computer systems by various firms. Many companies have computer systems that are outdated and unwieldy. If they could institute a new system from scratch, it would be more efficient. The old systems, however, grew up gradually, and many standardized ways of working around them have been built into the company. All of the company's data and the training of its personnel are invested in them. To switch to a new system would involve complete retraining, stopping production and re-entering data. Many of these systems contain multiple "frozen accidents", in the sense that temporary, unofficial "work-arounds" became integral parts of daily work routines (Gasser 1986; see also Kling and Scacchi 1982). It would be too expensive to replace them since every aspect of the company's business is somehow and differently involved in the current system. Although scientists (and the management of the companies Becker describes) well realize that they are living with imperfect, often wrongly reified, results, they cannot afford to change them.

Theories are the end result of many kinds of action, all involving work approaches, strategies, technologies and conventions for investigation. The component parts of a theory become increasingly inseparable as it develops. Again, they become thicker, or "clotted". Events, observations or assumptions not logically or practically associated at the beginning of the theory's development come to be seen by participants as necessarily connected.

These open systems dynamics are the structural backdrop for some of the smaller-scale community problems in scientific problem solving. Let us turn now to a more detailed discussion of problem solving and cooperation.

3.7 The Heterogeneity of Scientific Work

Common myths characterize scientific cooperation as deriving from a consensus imposed by nature. But if we examine the actual work organization of scientific enterprises, we find no such consensus. Scientific work neither loses its internal diversity nor is consequently retarded by lack of consensus. Consensus is not necessary for cooperation or for the successful conduct of work. This fundamental sociological finding holds in science no less than in any other kind of work.

However, scientific actors themselves face numerous problems in trying to ensure integrity of information in the presence of such diversity. One way of describing this process is to say that the actors trying to solve scientific problems come from different communities of practice and establish a mutual *modus operandi*. A university administrator in charge of grants and contracts, for example, answers to a different set of audiences and pursues a different set of tasks, than does an amateur field naturalist collecting specimens for a natural history museum.

When the worlds of these actors intersect a difficulty appears. The creation of new scientific knowledge depends on communication as well as on creating new findings. But because these new objects and methods mean different things in different worlds, actors are faced with the task of reconciling these meanings if they wish to cooperate. This reconciliation requires substantial labour on everyone's part. Scientists and other actors contributing to science translate, negotiate, debate, triangulate and simplify in order to work together.

The sociologists Latour, Callon and Law have described a process in scientific problem solving that is central to this kind of reconciliation (Callon and Law 1982; Law 1987). In order to create scientific authority, entrepreneurs gradually enlist participants (or, as Latour puts it, "allies") from a range of locations, re-interpret their concerns to fit their own programmatic goals, and then establish themselves as gatekeepers (in Law's term, as "obligatory points of passage"). This authority may be either substantive or methodological. Latour and Callon have called this process "interessement", to indicate the translation of the concerns of the non-scientist into those of the scientist.

Yet, a central feature of this situation is that entrepreneurs from more than one community of practice are trying to conduct such translations simultaneously. It is not just a case of *interessement* from non-scientist to scientist. Unless they use coercion, each translator must maintain the integrity of the interests of the other audiences in order to retain them as allies. Yet this must be done in such a way as to increase the centrality and importance of that entrepreneur's work. The *n*-way nature of the *interessement* (or, let us say, the challenge intersecting communities of practice pose to the coherence of translations) cannot be understood from a single viewpoint. Rather, it requires an ecological analysis of the sort intended in Hughes' (1971, p. 62) description of the ecology of institutions:

> In some measure an institution chooses its environment. This is one of the functions of the institution as enterprise. Someone inside the institution acts as an entrepreneur . . . one of the things the enterprising element must do is choose within the possible limits the environment to which the institution will react, that is, in many cases, the sources of its funds, the sources of its clientele (whether they be clients who will buy shoes, education or medicine), and the sources of its personnel of various grades and kinds. This is an ecology of institutions in the original sense of that term.

An advantage of the ecological analysis is that it does not presuppose an epistemological primacy for any one viewpoint: the viewpoint of the amateurs is not inherently better or worse than that of the professionals, for instance. The important questions are always about the *flow* of objects and concepts through the *network* of participating allies and communities of practice. The ecological viewpoint is anti- reductionist in that the unit of analysis is the whole enterprise, not simply the point of view of the university administration or of the professional scientist. It does, however, entail understanding the processes of management across worlds: crafting, diplomacy, the choice of clientele and personnel. This approach thus differs from the Callon–Latour– Law model of translations and interessement in several ways.

First, their model can be seen as a kind of "funnelling" – that is, reframing or mediating the concerns of several actors into a narrower passage point. The story in this case is *necessarily* told from the point of view of one passage point, usually the manager, entrepreneur or scientist. The analysis we propose here still contains a managerial bias, in that the stories of the museum director and sponsor are much more fully fleshed out than those of the amateur collectors or other players. But it is a many-to-many mapping, where several obligatory points of passage are negotiated with several kinds of allies, including manager-to-manager types.

The coherence of sets of translations depends on the extent to which entrepreneurial efforts from multiple worlds can coexist, whatever the nature of the processes that produce them. Translation here is indeterminate. There is an indefinite number of ways entrepreneurs from each cooperating community of practice may make their own work an obligatory point of passage for the whole network of participants. There is, therefore, an indeterminate number of coherent sets of translations. The problem for all the actors in a network, including scientific entrepreneurs, is to (temporarily) reduce their local uncertainty without risking a loss of cooperation from allies. Once the process has established an obligatory point of passage, the job then becomes to defend it against other translations threatening to displace it.

It is normally the case that the objects of scientific inquiry inhabit multiple communities of practice, since all science requires collective work. Varying degrees of coherence obtain both at different stages of the enterprise and from different points of view in the enterprise. However, one thing is clear. Because of the heterogeneous character of scientific work and its requirement for cooperation, the management of this diversity cannot be achieved via a simple pluralism or a *laissez-faire* solution. The fact that the objects *originate in*, and continue to inhabit, different worlds reflects the fundamental tension of science: how can findings which incorporate radically different meanings become coherent?

3.8 Heterogeneous Problem Solving and Boundary Objects

In the face of the heterogeneity produced by local constraints and divergent viewpoints, how do communities of scientists reconcile evidence from different sources? The problem is an old one in social science; indeed one could say it reflects the core problematic of sociology. One major concern of early sociologists such as Robert Park and Georg Simmel was to describe interaction between participants from groups (or "worlds") with very different "definitions of the situation". This concern gave rise to a series of case studies of ethnicities, work groups and subcultures now loosely grouped under the rubric "Chicago school sociology". Hughes, a leader of this group, argued for an ecological approach to understanding the participation of heterogeneous groups within a work-place, neighbourhood or region (Hughes 1971). By this he meant that the different perspectives, or viewpoints, of the participants need to be understood in a *sui generis* fashion, not simply as a compilation of individual instances, and as situated action.

Some findings from my studies of scientists of potential interest to CSCW are that scientists (i) cooperate without having good models of each other's work; (ii) successfully work together while employing different units of analysis, methods of aggregating data, and different abstractions of data; and (iii) cooperate while having different goals, time horizons and audiences to satisfy.

They do so by creating objects which serve much the same function as the "blackboard" in distributed artificial intelligence systems. I call these boundary objects, and they are a major method of solving heterogeneous problems. Boundary objects are objects that are both plastic enough to adapt to the local needs and constraints of the several parties employing them, yet robust enough to maintain a common identity across sites. They are weakly structured in common use, and become strongly structured in individual site use.

Like the blackboard, a boundary object "sits in the middle" of a group of actors with divergent viewpoints. Crucially, however, there are different types of boundary objects depending on the characteristics of the heterogeneous information being joined to create them. The combination of different time horizons produces one kind of boundary object; joining concrete and abstract representations of the same data produces another. Thus, this chapter presents not just one blackboard, but a *system* of blackboards structured according to the dynamic, open systems requirements of the community (including both machines and humans).

3.9 Types of Boundary Objects

In studying scientists, I became fascinated with heterogeneous subgroups within the scientific work-place. The analysis of boundary objects presented here draws on two case studies that incorporated radically different viewpoints in the conduct of work. First, I conducted a study of a community of neurophysiologists at the end of the nineteenth century in the United Kingdom. This group included both clinical and basic researchers, as well as hospital administrators, attendants, experimental animals, journalists and patients (Star 1989a). Second, with my colleague James Griesemer, I conducted a study of a zoological museum from 1900 to 1940 at Berkeley, California (Star and Griesemer 1989). This group included professional biologists, amateur collectors, university administrators, animals, local trappers, farmers and conservationists.

What is interesting about these studies from the point of view of CSCW is that the structure and attributes of the information brought in from the different participants were distributed and heterogeneous, yet were successfully reconciled. Space prohibits a detailed discussion of all the differences in viewpoint, but two salient ones are summarized below:

1. In comparing clinical and basic research evidence, the following differences obtain: clinical research operates with a much shorter time horizon (cure the patient, not find the theoretical generalization) than basic

research; the case is the unit of analysis for clinicians (an instance-based form of explanation), whereas for basic researchers it is analytic generalizations about classes of events. In clinical research, attention is directed toward concrete events such as symptoms, treatments and patient trajectories. Diagnosis draws on medical theory to validate concrete observations of this nature. In basic research, attention is directed toward analytic generalizations such as refinements to other theories and statements about the applicability of an experiment to a larger body of knowledge. Work proceeds from the experimental situation and is directed outwards toward a body of knowledge. Finally, for the clinician, interruptions to work come in the form of complications, which are "side effects" to be dealt with locally and discarded from the body of evidence (they never make their way into publication of the cases). Interruptions to work for the basic researcher come in the form of anomalies that must be accounted for in the body of evidence, either by controlling them or introducing them into the findings.

2. In the world of the natural history museum, one primary source of comparison is between amateur and professional biologists. There are some similar differences as between clinicians and basic researchers. For the amateur collector of specimens, the specimen itself is the unit of analysis – a dead bird or a bone found in a specific location. Collecting, like clinical work, is the art of dealing on an instance-by-instance basis with examples and local contingencies. For the professional biologist, on the other hand, the specimens collected by amateurs form a part of an abstract generalization about ecology, evolution or the distribution of species. The particular bug or beetle is not as important as what it represents. Furthermore, the work organization was highly distributed, ranging from the museum in Berkeley to various collecting expeditions throughout the state of California.

In analysing these types of heterogeneity, I found four types of boundary objects created by the participants. The following is not an exhaustive list by any means. These are only analytic distinctions, in the sense that we are really dealing here with systems of boundary objects that are themselves heterogeneous.

1. *Repositories*. These are ordered "piles" of objects that are indexed in a standardized fashion. Repositories are built to deal with problems of heterogeneity caused by differences in the unit of analysis. An example of a repository is a library or museum. It has the advantage of modularity.

2. *Ideal type or platonic object*. This is an object such as a map or atlas which in fact does not accurately describe the details of any one locality. It is abstracted from all domains, and may be fairly vague. However, it is adaptable to a local site precisely because it is fairly vague; it serves as a means of communicating and cooperating symbolically – a "good enough" road map for all parties. Examples of platonic objects are the early atlases of the brain

which in fact described no brain, which incorporated both clinical and basic data, and which served as a means of communicating across both worlds. Platonic objects arise with differences in degree of abstraction such as those which obtain in the clinical/basic distinction. They result in the deletion of local contingencies from the common object, and have the advantage of adaptability.

3. *Terrain with coincident boundaries.* These are common objects which have the same boundaries but different internal contents. They arise in the presence of different means of aggregating data and when work is distributed over a large- scale geographic area. The result of such an object is that work in each site can be conducted autonomously, but cooperating parties can work on the same area with the same referent. The advantage is the resolution of different goals. An example of coincident boundaries is the creation of the state of California itself as a boundary object for workers at the museum. The maps of California created by the amateur collectors and the conservationists resembled traditional road maps familiar to us all, and emphasized campsites, trails and places to collect. The maps created by the professional biologists, however, shared the same outline of the state (with the same geopolitical boundaries), but were filled in with a highly abstract, ecologically-based series of shaded areas representing "life zones", an ecological concept.

4. *Forms and labels.* These are boundary objects devised as methods of common communication across dispersed work groups. Both in neurophysiology and in biology, work took place at highly distributed sites, conducted by a number of different people. When amateur collectors obtained an animal, they were provided with a standardized form to fill out. Similarly, in the hospital, night attendants were given "fits sheets" on which to record data about patients' symptoms of epileptic fits in a standardized fashion; this information was later transmitted to a larger database compiled by the clinical researchers attempting to create theories of brain and nervous system function. The results of this type of boundary object are standardized indexes and what Latour would call "immutable mobiles" (objects that can be transported over long distances and convey unchanging information). The advantages of such objects are that local uncertainties (for instance, in the collecting of animals or in the observation of epileptic seizures) are deleted. Labels and forms may or may not come to be part of repositories.

3.10 Conclusions

What are the implications for CSCW of understanding the creation of boundary objects by scientists? First, boundary objects provide a "powerful abstraction" of the sort called for by Chandrasekaran (1981) to organize blackboards. They are, to use his terminology, neither committee nor hierarchy. They bypass the problems of combinatorial explosion and also bypass hierarchical delegation and representation. Unlike Turing's universal computer, the creation of boundary objects both respects local contingencies and allows for cross-site translation. Instead of a search for a logical Esperanto, already proved impossible in a distributed open systems context, we should search for an analysis of such objects. Problem solving in the contexts described above produces workable solutions that are not, in Simon's terms, well-structured. Rather, they are ill- structured: they are inconsistent, ambiguous and often "illogical". Yet, they are functional and serve to solve many tough problems in CSCW.

The problems of instantiating descriptions in distributed systems (Pattison et al. 1987) require a device similar to the creation of boundary objects for accounting for shifting constraints and organizational structures. Durfee et al. (1987) suggest a system that relies on cooperation and "plan-based nodes" that arrive at "locally complete" solutions for distributed problem solving. Again, the notion that systems of actors create common objects that inhabit different nodes in different fashions, and are thus locally complete but still common, should be useful here.

Future directions for research on these questions would include:

1. Expanding the taxonomy of boundary objects and refining the conceptions of the types of information used in their construction.

2. Examining the impact of combinations of boundary objects, and beginning to develop a notion of systems of such objects.

3. Examining the problem of "scaling up" or applying an ecological, human–machine analysis to what Gasser et al. (1986) call "multi-grained systems".

Cooperation need not rely on consensus, even for tasks like scientific problem solving. Boundary objects are one means by which such cooperation can be achieved. That is, the construction of such objects is a community phenomenon, requiring at least two sets of actors with different viewpoints. Analysis of the use of such an object at only one point in the system, or apart from its relationship to other nodes, will produce a systematic reductionist bias of the sort described by Wimsatt (1980). Heuristics used in such a fashion will reflect the neglect of the *sui generis* nature of the system. Furthermore, if the ecological unit of analysis recommended here and elsewhere in CSCW is adopted, it should be noted that human designers, users and modifiers of the computer systems involved will make boundary objects out of the information systems at every stage of the information processing trajectory.

Acknowledgements. The analysis of boundary objects in this paper was done jointly with James Griesemer, as reported in Star and Griesemer (1989). His contribution and work is gratefully acknowledged.

Chapter 4

Resolution of Inter-Individual Conflicts: A Mechanism of Learning in Joint Planning

R. Joiner

4.1. Introduction

In this chapter, it is argued that certain ways of resolving certain types of conflicts will lead to learning, and evidence is presented in support of this view. Thus, this chapter views certain types of conflict as productive and argues that they should be supported and promoted in computer-supported collaborative learning (CSCL).

The resolution of inter-individual conflicts has been proposed as an explanation of learning. Piaget in his early writings stressed the importance of peer interaction in cognitive development because it fosters conflict, but it was left to Doise and Mugny (1984) in their theory of sociocognitive conflict to elaborate on his ideas. However, they do not provide a detailed account of the processes involved in the resolution of inter-individual conflicts and this limits the ability of their theory to inform design of CSCL systems.

In this chapter, a model of the dialogue processes involved in the resolution of inter-individual conflicts is proposed as an explanation of cognitive change in joint planning, in an attempt to overcome the limitations of Doise and Mugny's theory. It has several implications for the design of CSCL. It is based on research into discourse understanding. An important idea in this research is focus and this is incorporated in to the model by making an important distinction between the dialogue focus, the task focus and the task representation. From this distinction three types of inter-individual difference are derived: dialogue focus differences, task focus differences, and task representation differences. It is argued that only the resolution of the latter two can lead to cognitive change. Evidence has been found to support the existence of the three inter-individual differences identified in the model, and the claim made about the resolution of task focus difference. The chapter concludes that designing CSCL systems to support the resolution of task focus and task representation differences could promote cognitive change.

4.2 Sociocognitive Conflict

Doise and Mugny claim in their theory of sociocognitive conflict that the resolution of inter-individual conflicts can lead to cognitive change, through the integration of two contradictory viewpoints: "given appropriate conditions the confrontation of these different approaches may result in them being coordinated into a new approach" (Doise 1990, p. 50).

The beneficial effects of sociocognitive conflict, according to Doise and Mugny, are dependent on how the conflict is resolved. Inter-individual conflicts can be resolved either in purely social terms (i.e. when one child complies with the other's point of view) or they can be resolved by the participants integrating their conflicting viewpoints. It is only the latter method of resolution which, Doise and Mugny claim, will lead to cognitive change.

The resolution of inter-individual conflicts is most applicable as an explanation of cognitive change in planning/problem solving tasks. Although a lot of evidence for the theory of sociocognitive conflict comes from work by Perret-Clermont (1980) on conservation of liquid and that of Doise and Mugny (1984) on experiments on the conservation of length, it has recently been argued by Light and Perret-Clermont (1989) that the cognitive change observed in these experiments may not be the result of the resolution of inter-individual conflicts but may be due to the supportive function of the social context. More consistent evidence comes from Glachan and Light, who found that the resolution of conflicts in a problem solving task was positively related to cognitive change (Glachan and Light 1982; Light and Glachan 1985).

A major problem with Doise and Mugny's theory is that it does not provide a model of the process of conflict resolution that could be used to inform the design of CSCL. It is not even clear what a sociocognitive conflict is in the context of joint planning (Blaye 1988). Also, Doise and Mugny suggest that cognitive change occurs when the participants coordinate their different viewpoints, but they do not explain how this process take place. A model of the resolution of inter-individual conflict is proposed in this chapter as a model of cognitive change in joint planning. It attempts to overcome some of the problems in Doise and Mugny's theory, and, because of this, has important implications for the design of CSCL.

4.3 Focus in Discourse

The model proposed in this chapter is based on research into discourse understanding. An important idea in this research is focus. It has been used in models of dialogue to interpret definite noun phrases (Grosz 1977). A focus-based model of the generation of first-use referring expressions has been developed by Appelt and Kornfield (1987). Focus is also a major component in several theories of discourse structure (Grosz and Sidner 1986; Reichman 1984; 1985) and more recently it has been used in models of plan recognition in extended dialogues (Carberry 1988; Litman and Allen 1987; 1990).

An important distinction made in all these models is between global and local focus. Local focus consists of the utterances making up the current topic of conversation. Global focus is the set of related topics to the current focus of attention, which have already been discussed.

Another important distinction is made by Grosz (1977; 1978; 1981). She distinguishes between implicit and explicit focus. Explicit focus is a representation of the items explicitly mentioned in the utterances making up the local focus. Implicit focus is a representation of items associated with items in explicit focus. The items in implicit focus are dependent on the items in explicit focus. If an event is in explicit focus then its subevents are in implicit focus. Likewise, if a physical object is in explicit focus, its subparts will be in implicit focus.

These models make a number of assumptions. Models that have dealt with the relationship between the discourse focus and the task representation always assume, for simplicity's sake, that participants share the same task representation. This assumption is obviously incompatible with a model of the resolution of inter-individual conflicts. Therefore, the model proposed in this chapter is not based on this assumption, but incorporates the idea of focus by making an important distinction, which is discussed in the next section.

Part of the power and usefulness of focus in discourse analysis is due to the assumption that participants always share a common dialogue focus. However, it will be shown later in this chapter that this assumption is not always true and although people believe they have a common focus, they in fact sometimes have different dialogue foci and, again, this difference can lead to inter-individual conflicts.

4.4 Components of the Model

The dialogue model proposed in this chapter is a focus-based model. Section 4.3 reported that focus is an important feature in several theories and models of discourse understanding. To allow for inter-individual conflicts between participants, an important distinction is made in the model between the dialogue focus, the task focus and the task representation.

4.4.1 Dialogue Focus

The *dialogue focus* is defined as the representation of the objects and events explicitly mentioned in the discourse that are relevant to the current topic of conversation. As with previous focus-based models, there is a distinction made between global and local focus. Local focus is a representation of the items that are explicitly mentioned in the current topic of conversation. Global focus is a representation of all the items mentioned in topics related to the current topic of conversation. Also, like previous models, participants assume they have a common focus, but unlike previous models this assumption is not always true. In Section 4.4.5, conflicts that resulted from participants unwittingly having different foci are reported.

4.4.2 Task Focus

The *task focus* is defined as the subset of knowledge relevant to the purpose of the active focus space. It is similar to Grosz' (1977) notion of implicit focus. The difference between Grosz' implicit focus and task focus is that implicit focus, unlike task focus, is assumed to be the same for both participants, whereas the participants' task focus can be different. (i.e. what one person thinks is relevant may not be what another person thinks is relevant).

4.4.3 Task Representation

The *task representation* is the representation of the objects, beliefs and actions the participant has about the task. Unlike previous work on focus, participants can have different task representations. Each item in the task representation is associated with other items. For example the goal "making a cup of tea" is associated with its subgoals "put tea-bag into cup", "pour hot water into cup", "take tea-bag out", "pour milk into cup".

Items in the task representation also have a measure of confidence associated with them. This measure attempts to represent how confident a particular individual feels about an item. A person's confidence in an item is in part determined by the origins of that item. A person will be very confident in an item derived from direct perception but may not feel very confident in an item derived from other items in which she is not very confident. This measure of confidence will vary depending on its consistency with everyday events.

Another property of the task representation is that it is distributed. A distributed representation can allow for the fact that participants may have several different task models. They may have different models representing different aspects of the task, and they may also have several different models of the same aspect of the task. This part of the model is based on Di Sessa's (1986) work on users' understanding of complex devices. A further property essential for representing intra-individual conflicts is that the task representations allows for inconsistencies. Inconsistent beliefs are represented as conflicting beliefs in different task models.

4.5 Inter-Individual Differences

One of the problems with Doise and Mugny's theory is that it is not clear what a sociocognitive conflict is in joint planning. In the model proposed in this chapter inter-individual conflicts are perceived when one participant perceives an inconsistency or contradiction between their dialogue focus and their task focus. They are caused by three types of inter-individual difference: (i) dialogue focus differences, (ii) task focus differences and (iii) task representation differences. These differences are derived from the distinction made in the previous section.

4.5.1 Dialogue Focus Differences

The first type of inter-individual difference derived from the model is *dialogue focus difference*. This difference occurs when participants unknowingly do not have a shared dialogue focus (see Fig. 4.1).

In an earlier model (Joiner 1991) it was assumed these differences did not occur, but recent investigations have found several inter-individual conflicts that were the result of the participants having different dialogue foci. They have also been observed by Grosz (1981), who reports that they

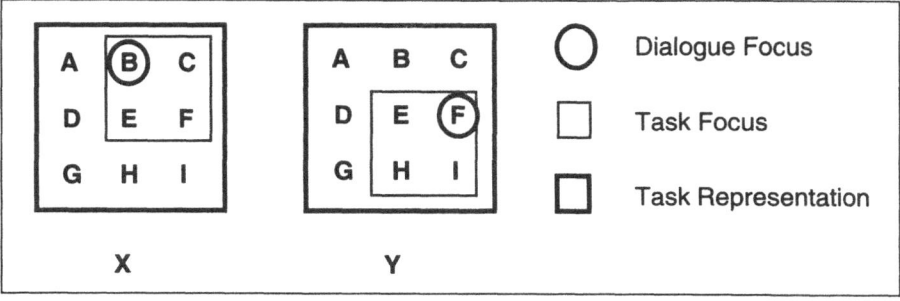

Fig. 4.1. Dialogue focus differences.

often go unnoticed and are difficult to detect by the participants. They are mainly the result of participants using the same term to refer to different things. An amusing example is found in Umberto Eco's *Name of the Rose*. In this example, the main character, Severinus, is talking about truffles:

> a lord in my country knowing I was acquainted with Italy, asked me why, as he had seen down there, some lords went out to pasture their pigs; and I laughed realizing that on the contrary, they were going in search of truffles. But when I told him that these lords hoped to find the "truffle" underground to eat it, he thought I said they were seeking "der teufel", the devil, and he blessed himself devoutly, looking at me in amazement. Then the misunderstanding was cleared up and we both laughed at it. (p. 288)

The resolution of these differences does not lead to cognitive change but to the maintenance of a common dialogue focus, an outcome which makes communication possible.

4.5.2 Task Focus Differences

The second type of inter-individual difference is *task focus difference*, which occurs when both participants have a common dialogue focus and the same task representation but different task foci. In Fig. 4.2, both participants have nine items in their task representation, which are identical. However, they have different items in their task foci.

An example is given below of an inter-individual conflict which is the result of a task focus:

001	X	Let's go to Croydon on the train today
002	Y	We can't, there's a train strike
003	X	Oh yeah

In this example X's proposal brings into Y's task focus the belief that there is a train strike which is inconsistent with X's proposal. Y communicates this to

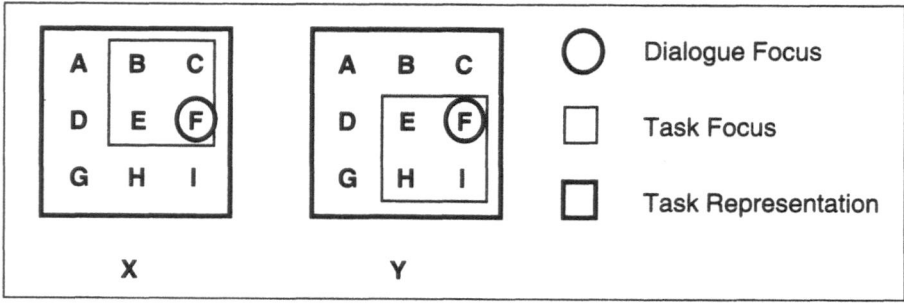

Fig. 4.2. Task focus differences.

X. It brings the same belief into X's task focus, which makes X see the proposal is invalid and therefore accept the challenge. It was a task focus difference because both believed that there was a train strike but Y was the only one to have it in her task focus when X made the proposal.

The resolution of task focus differences, it is claimed, can lead to cognitive change, because of the nature of individual planning. Young and Simon (1987) note that in an unknown and unpredictable world (which is the case when learning a task) it makes little sense to construct a detailed plan before execution. Also, constructing such a plan and imagining future states places a heavy demand on working memory. Therefore, they claim, it makes more sense to make a partial or incomplete plan. Plans can be incomplete in one of two ways: either horizontally incomplete if only a few steps of a multi-step plan are specified, or vertically incomplete if the lower levels of the plan are not specified. In joint planning the participants can construct different parts of the plan and therefore overcome the working memory limitations. The participants' different task foci can also mean that in joint planning harmful interactions between different parts of the plan can be detected before carrying them out, thus cutting down on the time needed to detect the interaction and correct it. Early detection of these types of errors makes learning more effective because it prevents students stumbling along with incorrect solutions, and avoids the extreme frustration that can build up as students struggle to locate the error and repair it (Anderson et al. 1990).

4.5.3 Task Representation Differences

The third type of inter-individual difference is *task representation difference*. In Fig. 4.3 both X and Y have four items in their task focus, but this time X and Y have a different representation of G in their task focus.

An example of a task representation difference is given below. The participants have conflicting beliefs about where Jo was yesterday:

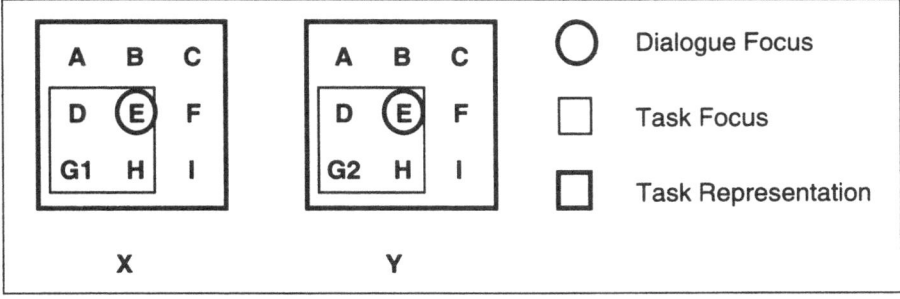

Fig. 4.3. Task representation differences.

```
001   X   I saw Jo in Milton Keynes yesterday
002   Y   She couldn't have: I saw her in Croydon
```

When X says Jo was in Milton Keynes yesterday it brings into Y's task focus her own belief that Jo was in Croydon. Y challenges X by saying that she saw Jo in Croydon. Neither participant believes that the other's view is correct.

There are several different ways in which this type of difference can be resolved positively (i.e. not by compliance). One way is when one participant makes a new proposal which coordinates the mutually opposing views into a framework where both are valid. Another method is by testing the two contradictory beliefs, either by asking someone, testing one of the beliefs in the real world or by finding some relevant information. A further method is if one participant accepts the other person's belief because she sounds more confident. This method can lead to regression (Tudge 1985; 1989).

The resolution of task representation differences, it is argued, can facilitate cognitive change. Below is another example of a task representation difference that illustrates this argument:

```
001   X   Shall we go to Thorpe Park on Sunday?
002   Y   We can't, no trains run on Sunday
003   X   I'm sure they do to Thorpe Park
004       Shall we check the train timetable?
005       ( X and Y look at train timetable)
006       See, no train service on Sunday
```

As the example above shows, the resolution of this type of difference can often lead to participants revising their beliefs about facts in the world. Such revisions are beneficial to subsequent individual planning.

4.6 First Study

A series of experiments was carried out to investigate the model proposed in this chapter. The aim of the first study was to investigate whether the inter-individual differences identified in the model occurred in joint planning (Joiner 1991).

4.6.1 Method

In this study three pairs of children aged between 11 and 12 years were video-taped attempting to solve a planning problem in the form of an adventure game called "The Muksters". The game was specially developed for the study in Hypercard and was set in the imaginary world of "Mukland" (see Fig. 4.4).

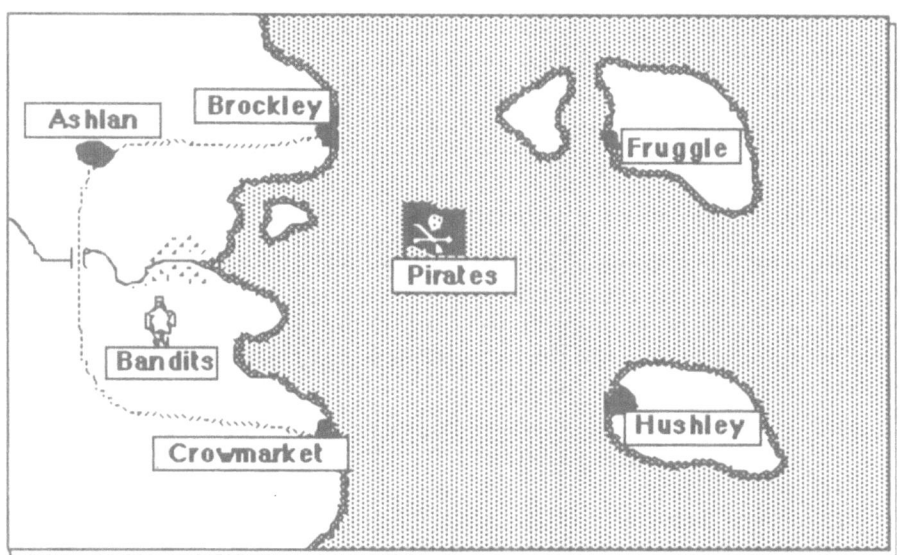

Fig. 4.4. Mukland.

The goal of the task was to help the Muksters return the crown to the king at Ashlan with all his subjects. There were four Muksters (a driver, a captain, a pilot and a guard) and four means of transport (a car, two ships and a plane). At the start of the game the Muksters were all at Ashlan. Each one had a particular role to play in the game. The driver was needed to drive the car, which was at Ashlan. The pilot was needed to fly the plane, which was at Hushley, and the captain was needed to sail the boats, which were at Crowmarket and Brockley. The crown was initially at Fruggle.

The task was made difficult by the presence of the pirates, who would steal the crown if the children tried to take it across the sea in either of the ships. This constraint prevented the children from using the most direct route, which was to go from Ashlan to Brockley in the car with all the Muksters, take one ship from Brockley to Fruggle; pick up the crown and then return to Ashlan the same way. The optimal route was to go to Crowmarket with all the Muksters in the car, take one of the ships to Hushley with the pilot and the captain, then use the plane to go from Hushley to Fruggle with the captain and the pilot, pick up the crown, return to Crowmarket in the plane with the pilot and the captain and finally return to Ashlan with all the Muksters and the crown in the car.

4.6.2 Results

The first 200 utterances of each pair were analysed. In total, 34 inter-individual conflicts were identified in this analysis and 29 of them could be successfully identified by the model proposed in this chapter. Of these conflicts, 19 were identified as task focus differences, 9 as task representation differences and 1 was recognized as a dialogue focus difference. The remaining 6 could not be explained within the model.

4.6.2.1 Task Representation Differences

Below are two examples of task representation differences found in the transcripts. They all reveal different methods of resolving these inter-individual differences. In the first example, the disagreement (in bold) is over how many people the car can take and it is resolved by the children finding some relevant information:

006	A	I say we get information first
		[goes to information]
007	B	mm yep
008	A	its best to
009		get information on the ships
		[B shakes his head]
010	B	they can carry as many people as they want
011	**A**	**Oh, they can have three on the car I think**
012	**B**	**The car can carry the driver and three passengers**
013	**A**	**Shall we check?**
		[checks to see how many people the car can carry]
014	**B**	**Four people together**

In this example A changes the dialogue focus to "car can carry three people" (utterance 011). This change brings into B's task focus the contradictory belief that the car can carry the driver and three passengers. Evidence for this comes from line 012 when B communicates this contradiction to A. They resolve this conflict by searching for some information (utterance 013) about the car and finding out that the car can take four people.

The second example concerns a disagreement over whether the car can take everybody. It is resolved when A tries to see how many people she can fit into the car and finds out she can put everybody in it:

180	A	Right then, everybody on
181	**B**	**We can't fit them all on**
182	A	Oh yes we can
		[attempts to load everybody onto the car, and succeeds]
183		**Right then**

In this example A changes the dialogue focus to "right, everybody on the car". This change brings into B's task focus the contradictory belief that "the car can't take everybody". Evidence for this comes from line 181 when she communicates this belief to A. They resolve this conflict by trying to see how many people they can fit into the car, and finding they can fit everybody.

4.6.2.2 Task Focus Differences

Below is an example of a task focus difference which shows one participant correcting the other child's plan. The disagreement (in bold) is about whether they need to take the guard on the plane when returning with the crown:

060	B	Right then, we need who off the car?
063		the pilot and the captain I think
064	A	the pilot
065	B	and the captain I think
066	**A**	**take the guard with us for the plane**
067	**B**	**no, because no one can attack us up there**
068		**anyway we'll take**
069	A	Oh yeah

In this example A proposes they take the guard on the plane in line 066. The reason for this is to protect the crown from the pirates, although this is never said. B changes her task focus accordingly to reveal her belief that the pirates can't attack them in the plane, and therefore there is no need to take the guard. Evidence for this comes from line 67 when B challenges A's proposal. A changes her task focus to correspond with B's challenge. This change reveals her belief that the pirates can't attack the plane and she therefore accepts A's challenge that there is no need to take the guard on the plane, as evidenced in line 069.

4.6.2.3 Dialogue Focus Differences

This is the only example of a dialogue focus difference found in the transcripts. The children are at the start of the game, trying to decide where to go, when they realize they do not have enough information. The disagreement (in bold) is about whether they should go to Hushley:

024	A	How about getting the driver, the pilot, the guard and the captain on the car and get it to
025		where's
026	B	where's plane?
027		where's ship?
028		shall we check?
029	A	ship1's at Brockley
035		ship2's at Fruggle I think
		[finds out that ship2's at Crowmarket]
036	B	Crowmarket
037	A	Oh

038	B	it's at Crowmarket
039	A	and we can go to Hushley
040	B	o but we went to Brockley last time
041	A	we have to get the boat to Hushley
042		that's where the plane goes
043		and they'll carry the extra passengers
044		that can't go in the plane
045		the plane will carry the pilot and one other person

In this example A changes the dialogue focus to "and we can go to Hushley" in line 039. B perceives the change as a proposal "to go to Crowmarket from Ashlan and then go to Hushley". She changes her task focus accordingly and this reveals the inconsistent belief that they did not go to Crowmarket from Ashlan last time. Evidence for this interpretation comes from her challenge in line 040. However B's perception of the dialogue focus is not what A intended. A was not proposing they should go to Crowmarket from Ashlan and then go to Hushley; instead she was suggesting they could go to Hushley from Crowmarket to pick up the extra passengers who can't come back on the plane when they have picked up the crown. Evidence for this interpretation comes from lines 42–45.

4.6.3 Discussion

The aim of the first study was to investigate whether the three inter-individual differences proposed in the model were present in joint planning, and to a certain degree it was successful. All three inter-individual differences were identified in the experiment. There were twice as many task focus differences found as task representation differences. The probable reason for this finding was that both members of the pair were new to the task, and because they were working together on the task would have had virtually the same experience of it. Thus, there was very little chance of them developing different conceptions of the task. Only one dialogue focus difference was found in this study. Again, this could have been due to the participants' similar experience of the task. In tasks where they have different perspectives, there would be more chance of the participants having dialogue focus differences.

4.7 Second Study

A second study investigated the claims made in the model about the resolution of task focus differences (Joiner, unpublished work). Luchins' (1942) water jugs problem was used in this experiment. This involves emptying jugs and filling them to obtain a desired amount of water.

Task focus differences in this problem corresponded to the participants having different cognitive sets, where a cognitive set is taken to be a strong prior preference for using one particular strategy for solving the problem. Each participant has in effect has focused on one strategy. It is not the case that they are using different strategies because they have conflicting beliefs about which one to use (i.e. a task representation difference), rather it is just that they are not aware of the other participant's strategy.

Different task foci or cognitive sets can be generated in the water jugs problem by giving the participants different training programmes. Luchins showed that giving a child problems that can be solved only by adding the contents of the smaller jugs to the larger one generates in that child a strong preference for using an adding strategy. Alternatively, giving the child problems that are solved by subtracting the contents of the smaller jugs from the larger jugs creates a strong preference in that child to use a subtractive strategy.

4.7.1 Method

In this study children ($n = 56$) aged between 9 and 11 years tackled three different water jugs problems in pairs. The task used was a computerized version of Luchins' water jugs problem. There were three sessions: a training session, an interaction session and a post test. The children were split into two groups, a mixed training group and a same training group. In the mixed training group one member of each pair was trained to use the adding strategy and the other was trained to use the subtractive strategy. In the same training group each member of the pair was trained to use the adding strategy.

The interaction session immediately followed the training session, and the children in this session worked in pairs to solve three problems: one problem that could be solved using the adding strategy and two that could be solved using the subtractive strategy. The post test was immediately after the interaction session and, again, the children had three problems (two subtractive problems and one adding problem) to solve but this time on their own.

4.7.2 Results

In this experiment a task focus difference was assumed to have occurred when one of the pair proposed a subtractive strategy. Those children whose partner proposed a subtractive strategy were put into the task focus group ($n = 24$). Primarily, this was children from the mixed training group. All those children whose partner did not propose a subtractive strategy and who had not been trained to use one were put into the control group ($n = 17$).

To test whether the resolution of task focus differences in joint planning leads to learning, two measures were used. The first measure was to compare the success rate on subtractive problems of children in the task focus group with the success rate of children from the control group. In the task focus group 62.5% solved both subtractive problems compared with only 35% in the control group. The second measure used in this study, and a truer indicator of learning, concerned the use by the children in the post test of the subtractive strategy. Only 35% of children in the control group used the subtractive strategy compared with 87.5% of the children in the non-insight group. This difference is significant.

4.7.3 Summary

In summary, evidence was found which suggested that the resolution of task focus differences in joint planning can lead to learning. The children who resolved the task focus difference, which was engendered in this study, were more likely to succeed on problems they had not been trained on, and were more likely to use a strategy thay had not been trained to use.

4.8 General Discussion

This chapter argues that designing CSCL systems to support the resolution of certain types of conflict could facilitate cognitive change. A dialogue model of the resolution of inter-individual conflicts is proposed as a model of learning in joint planning. A key distinction is made in the model between the dialogue focus, the task focus and the task representation, and it is proposed that inter-individual conflicts are caused by three different types of inter-individual difference: dialogue focus differences, task focus differences and task representation differences. The resolution of dialogue focus differences, it is claimed, leads only to the maintenance of a common dialogue focus, whereas the resolution of the other two inter-individual differences can lead to learning. Evidence reported in this chapter supports the existence of all three inter-individual differences and shows that the resolution of task focus differences can lead to learning.

An important implication of this model is that supporting the perception and resolution of task focus differences and task representation differences in CSCL could promote learning. Using the examples found in the first study, it is possible to see how computers can be designed to support the resolution of task representation differences. In the first example, the conflict was resolved by one participant finding some relevant information confirming one of the children's positions. The important implication from this example is that participants should be able to access all the relevant information. In the second example, one participant resolved the conflict by just trying something out. This method of resolution is ideally suited to the computer because ideas can be tested that may be difficult or impossible to test in the real world. A prime example of this is Sharedark (Smith et al. 1991), which makes it possible to change the laws of physics. The perception of task focus differences could also be promoted in a CSCL system. It is proposed in the model that the task focus contains all the information relevant to the dialogue focus. Therefore, to engender task focus differences it is necessary to manipulate what each participant thinks is relevant. One method would be to give the participants different roles, which would alter what each participant thought was relevant.

The resolution of dialogue focus differences, it is claimed in the model, would lead to the maintenance of a shared dialogue focus. A shared dialogue focus enables effective communication, which is essential for successful joint problem solving. In a recent investigation into CSCW, Tatar et al. (1991) reported that participants using Cognoter had difficulties maintaining a shared dialogue focus. It is therefore important both for CSCL and computer-supported cooperative work (CSCW) that systems that do not lead to dialogue focus differences are developed. It may not be possible to prevent dialogue focus differences completely, but when they do occur systems should be designed to support their early detection and resolution.

Chapter 5

Cooperation and Conflict in Knowledge-Intensive Computer Supported Cooperative Work

C. Hutchison and D. Rosenberg

The aim of this paper is to outline a method of analysis that can be incorporated into the procedures and practices of systems design in the framework of computer supported cooperative work (CSCW) in complex, information-rich environments. Any theoretical background to CSCW must be fundamentally interdisciplinary, drawing input from social psychology, organization theory, anthropology and linguistics, as well as from more computer-orientated disciplines, such as systems theory and design, knowledge engineering and so on. Consequently, it is clearly important to establish the boundaries for CSCW both as a coherent field of study and also as empirically observable human activity amenable to formal characterization. The present study is intended to illustrate what a CSCW-type analysis might look like under the constraint that it is more focused on the social nature of the human activity than, say, systems design; while at the same time being more strongly orientated towards the provision of a computationally-relevant framework than a social science description.

5.1 Introduction

The immediate industrial motivation for this study has been the application of knowledge-based techniques and natural language understanding in advanced manufacturing systems, specifically to support the integrated and collaborative aspects of human activities in manufacturing. The material presented in this paper is largely based on a feasibility study carried out by Rosenberg in the purchasing department of a computer manufacturing organization. The results of the study were also confirmed against selected activities (fault repairs and fault reporting) in other comparable manufacturing organizations.

The main function of the department as a whole is to purchase from outside vendors the peripheral components, such as printers, tape or disc drives, to be integrated with the firm's own "total system" that is sold to customers. One of the major collaborative tasks for the staff of the department involves the selection of peripherals suitable for such integration. The selected peripherals must satisfy a number of distinct constraints, ranging from engineering features such as compatible interfaces between the bought-in peripheral and the firm's own host system, to the financial viability of the vendor organization, particularly if their products are required in large quantities.

The decisions are made collaboratively in the context of a procedure called design review, and are based on a number of criteria that are technical, financial and commercial in nature. They are the result of a complex interplay between the priorities of the manufacturing activity in general (for example, to reduce lead time between receiving a customer order and dispatching the finished product to the customer) and the firm's own policies (for example, strict quality control over all products in order to remain competitive in the market, as well as reducing costs of after sales maintenance). There are also further criteria that reflect the experts' personal experience of working with a particular vendor and a particular product.

The collaboration between human experts in the process of design review amounts to working towards the same goal – that is, successively shortlisting the number of candidate products and vendors – where each expert is a specialist, providing information and advice from her own domain. Thus, for example, experts from the engineering section of the department report to the design review committee on the quality of samples of peripherals under consideration and on their compatibility with the host system from a technical point of view. Financial experts report on the vendor organization, their position on the market and the cost and quality of their product in comparison with the alternatives available on the market. Customer service staff report on the cost of maintenance and repairs of peripherals bought previously, in so far as this information may influence decisions to buy again from a particular vendor.

Maintenance of computer systems at customer sites is one of the areas of departmental activity which relies most heavily on cooperation between experts working in different domains. The activity requires deployment of a number of human experts, including field engineers who carry out repairs in the field, diagnostic engineers who focus on difficult faults that cannot be repaired on site, customer service staff who monitor the cost of maintenance and repairs, and quality control who provide an overview of the activity (for example, in the form of statistical data about field repairs). Feedback from this activity is also required by other departments responsible for the provision of spare parts, the design of new products, and so on.

According to the development team of expert system designers and artificial intelligence (AI) researchers, the most promising application of expert systems in this context seems to involve installing an advisory system to assist human experts in fault diagnosis. Such systems have already been developed and installed in a number of industrial establishments, so that "diagnostic knowledge systems are indeed the most common AI systems in use today" (Rauch-Hindin 1988, p. 292). Their feasibility in the areas of troubleshooting, preventative maintenance or repairs, fault monitoring and other related areas is evidenced by systems currently in industrial use: for example, CATS-1 used at locomotive minor-maintenance repair shops; PDS, which diagnoses faults in steam turbine generators on the basis of sensor data; SPEAR, a remote tape-drive diagnostic system which analyses error logs; ACE, which analyses cable trouble in telephone networks.

These systems incorporate some aspects of the collaborative nature of human activity related to faults and repairs. They do so largely because they have access to and make use of the information from a number of sources that can be seen to represent collaborating agents. In the case of ACE, knowledge engineers developed the system knowledge base using knowledge about cable analysis from the perspectives of theoreticians, operating analysts and developers of automated complaint tracking systems, as well as from textbooks on telephone cable analysis.

Other features that resemble collaboration in the context of fault diagnosis have also been incorporated, for example in SPEAR and ACE. Both utilize the information provided by the error logs, databases on maintenance and repair of the respective equipment they know about, and other "historical" data in order to make the fault diagnosis more accurate and more efficient. This information is also used to predict likely trouble spots and to advise on preventative, as well as corrective, action. In this respect, the system performance combines analytical tasks normally carried out by diagnostic engineers engaged in preventative maintenance with the diagnostic tasks of field engineers who carry out actual repairs.

Therefore, it seems reasonable to suppose that a knowledge base system introduced primarily to aid fault diagnosis could subsequently be expanded even further, to aid other collaborative aspects of the activity in the purchasing department. This may be achieved, for example, by recording information about fault repairs and preparing it for statistical presentation, thus assisting quality control. This information could also be used as the basis for the assessment of maintenance cost relevant to the customer service sector of the activity.

5.2 Cooperation and Conflict in Practice

Thus, from a knowledge engineering point of view, a diagnostic expert system can be developed using knowledge about the structure of computer systems sold to customers, their normal operating behaviour, and types of faults and faulty behaviour, as well as related knowledge provided by error logs and so on. The system would also know how to manipulate knowledge from the multiple sources outlined above in the context of a specific problem solving situation in order to arrive at an optimal solution to the problem. The optimal solution in this sense is based on the factual and operative knowledge an individual expert has of her domain.

However, from an application point of view, individual experts' domain knowledge is often not sufficient to provide an optimal solution. In the context of practical human reasoning, both the individual and the social aspects of experts' behaviour are crucial for adequate modelling of problem solving strategies that may lead to truly optimal solutions. An "optimal solution" in the context of expert systems is most frequently taken to be an optimal *technical* solution, rather than one which takes into account the multiplicity of *personal* goals and interests of individuals in the cooperative work activity.

To give a particular example (one of the rare ones that does not require extensive explanation of technical detail), in the course of repairing a computer printer the most effective individual strategy is for the field engineer (and for the expert system assisting him) to identify the smallest replaceable unit of a faulty computer, replace it with a new one and move on to the next customer site. However, according to the other experts involved in the activity, this is the least effective strategy for the purchasing unit as a whole, since it is the most expensive in terms of staff deployment (field engineers visit more customers and are thus better paid, while real fault diagnosis is carried out by more expensive diagnostic engineers), spares cost more, and so on.

As this example illustrates, the personal goals and interests of individuals may in fact conflict with the assumed common goal and interests of the unit as a collaborative whole. Put differently, in collaborative problem solving the participants do not always move directly and smoothly towards this common goal, but sometimes have to negotiate a compromise solution that takes account of conflicting interests of individual participants involved in the collaboration.

Because human experts have somehow managed to establish a balance between cooperation and conflict in such socially significant situations, the application of an expert system in this organization may affect this balance if the system is not sensitive to this aspect of human expertise. In the best possible scenario, the expert system which advises a field engineer to locate the smallest replaceable unit and replace it with a new one will be ignored if this advice cannot, for whatever reason, be followed in practice. In the worst possible scenario, such a system would serve to aggravate the possible conflict of interests implicit in the situation, so that the department may even be better off without it.

Thus, existing expert systems may indeed be sophisticated and complex, but are still basically stand-alone specialist systems that can only be used in a restricted domain for a specific purpose (for fault diagnosis), and, even more importantly, by a single user-type. Although they use information from various sources, this is done to improve the efficiency of the basic activity, namely diagnosing faults in the equipment the system knows about. This information is not used to integrate fault diagnosis with the rest of the global organization of human activity related to maintenance and repairs of a given type of equipment, which is intrinsically social and collaborative in nature.

In our view of collaboration, based primarily on the study of human activities, expert systems (even the most recent or the most sophisticated ones) have provided only limited support for the integration of human activities in an industrial context such as manufacturing. In this chapter we suggest several reasons why this is the case, as well as discussing possible ways of addressing the issues that arise in this context, focusing on the management and use of expert systems in complex cooperative working environments. On the one hand, it is now a commonplace and uncontentious fact that expert systems, including diagnostic systems, really do play a vital role in industry and by and large perform well the tasks they are designed to perform. On the other hand, we know that people, whether or not it is formally acknowledged in the organizational context in which they work, actually do work collaboratively and cooperatively. Moreover, they do so in highly complex and often unexpected ways. Much of the character of this cooperative and collaborative work may be implicit rather than overtly specified in, for example, specific task assignments or more generally in organizational charts or in employees' conditions of service.

Until now, knowledge base systems design and cooperative working have been two separate issues in separate disciplines. We are now proposing to bring them together in the framework of multi-agent knowledge engineering. Since the way real people work together in real industrial situations should be brought into the equation, we necessarily have to look at issues that have both a technical and a cultural-political dimension. At the same time we recognize that technical solutions will not solve political problems, and that, indeed, they may aggravate them.

We will argue that it may be a misconception of the role of expert systems to perceive them solely as technical tools; that is, to adopt a strictly technological-physicalist rather than a more broadly functional-cultural perspective on the technology. In the context of CSCW, the development and integration of expert systems into the industrial environment may imply a radical shift of perspective on such systems. That shift will be away from the image of the stand-alone, social aid to (or surrogate for) the human expert, operating within clearly specified "knowledge" boundaries, and towards an image of the machine simply as a functional component, albeit an important one, of a broader "open" system that includes not only the user but also the work group[1] of which the user is a part. A maximally effective expert system, in other words, will not necessarily be coincident

Fig. 5.1. Hierarchical representation of the work group, with reductionist model of the expert system as self-contained unit.

with the way we conventionally look at it – as a physically bounded piece of technology that is within the sphere of responsibility and control of some specific individual user who may consider that she has proprietorial rights over the technology and, more importantly, over the information that that technology generates, as caricatured in Fig. 5.1.

We shall be looking at how expert systems may be more successfully integrated into the real-life industrial environment, where ultimately all expert systems operate; the expert "system" will be viewed as a part of a more global system involving not only the direct user of the system but also the other collaborative agents in the organization. Therefore, our analysis will by necessity have to include those aspects of human expert behaviour that make the expert a part of a social structure. The expert systems will effectively no longer be saying "I know everything within my world and my user is the sole owner of that knowledge". Instead, it will, in its design, reflect the organization of the community which shares a body of knowledge required for knowledge-based activities (Fig. 5.2).

5.3 The "Organization" of Organizations

What is an "organization"? We believe that there is no single, straightforward answer; what it is will depend on who is asking and why they are

Fig. 5.2. Heterarchical representation of the work group, with holistic model of the expert system as participant in the group-wide knowledge and information flow.

interested. We shall endeavour an answer, then, that satisfies our own theoretical interests. To make the following argument clearer, we will for the time being informally broaden our notion of what counts as an organization to include not merely commercial and industrial entities, but also such socially cohesive groupings as squash clubs, political parties, school choirs and the local branch of Alcoholics Anonymous. (Huczynski and Buchanan 1991 list other plausible candidates.) One way of characterizing an organization is simply by locating it within a recognizable (super-)class: for example, one way of characterizing a saloon car is to say that it's a type of vehicle; of chess, that it's a board game; of the local branch of Alcoholics Anonymous, that it's a self-help group for compulsive drinkers and their families. This serves to indicate what *kind* of thing it is, but does not get us very far towards understanding what it is about the *nature* of the entity that enables us to locate it within its class in the first place. What, then, are the necessary conditions some complex entity must satisfy for it to be considered an organization? Consider the following definition: "*Organizations* are social arrangements for the controlled performance of collective goals" (Huczynski and Buchanan 1991, p. 7).

So far as it goes, we endorse this definition, and consider each of the constituent phrases of the definition to be crucial. Organizations are collections of people who interact with each other as a group for the purpose of performing tasks that are set and monitored by the organization itself;

moreover, membership of the group is controlled within and by the organization.

We believe, however, that a proper understanding of organizations, and in particular of the impact of knowledge-based systems on the performance of organizations requires a richer and more abstract characterization.[2] We shall hereafter use the term "organization" with a "systematic ambiguity" (to use Chomsky's phrase), to refer not only to concrete commercial entities as characterized in the above definition, but also to the network of abstract dependency relationships between functional parts – what in structuralist discourse is called a "system of differences" (de Saussure 1916) – by virtue of the presence of which that organization is just *that* organization, as a stable and coherent whole. By way of comparison, consider other questions of the same kind: "What is a car?" or "What is a chess set?" For us to judge an object to be a car, there must exist a certain specific and invariable relationship between parts we call wheels, transmission shaft, engine, seats, steering wheel and so on, in such a way as to make its use *as a car* possible. Similarly, for some ensemble of objects to be a chess set it must comprise just the number of pieces of just the right kinds for us to be able to use it in the normal way to play a recognizable game of chess.

The fact that, in an industrial organization, O'Mara is a sales engineer, that Patel is an audit clerk, or that Toby is the tea- boy, or that Toby has green eyes and weighs ten stone, is, from this perspective, irrelevant to the organization, just as, in the case of a chess set, that the pieces are made of wood or onyx is irrelevant for the purpose of playing a game of chess (cf. de Saussure 1916, p. 110), and has nothing to do with our classifying the ensemble as a chess set. Now consider that seven of the pieces are missing; as a chess set the organization has ceased to exist, though one may functionally bring it back into existence by, for example, using buttons or coins in the place of the missing pieces. Consider also that if the ensemble consists of, say, 43 pieces, 17 of which are pawns and 5 of which are splidgets, and that the single Queen can move forward only one square at a time, then whatever that ensemble is, it is not a chess set.

One very crucial fact that distinguishes organizations, as, for example, characterized above by Huczynski and Buchanan, from cars and chess sets is that the former alone have an autonomous internal dynamic that under normal circumstances serves to perpetuate their own existence. Or, to put it another way, it is the existence of the organization that determines the activities undertaken by the organization; while, at the same time, it is the performance of these very activities that determines the continued functioning of the organization. Thus, for example, it is the collective complementary activities of groups of individuals working towards the common purpose of producing and selling goods that defines their collectivity as a manufacturing organization, while the existence of the organization in which they participate defines the nature of the activities that they perform. Moreover, such an organization will quickly cease to exist if it ceases to manufacture; in that sense, an indirect but seminal product of the organization is the organization itself.

If some new element – for example, an expert system – is introduced into the organization, the result of the incorporation of this element is by no means uniquely determined by the inherent properties of the element in itself; rather, by the manner in which that element is assimilated into the organizational context. Specifically, the changes that occur in the organization will principally be those occasioned by the perceptions that the work groups concerned have of the new element in itself, by their interpretations of the proposed relationship that the element will have with existing elements in the working unit – for instance, with other members of the group – and by the actions subsequently taken by those members, either individually or collectively, to accommodate the new element.[3] For example, if we attempt to introduce a fault diagnosis expert system into an organization, our first frame of reference must be the organizational structure, as conventionally understood, which enables us to locate that part of the organization where fault diagnosis is carried out and the people who do it. This information will allow the designer to identify those individuals who will therefore become the experts with whom she begins the knowledge engineering activity and those who are likely to be the direct end users of the system. But from this point onwards the process of accommodation will be shaped by a number of factors, including:

- Assumptions regarding who owns and controls the relevant expert knowledge prior to the introduction of the expert system

- "Folkloric" assumptions with regard to what exactly an expert system is, what it is capable of, and what consequences its introduction will have for the working practices of members of the organization

- The routinized day-to-day activities not only of the individual user herself but also of other members of the immediate work group who are affected in some way by those activities

To understand how this process of accommodation happens, we shall distinguish between the "organization" of an organization and its "structure". Whereas the "organization" is the network of formal dependency relationships that define in the abstract the social grouping as an organization, the structure is the physical actualization of that network. So, for example, if the sales engineer O'Mara leaves and Cohen is recruited to take over his role, the organization does not change, but the structure does. Similarly, if Cohen spends a great deal of time talking to the service staff, while O'Mara did not, the structure changes, though the organization remains the same. We shall provisionally think of the structure, then, as the network of *actual* relationships – paths of communication and affiliation – that members of the work group, as individuals, contract with others in the organization.

But the organization itself also specifies formal paths of communication – who reports to whom, who delegates what to whom, who liaises with whom for what purpose – and these paths are enshrined in, for example, organizational charts. It may very well happen, and is in fact probably the normal state of affairs, that there is at least a partial mismatch between the paths represented in the organizational chart and those which are ongoingly negotiated between actual individuals. Formal relationships of authority and responsibility will still ordinarily be – indeed, must be – observed if the organization is to maintain its internal integrity. However, by virtue of the fact that the organization is constituted of individuals with their own personalities, interests and goals, the actual (and usually unintended) structure that emerges naturally from the dynamics of interpersonal behaviour will be far richer and denser than that formally represented in the organizational chart. By way of illustration, Fig. 5.3 shows a typical organizational chart for a fictitious company; in Fig. 5.4 the chart is augmented to show the actual network of communication between individuals in the specific context involving the maintenance of computer systems.[4]

Let us, then, say that the basic organizational chart envisions the *overt* structure of the organization; the augmented chart traces the *covert* structure. A down-to-earth example of the difference between overt and covert structure in a different domain might illustrate the point: in an American

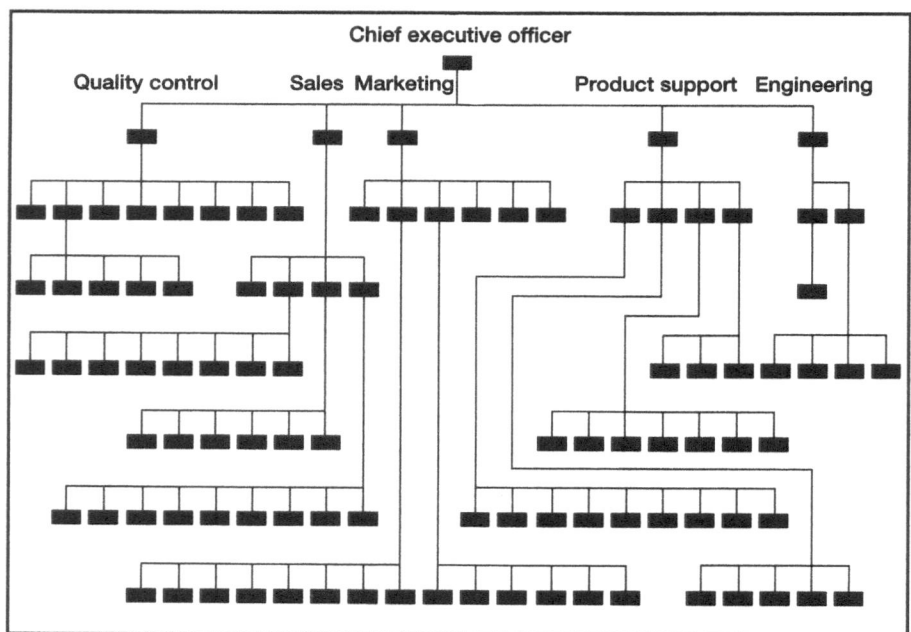

Fig. 5.3. Formal organization chart.

study of sentencing drunks (Spradley 1970), judges were found to be using the following rule in passing sentence: "Drunks who admit they have a drinking problem and desire professional help should be sentenced to the treatment centre rather than gaol". This is clearly a prescription at the level of overt structure. A concurrent study of the cultural knowledge of the drunks themselves, on the other hand, showed them to be using different rules from that of the judge: "In order to do easy time, convince the judge you have a drink problem and want professional help". The reasoning of the drunks evidences a covert structure of the situation. The social perspectives and goals of the judge and the drunk, while quite different, converge, with the same real-world result: the drunk is sentenced to the treatment centre rather than prison, to the satisfaction of both parties involved.

However, to talk about overt and covert structure rather oversimplifies what we mean by "structure". In many respects, we view the structure of the organization as similar to, but not fully congruent with, what other writers (e.g. Flood and Jackson 1991; Hellriegel et al. 1989; Kilmann et al. 1985) have called the company "culture". The "culture" of an organization is most easily thought of as the complex fabric of shared beliefs, values, behavioural norms, expectations, sometimes even company- specific jargon for naming jobs, processes and products, the socialized sense and cognitive style of "who we are" and "how we do things". It will very often happen that, whether from an historical perspective it has been consciously

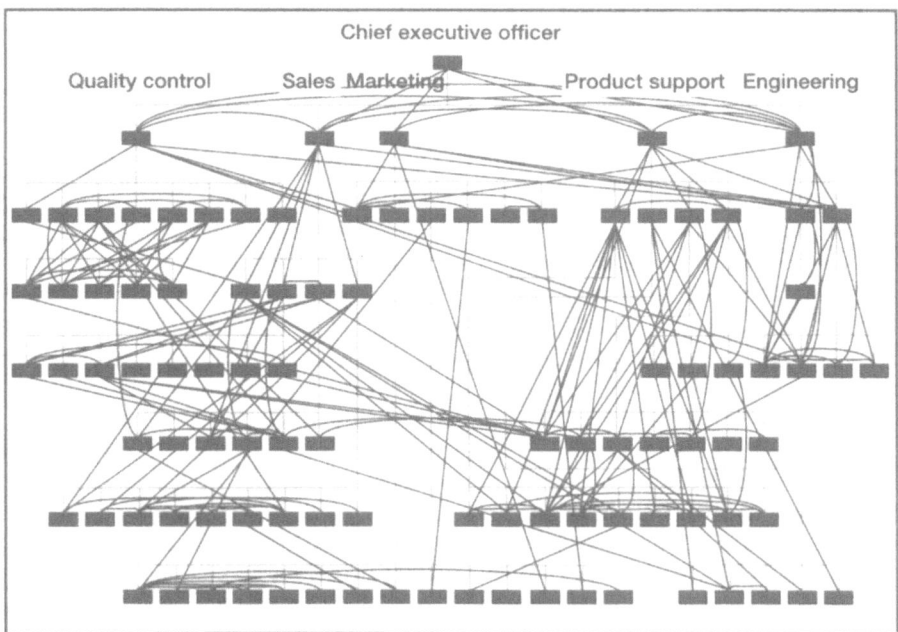

Fig. 5.4. Formal organization chart, augmented to show the actual network of communication.

engineered or not, a specific culture is fostered by the company itself, in so far as it serves as cognitive support for company goals. Cultures are themselves the products of, and sustained by, activity at a more fundamental level, however: that of talk. We have already pointed to the webs of communication and affiliation that criss-cross the organization; a more fine-grained analysis will examine the substantive linguistic *content* of communicative acts between individuals for a principled description of the interactions out of which the culture emerges as a symbolic universe. We take this up again briefly in Section 5.4, though a detailed analysis is the subject of another discussion (Rosenberg and Hutchison 1992). For the present, we shall simply note that it is misleading to speak as though there were a homogeneous monolithic company culture that can be identified uniquely with the overt structure of the organization. While the "official" culture is to some extent amenable to management and controlled change (Hellriegel et al. 1989), subcultures may also emerge naturally from informal patterns of talk between individuals. (In unionized organizations, for example, a particularly salient subculture will be that which emerges from union activity.) When a specific subculture becomes significant enough to affect the actual performance of work groups within the organization, it will approximate to what we are calling the covert structure.

It is the covert structure which, representing the actual dynamics of human activity, determines the performance of the organization. Moreover, significant activity within the covert structure can, when it is perceived to coincide with the corporate goals recognized in the overt structure, lead to a modification both of the organization (in terms of abstract roles and responsibilities) and of the overt structure (in terms of who is sanctioned to do what).

An example will serve as an illustration. The manufacturing organization which provided the basis for the feasibility study had bought a large quantity of tape-drives from a vendor whose main activity is the manufacture of tape-drives. One aspect of the collaboration between the purchasing department and the vendor organization was focused on fault repairs and fault reporting, since there was a significant number of intermittent faults in the vendor's tape-drives. The repair of such faults was as a rule in the first instance attempted by the field engineer on customer site. Since this action did not solve the problem, the faulty units were brought into the manufacturing organization for testing in their diagnostic laboratory. Vendor participation in the diagnostic process was also required, as there was not sufficient information available from the field engineer about the system behaviour at the time of breakdown. Most of the tests yielded negative results, that is, no faults were found in the tape-drives tested, and in such cases, this would be dubbed "NFF- type failure" (i.e. "no fault found"). The established practice was to return the units to the spares section, put them back into customer systems, where they would eventually break down again, come back to the diagnostic unit and the cycle would then repeat itself at great expense and inconvenience to the manufacturer, the original vendor and the customer. Within the overt structure – the routinized test–result–act cycle – the sanctioned interpretation of NFF-type failure was that nothing was wrong with the tape-drives. In this particular case, however, a covert structure of concern and action emerged from informal cooperative reasoning on the part of the diagnostic engineer and the vendor that enabled the interpretation of NFF-type failure as evidence of a possible inadequacy in the testing procedures themselves. It was therefore possible to expand this cooperation in order for both parties to sharpen up their testing and quality procedures. The end result of this collaboration has been that the vendor organization has become a major repair centre within the manufacturing organization, specializing in quality control and diagnostic testing of the faulty units that are brought back from the field. The example clearly illustrates the way in which the responsiveness of the organization to a provenly effective emergent covert structure led to a (localized) redefinition of the overt structure and the organization of the company. (In an alternative scenario, a lack of such responsiveness could well have ensued in a conflict between the overt and covert structure.)

Changes to the organization such as the one instanced above appear to be engendered by the internal dynamics – specifically, the covert structure – of the organization. The salient differences between the overt and covert structures may be characterized as follows. In the example that we are using, of the work group engaged in purchasing peripherals, the overt organizational structure (Fig. 5.5) shows all the areas in which information about vendors is located. This information is here represented in the systemic net formalism, the net having been generated as a mediating representation in and by the early stages of the knowledge elicitation process.[5] In this instance it is used to capture the differences between overt (Fig. 5.5) and covert (Fig. 5.6) organizational structure.

The systemic net formalism has been used here because it provides "content-free" notation, which can form the basis for a uniform representational framework that depicts the systems of choices allowed by the two kinds of structure. The formalism itself depicts functional relationships among structural elements, which have been classified (along the vertical axis, following the standard definitions used by the organization) into departments and sections with associated roles and job descriptions that determine individual and group participation in an activity such as "product support".

From this perspective the overt organizational structure may be seen as the framework of constraints which determines the structural "location" in which an activity is carried out. It can be described as a configuration of elements which stand in hierarchical relationship to one another, where the line relationships in the hierarchy depict relations of authority, responsibility and accountability between those elements, as shown in Fig. 5.3. Representation in the form of a systemic net, on the other hand, is a

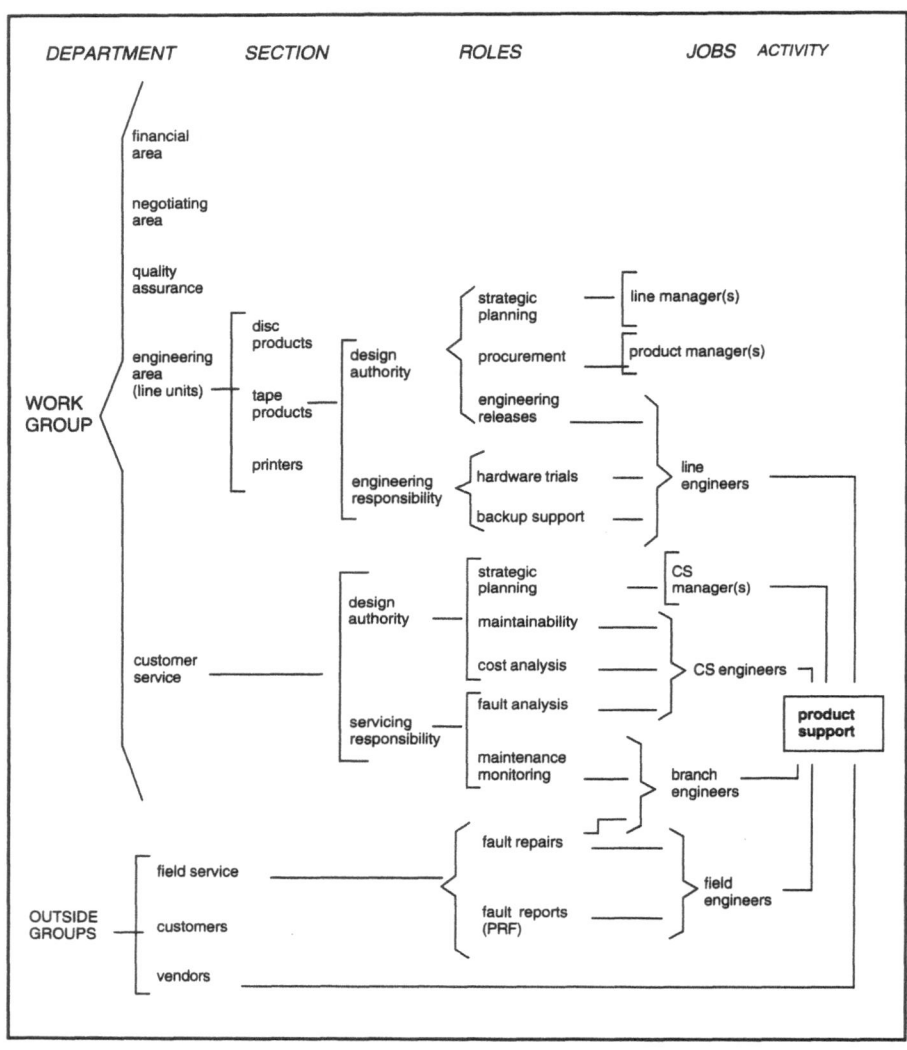

Fig. 5.5. The overt organizational structure.

translation of the structural information into a specification of the system of choices by which those relationships are organized and realized in practice. Thus, for example, the work group consists of seven areas, all of which simultaneously contribute to the working of the group. Another system of choices is shown in the engineering area, which is subdivided into three distinct sections, each section being responsible for a different kind of product (discs, tapes, printers and so on). Further realization of this structure is exemplified by the engineering (tape products) perspective, showing the

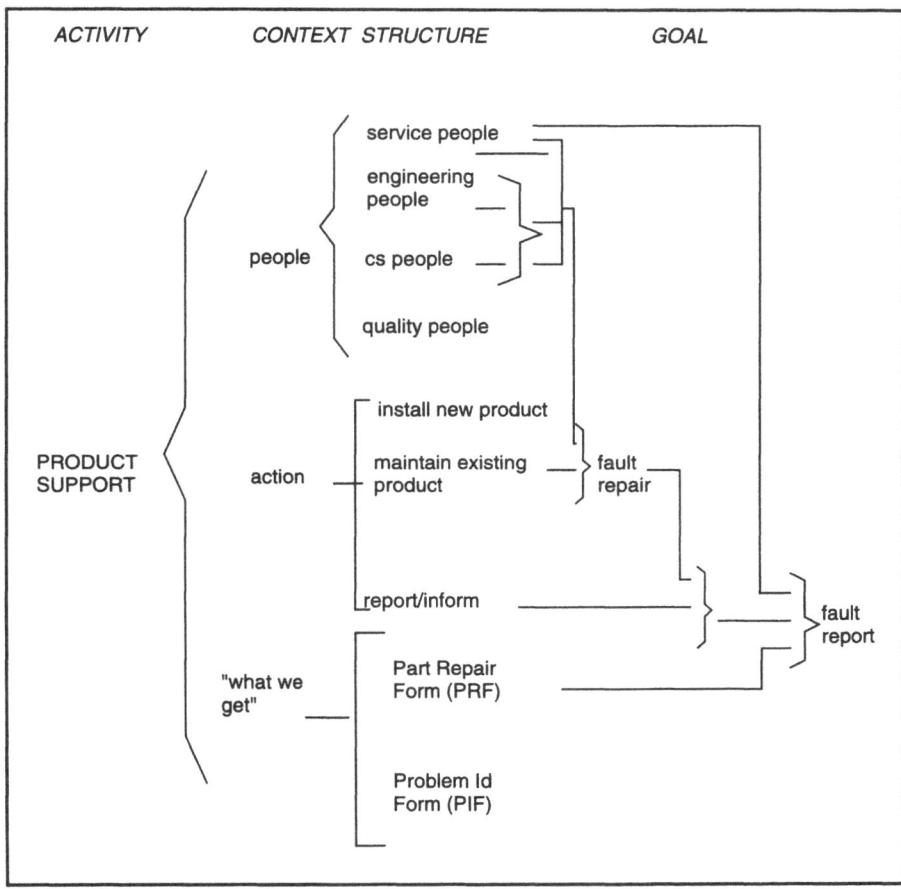

Fig. 5.6. The covert organizational structure.

major roles and responsibilities of that section, related to the people who are responsible for the performance of those functions.

In this way each structural element in the network is deemed to perform a specific function which is closely associated with its place in a hierarchical structure. The network read from left to right shows how structural elements are related functionally, in the sense that it specifies whether in a given system of choices all elements occur together, or function as alternatives. Thus, for example, in Fig. 5.5, the work group can be defined as consisting of five areas which are all involved in its function as a department, whereas in the engineering area the work of an individual section involves either disc products, tape products or printers, but not all together in the same section. Reading from right to left, this network generates several paradigms; for example, the activity "product support" requires participation of all of the following:

line engineers
  who are involved in both engineering releases
    in their role as a design authority
      and hardware trials
      and backup support
    both being a part of engineering responsibility ...
and one of CS managers ...
and CS engineers ...
and branch engineers ...
and field engineers ... who are members of outside groups
and vendors ... who are members of outside groups

There is no conflict inherent in this structure *per se*. Conflict arises out of the actual behaviours of each structural element, out of the content of her activities in the context of the activities and perceptions of others, rather than in consequence of her overt relation with the rest of the structure. A role assumed in covert structure, unlike an element in the overt structure, is always related to messages, discourses or behaviours whose occurrence and content are inherently unpredictable, and only ever contingently related to the organizational structure. Thus the information given in Fig. 5.6 shows that the activity "product support" has the goals of producing a fault repair or a fault report.

The context in which this activity can result in the given goals has been structured in terms of participants or agents ("people"), what they do ("action") and outcomes of their action ("what we get"), where each element in the network is labelled with the terms and phrases actually used by expert informants in interviews with knowledge engineers. This makes our notion of covert structure inherently situated, in so far as the relationship between the activity and the associated goals is determined by the information about a specific configuration of agents, their actions and the outcomes of those actions.

In Section 5.4 we develop this notion of "situatedness" by first sketching out a picture of expert system design uninformed by the concepts of overt and covert structure, and subsequently showing how these concepts help to embed a description of expert domain knowledge into a wider social context of its application. It is our view that this is where conflicts arise, should be acknowledged, discussed and allowed to inform design.

5.4 Experts as People

Although the organization itself is a coherent unity, it exists in an environment which perpetually impinges upon it and with which it perpetually interacts. The performance of other similar organizations, national and global economic and political changes, and technological developments may all influence the behaviour of the organization to the extent that it perceives their relevance to its own goals.

Developments in information technology, for example, have in recent years had a considerable impact on the way people work. Expert systems are a special case of this, in so far as, unlike conventional information technology (IT) systems (e.g. word processors, spreadsheets, databases) which are unpretentiously tools devoid of agentivity, it is implicit in the design of expert systems that, more than merely technological innovations, their design crucially and explicitly includes reference to abilities that have traditionally been seen as exclusively human, such as knowledge processing, intelligence, expertise and problem solving, as well as the products of these abilities such as problem solutions, explanations, justifications and so on.

We shall argue that one of the more important reasons for the frequently unsuccessful integration of expert systems into organizations is in consequence of a misconception of the nature of the knowledge and behaviour of human experts and expert systems alike. The conventional simplistic understanding runs something like this:

Technocentricity. Human expert knowledge relevant to industrial applications is uniquely technical in character, orientated solely towards the optimal solution of complex technical problems.

Realism. Objects and processes in problem domains can be objectively and exhaustively described, the "real" properties and behaviours determined independently of the observations and interpretations of observers and participants. Such descriptions are called "facts"; possession of these facts is called "knowledge".

Scientism. Human experts are scientists, and their intervention in the problem solving is independent of the broader industrial context: given the same "objective" description of the domain, the same problem, and the same problem solving expert knowledge, the same results will be repeatable in any context.

Epistemic integrity. Human expert knowledge is stable and "complete" – an essentially declarative and propositional knowledge encoded in long-term memory is sufficient for the solution of the problem, and is not significantly brought into question or modified by the active process of problem solving.

Modularity. Such knowledge can in principle be – and is for practical purposes generally assumed to be – neatly compartmentalized, without loss, in discrete (modular) packages.[6]

Formalisability. Such knowledge can be exhaustively described and fully formalized in some appropriate notation, paradigmatically in the form of antecedent-consequent rules, without loss of information relevant to performance.

Portability. Human expert knowledge, thus captured, can be implemented in a computer program.

Replicability. The performance of the computer program in some appropriate problem solving task is isomorphic with the performance of the human expert.[7]

In short, the popular conception is inherently *reductionist*. Moreover, designers of expert systems seem frequently to be infected by the same reductionist spirit, for while customizing the system to the context to the extent that they are properly capturing domain-specific expertise in a narrowly technical sense, their observance of the above credenda lead to the design of a system that is perceived by the work group to be "alien" to the environment. There is a tendency to see the expert system as a generic "spare part" which in turn provokes "the rejection of what people feel is an 'alien' system that is being imposed upon them. People refer to the 'Not Invented Here' or NIH syndrome – it is an effect of the feelings of alienation that can develop when outside solutions are imposed on people who have yet to recognize a problem" (Bell and Hardiman 1989, p. 55).

Indeed, in manufacturing parlance, we end up trying to install ill-fitting expert systems that may well turn out to be "solutions looking for problems". We made reference earlier in this chapter to the "corporate culture" of an organization, the tissue of beliefs, values and so forth, that instil the work groups with their sense of "who we are". Cultural rejection is as much a feature of industrial organization as it is of transplant surgery or national chauvinism. The chances of such cultural rejection are increased if expert system designers ignore the complications engendered by the potential for conflict inherent in the nature of the problem domain.

We believe that, on the contrary, the knowledge and information that experts, as people, have and use are not and cannot be neatly contained in discrete packages, but rather carry indicators of the broader covert structure. As a simple example, there is a systematic variation in the way experts refer to and talk with employees of the organization and their colleagues. Thus, in the context of overt structure shown in Fig. 5.5, the people working in the department are referred to in terms of their purely structural roles in the hierarchy (job titles), as line managers, line engineers, branch engineers and so on, whereas in the context of covert structure (Fig. 5.6) the same individuals are referred to non-hierarchically as "people", that is, "engineering people", "CS people", "service people", and so forth, as front-line participants in the activities undertaken by the work group. (More significant indicators of covert structure that may be obtained from interview data are described in more detail in elsewhere: see Hutchison and Rosenberg 1992; Rosenberg 1988; Rosenberg and Hutchison 1992.)

It is on this level that expert knowledge is utilized, where the actual collaboration is practised, and where conflicts may arise and be resolved, as illustrated in Figs 5.7 to 5.9.

Fig. 5.7 displays a fragment of the technical domain knowledge that we would normally expect to elicit when interviewing an expert in fault repair. It shows that technical solutions are found when a unit has broken down

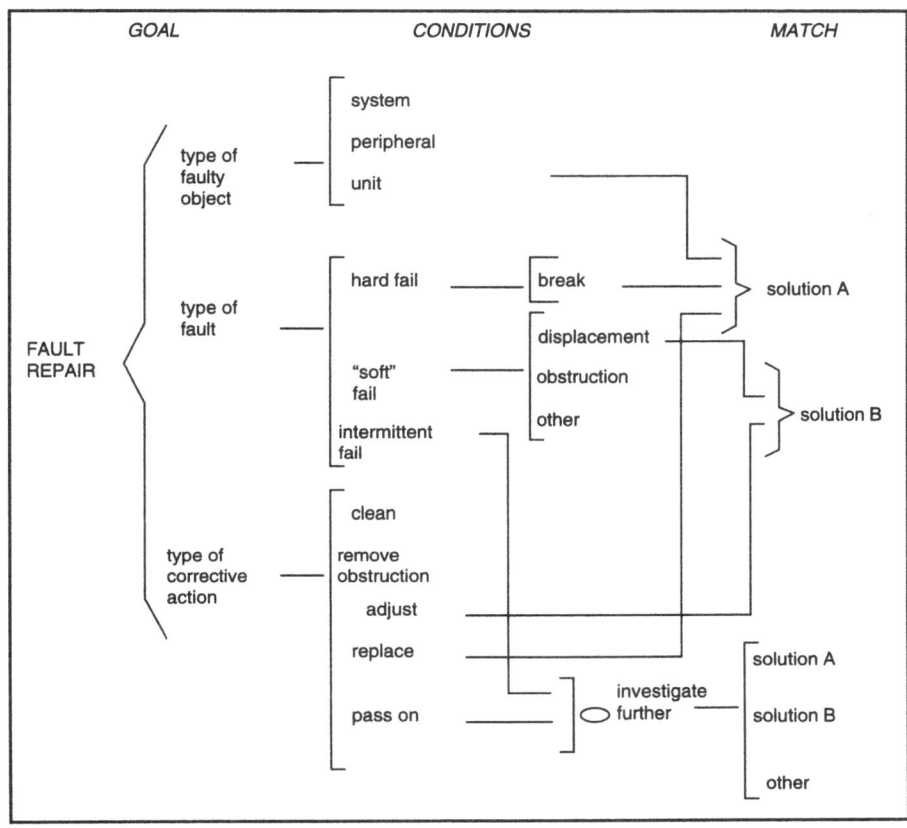

Fig. 5.7. Technical domain knowledge.

(which is an instance of hard fail) and has been replaced, thus yielding Solution A, or when some kind of displacement occurred in the faulty object, which is then adjusted (Solution B), or when there is an intermittent fault which requires further investigation in order to find the appropriate solution.

Fig. 5.8 augments the description by showing the constraints under which that knowledge can provide an optimal solution for the expert problem, not only in terms of its technical merit, but also incorporating the information about the most effective, established or even preferred course of action.

Thus, an operator task on site is to deal with obstruction type "soft" fail; examples of this include paper jams, cleaning tape heads and so on. Field engineers are expected either to replace a faulty unit if it is broken – that is, if it is an instance of hard fail possibly to be investigated further by diagnostic engineers – or to adjust a part which is misplaced. If they cannot

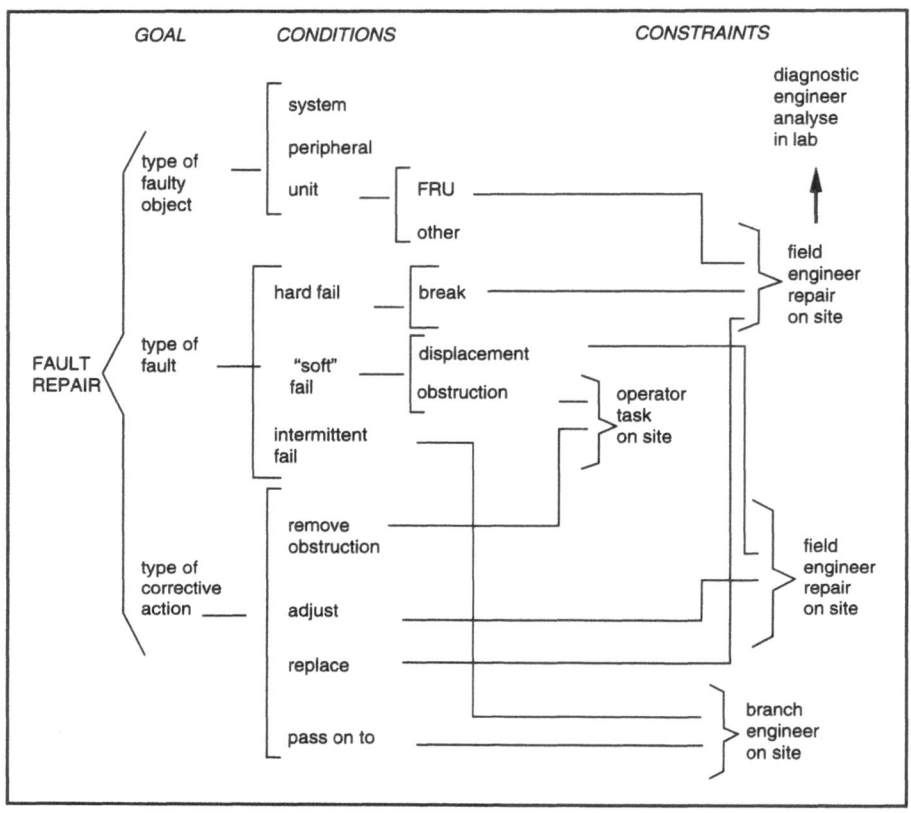

Fig. 5.8. Technical domain knowledge diagram augmented to show optimal solutions.

correct the fault themselves, as often happens in the case of intermittent fails, they are expected to pass the problem on to the branch engineer, who will then decide on the appropriate course of action. In this context of "normal" courses of action, a faulty unit that is brought to the diagnostic laboratory is assumed to be an instance of hard fail; in other words, it represents an example of technical Solution A as shown in Fig. 5.7. Fig. 5.9 shows under what conditions this solution may create conflict.

Since there is an ambiguity in the action of bringing a faulty unit into the diagnostic laboratory for further investigation, namely to establish why a particular break-type fault occurs, this process is obstructed if no break (or any other fault, for that matter, can be found). The miscommunication obstructs the expected information flow among different agents involved in the activity related to fault repairs and fault reporting, thus creating conflict in the actualization of their activities. The "smoothness" of the information flow is essentially determined by what the entire community knows to be

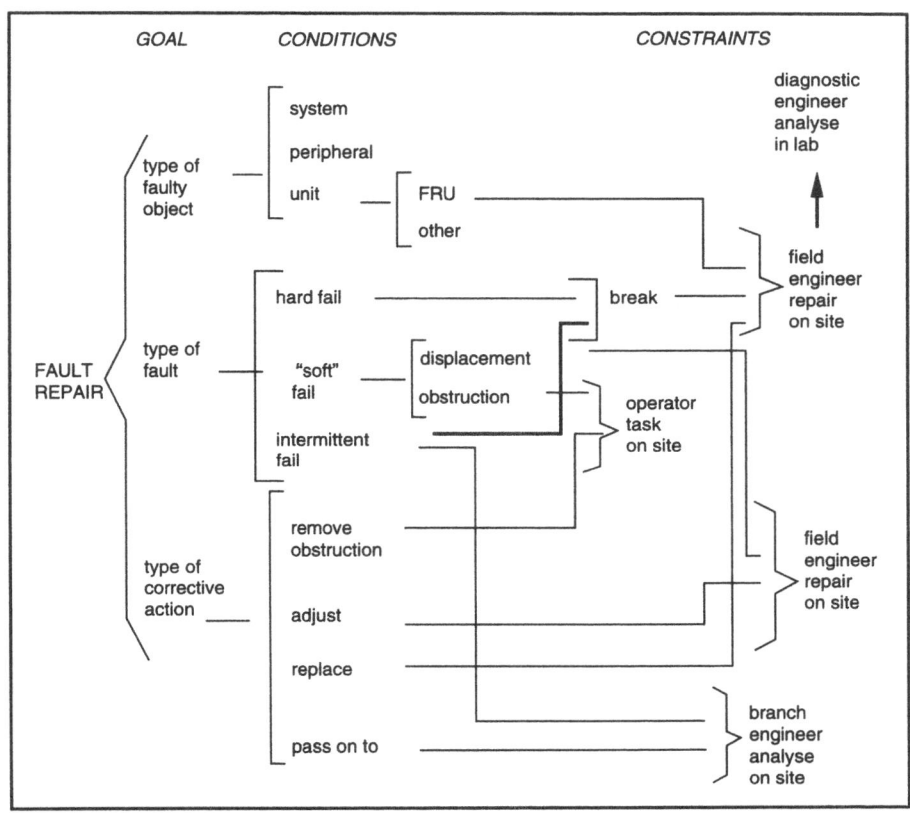

Fig. 5.9. Conditions which may lead to conflict.

"a normal course of action" on which rests the interpretation of its significance.

We shall now expand our characterization of the "organization" of organizations further. More than being simply "social arrangements" (Huczynski and Buchanan 1991), we view the integrity of organizations as coherent and cohesive unities to be sustained through continuous processes of transaction. All transactions are "historical" and serve to preserve the integrity of the organization over time. This will include not only such obvious commercial activities as purchasing, manufacturing and vending, but also less visible transactions such as external dialogue, through public relations and the advertising media, with targeted sections of the public, or internal dialogue in the recruitment and mobility of staff and so forth. Synchronically, dialogue is the principal medium through which members of the organization cooperatively construct and maintain the realities that bind them together in a common purpose.

The organization, that is, is pre-eminently a linguistic domain, its covert structure(s) being defined by flows of information between individuals. Our general claim is that what is known is known by communities rather than by individuals (or that individuals know what they know solely by virtue of their active participation in knowledgeable communities), that it is communities which legislate (on whatever grounds) on what will count as knowledge, and that it follows from this that it is not individuals (human or machine) who are intelligent systems but the communities to which they belong (or of which they are a functional part). Our particular claim is that the design of "expert systems" in the industrial environment will be tantamount to a tactical design of the entire work group of which the technology is merely a functional part. It is this view of the organization that Figs 5.2 and 5.6 endeavour to capture.

5.5 Conclusion

Pessimistic reports have appeared over recent years suggesting that possibly as many as 80%–90% of all expert systems commissioned are either not finally built or, if built, not used. In this paper, we have considered some of the reasons why this may be the case: (i) implicit assumptions that have hitherto guided the knowledge elicitation process and the design of expert systems – technocentricity, realism, scientism, epistemic integrity and so on; (ii) in consequence of these assumptions, an excessive focus on the exclusively technical issues in problem solving, at the expense of more socially relevant aspects of expertise.

We have introduced some novel theoretical concepts and dichotomies as an aid in understanding and representing what we perceive to be social and collaborative aspects of human expertise which play a crucial causal role in creating the organizational context in which the expert system is to be deployed. These are "organization" versus "structure", and "overt" versus "covert" structure. Of these, the most important for our present purposes is "covert structure", seen as an emergent property of individuals continuously engaged in interaction in their day-to-day working. We would therefore endeavour to describe the covert structure of a work group by analysing the flow of information at the fine-grained level of situated utterances and actions.

Finally, we would clarify some aspects of what we are intending to do. In the first place, we are not claiming that our notion of covert structure is an attempt to carry out organizational modelling in any conventional sense. Indeed, we do not consider this a necessary part of knowledge engineering practice. What we *are* claiming is that some specific kinds of information about organizations are relevant to knowledge engineering practice, and that our notion of covert structure enables us to pick out just that information.

In the second place, we are not proposing to provide expert systems with "social" knowledge or expertise; what we *are* proposing is that as knowledge engineers we need to develop conflict awareness in order to inform our knowledge engineering practice such that we can design expert systems for application rather than as exempla of merely technical virtuosity.

Notes

1 We recognize the following levels of description of organizational behaviour: the individual, the constituent work groups within the organization, the organization itself, and the broader external environment of which the organization is a part (cf. Mullins 1989, pp. 2–3).

2 Certain of the ideas in the following discussion have been loosely inspired by Maturana and Varela (1987).

3 In a more discursive survey of the impact of the introduction of information systems into companies, Toffler (1990) draws attention to relevant broader aspects which we do not consider in the present discussion; specifically, to "fights over information itself. Who gets what kind of information? Who has access to the main data base? Who can add to that data base? What assumptions are built into the accounting? Which department or division `owns' what data? And even more importantly, who dictates the assumptions or models built into the software? The conflicts over such questions, while seemingly technical, clearly affect the money, status, and power of individuals and businesses" (Toffler 1990, p. 143).

4 We thank Roger Stewart for providing the templates which formed the basis for Figs 5.3 and 5.4.

5 Use of systemic nets for representing ethnographic knowledge and for supporting the conceptualization stage of qualitative data analysis has a long history. The latter use has also recently been extended by Johnson et al. (1990; 1992) to knowledge engineering.

6 It is interesting to note that even an eminent a scientist as Ed Feigenbaum can, without any apparent sense of irony, write that "The Japanese are planning the miracle *product.* ... The miracle product is knowledge, and the Japanese are planning to *package and sell it* the way other nations package and sell energy, food, or manufactured goods" (Feigenbaum and McCorduck 1984, p. 24; our italics).

7 Cf. Collins (1990, pp. 3, 14–15): "Individual human beings participate in knowledge communities but they are not the location of knowledge"; "An artificial intelligence is a *social prosthesis* ... when we build an expert system it is meant to fit into a social organism where a human fitted before. An ideal expert system would replace an expert, possibly making him or her redundant. It would fit where a real expert once fitted without anyone noticing much difference in the way the corresponding *social group* functions."

Chapter *6*

Organizational Structures, Computer Supported Cooperative Work and Conflict

P. Thomas and J. Riddick

6.1 Introduction

The label "computer-supported cooperative work" (CSCW) has found numerous interpretations, reflecting the difficulty of establishing a baseline – in terms of concept, theory and investigative process – for a new discipline and a new application of information technology. The individual components – the C, S, C and W – of CSCW have been suggested to be only glosses, as has the range of applications that are considered "groupware"' (Bannon and Schmidt 1989; Bannon et al. 1988; Greenberg 1991; Greif 1988; Grudin 1991; Kraut et al. 1988).

In particular, the term "cooperative" is recognized as glossing a continuum of activities, relationships, behaviours, attitudes and perceptions. The "cooperation" that CSCW must seek to deal with may range from aggression, through collaboration, to tight organizational and social coupling. The continuum of cooperation can be expressed as follows:

aggression – conflict – coalition – collaboration – tight coupling

Increasingly, studies in CSCW have been concerned with the right- most end of this continuum. Research has focused on the possibilities of undercutting support for focused work activities by targeting non-formal unfocused interactions. Systems such as CRUSIER (Root 1988), TeamWorkstation (Ishii 1990), VideoWindow (Fish et al. 1990), VRooms

(Borning and Travers 1991), MERMAID (Watabe et al. 1990), CAVECAT (Mantei et al. 1991) and LiveWare (Witten et al. 1991) provide support for informal activities. The "media space" is one device to support a seamless transition between work and non-work and to blur the boundary between technology, people and work. Xerox's RAVE media space (Gaver 1991), for example, aims to support more than just intense collaborations on particular activities.

Other studies, focusing on the centre of the continuum, have investigated organizational settings in which cooperation is a prominent feature (Ciborra and Olson 1988; Engestrom and Engestrom 1988; Eveland and Bikson 1988; Linde 1988; Mackay 1988), one prominent area for research and development being support for focused cooperation in meetings (Mantei 1988; Olson and Bly 1991; Tatar et al. 1991; Valacich et al. 1991). The assertion of these studies is that the design of technology for cooperative working is only possible through close empirical examination of the nature of cooperative activity in varied organizational settings.

Our concern here is with the left-most end of the continuum of cooperation – that of conflict. In this chapter we will suggest that:

- Conflict is an inherent part of cooperative work

- Understanding sources of conflict can provide us with strategies to manage and exploit it effectively

- An understanding of conflict can provide a richer understanding of cooperative work

- This understanding is central to the design and construction of systems which aim to support cooperative working

Our perspective in this chapter is explicitly organizational: we focus on the work that constitutes the output of an organization and the organizational structures that support it rather than take "cooperation" itself as a topic of discussion. Our approach to these issues is through the examination of a particular type of organizational work which is collaborative in nature: design work in the construction industry. Our examination is not extensive, but allows us to illustrate some of the ways in which conflict is inherent in cooperative work, and to provide recommendations that are directly applicable to the design of systems to support cooperative working.

One obvious interpretation of "conflict" is that it arises from the interaction between individuals with divergent goals. An assumption we will make here is that conflict also arises between individuals with the same goals, but with different approaches to achieving those goals, and with fundamentally different skills and abilities. A major cause of conflict may thus be rooted in the nature of the capabilities of individuals in relation to their work. Conflict may arise at several loci: worker–worker, through the interaction between individuals of different capabilities; worker–task, through the interaction between the capabilities of the individual worker and the requirements of the task; and in terms of systems to support CSCW, technology– worker, through the interaction between the task or activity represented in the system, and the capability of the worker.

From this perspective, to manage and exploit "conflict arising from difference" requires an explicit focus on (i) the capability of the individual worker for various kinds of activity, and (ii) the character of work in terms of the required capability of the individual to undertake that work.

Our suggestion is that systems which aim to provide support for cooperative working must support relationships between individuals at various levels of capability, individuals' relationships to a particular task (and others' relationships, collaboratively, to that task), and the relationship between technology and worker.

6.2 Conflict in Cooperative Work

Work is characterized by a commitment to a planned or desired objective which is not yet material – the creation of "something out of nothing" (Stamp 1989). Because the "something" that the work is intended to produce is as-yet unrealized, individual workers may see the work in a different ways; they have their own "subjective realities" (views, priorities, schemes of action, perspectives) about what is required, and how best to achieve a desired outcome. Individuals' subjective realities are shaped by factors such as their organizational context, abilities and educational experiences.

When working cooperatively, these different subjective realities provide a rich source of variation – this is of course the *raison d'être* of cooperative work – but they are also the source of confusion, misunderstanding and disagreement. The problems which occur at the interfaces between individuals' subjective realities are what we may term "conflict". It is an inherent part of cooperation.

However, variation does not mean that workers can be put together in a random fashion to achieve a work objective. A legitimate concern in terms of supporting organizational work effectively – through technology or otherwise – is the understanding of systematic differences between individuals and the ways in which individuals can be allowed the freedom to use their abilities creatively. We will discuss the nature of these systematic differences by drawing on concepts from stratified systems theory (SST).

6.3 Stratified Systems Theory and "Levels" of Work

SST provides an account of the nature of individuals' skills and capabilities, and the relationships between individuals and tasks (Brown and Jaques

1965; Jaques 1976; 1989; Rowbottom and Billis 1977). It suggests that there are two factors that have created the phenomenon of the hierarchical organization:

1. The work that may be undertaken by an organization is greater than any individual can achieve alone: work is packaged and delegated so that managers are accountable for subordinates' output, and they are responsible to the manager.
2. There are differences in the capability and capacity of individuals for executive work and decision making (Brown and Jaques 1965; Stamp 1989).

SST identifies seven different levels of work equivalent to qualitative differences in individuals' capacity for executive work, decision making and exercise of discretion. The first five are considered relevant to our example, and are described below (after Rowbottom and Billis 1977):

1. *Level I: prescribed output* Working towards completely specified objectives, with no expectation of significant judgements about what the final output should be.
2. *Level II: situational response* Precise objectives have to be judged according to particular circumstances with no commitment on how future possible situations have to be dealt with.
3. *Level III: systematic service provision* Provision of services according to specific situation, with no expectation of making decisions on resource reallocation in future situations.
4. *Level IV: comprehensive service provision* Development of operating systems to meet changing objectives, with no expectation of making decisions on resource reallocation about completely new objectives.
5. *Level V: managing complex systems* Meeting strategic objectives through the integration of functional and operational requirements, with no expectation of making decisions about resource reallocation outside a specific service or product boundary.

The levels are characterized in terms of output (what the individual at that level produces) and discretion (the upper boundary of the decision making that characterizes the work).

Work is thus viewed as the exercise of discretion within prescribed limits. The capacity to make decisions represents the investment that an organization makes in an individual. The exercise of discretion is what contributes to the experience of the "weight" of work – mulling over ideas, using gut feel and intuition to make decisions. Prescribed limits are the rules, regulations and policies which bound the discretion that is appropriate for any given task.

The concept of level as described here has some immediate practical applicability. Empirical work in organizations (Brown and Jaques 1965) suggests an individual will feel comfortable if their manager operates at one qualitative level above the individual's own work level. This is because the manager provides the appropriate type of containment to the individual's decision making. If the manager is too close in capacity to the subordinate, the subordinate feels inhibited – as if the manager is attempting to do the subordinate's work. If the manager is too far from the individual in terms of capacity the amount of discretionary activity expected of the individual is too great. The individual may thus feel that they are assigned tasks they don't understand.

SST, focusing on the relationships between individuals in terms of the capacity for decision making, provides a framework that can capture significant features of the nature of work. We have suggested that the advantages of collaboration come from individual diversity, but conflict arises from a failure properly to realize and manage that diversity. We will attempt to apply this framework to the example of work in the construction industry, noting the conflict that is a part of cooperative work, and consider its implications for the design of systems to support cooperative working.

6.4 Cooperation and Conflict in Organizations: The Construction Industry

Design work in the construction industry we see as paradigmatic of work that is concerned with the delivery of a product or service, where this requires explicit contracted cooperation from members of different corporate organizations.

Project organizations in the construction industry are defined primarily by the requirements of the product they deliver, rather than by the skills and capabilities of the individuals involved. There are three broad reasons for this:

1. *Method of procurement.* The contract is considered to define the relationships between participants at the corporate level.

2. *Changing emphasis.* As a project moves from design to construction, the nature of the work changes and this leads to uncertainty over accountability.

3. *Diverse employment organizations.* Firms who provide different components need to interact with each other about their contribution.

For the purposes of this chapter, we draw upon the organization of the various design contributions to construction projects throughout the different stages involved – the central issue being the nature of the relationships between individuals and their approaches to work. We suggest that the important concern here is the nature of accountability and authority, which holds a project together – what work any individual is accountable for delivering, and to what extent this work can be allocated to others. The concept of accountability in this context is not concerned with "who is under contract to whom": the focus is not on which firm has responsibility for the finished product, or which has responsibility for delivering a product on time or within cost. Instead, the concern is with the nature of relationships between individuals working in a project organization.

6.5 Organizational Issues and Conflict in Design Construction

Within the design function of any construction project there are three distinct levels of work involved (Riddick 1991). These are (see Table 6.1):

1. Level IV: concept design.
2. Level III: system design.
3. Level II: detailed design.

Individuals at all of these levels are involved at every stage of the design contribution to the completion of a building project, and individuals at each level provide the major output at some stage. SST suggests that each of these different levels of work entails quite distinct approaches to design, and requires the involvement of individuals of distinct levels of capability.

These different levels of work are not only different stages in the design process. Rather, design work of this kind is intended to deliver different sorts of outputs at different stages. This means that there must be managerial relationships between higher and lower levels, to ensure that work is allocated and reviewed appropriately. For work of this kind, output has to come from all levels and there is thus a requirement that higher levels integrate the work of those working in lower levels to produce a more complex output.

6.5.1 Level IV: Concept Design

The highest level of design work, level IV concept design, emphasises the development of new solutions to meet changing criteria drawing on the internal resources of the design organization. The output here is a proposed plan of construction which fulfils various criteria of aesthetic appeal and client requirements for space, value for money and time of construction.

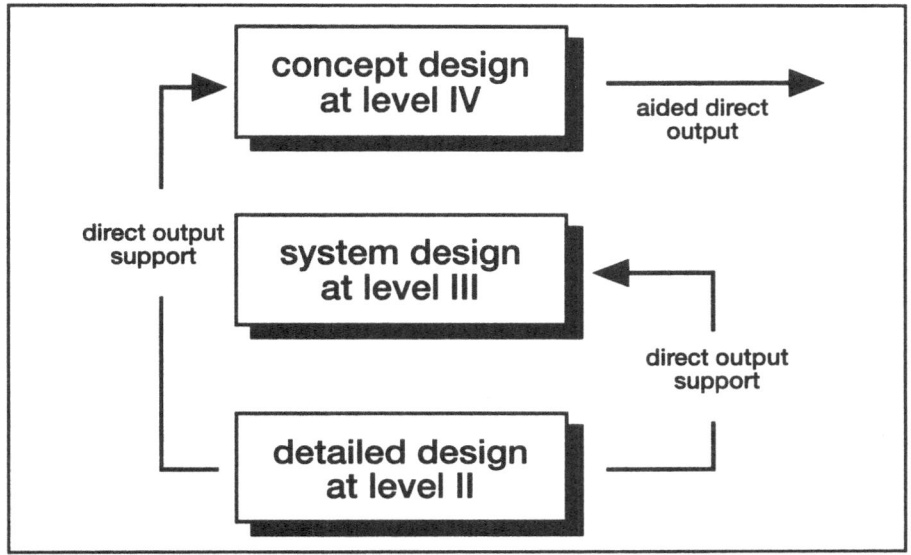

Fig. 6.1. Relationships of direct output support between levels II, III and IV.

To ensure that the design as described in the plan of construction will function, it is necessary for work to be allocated to individuals working at level II and level III to test that the design is actually implementable. This relationship between individuals at level IV, III, and II may be termed "direct output support" from levels III and II (the output of these levels is directly used in work at level IV). The output at level IV is thus "aided direct output" (see Fig. 6.1).

The nature of these relationships are such that conflict exists, since level IV concept design is very much the "high-status" aspect of design work and tends to overshadow other aspects of the work of producing the plan of construction. The result is that individuals working at level IV may overlook their management responsibilities to those below. As we will discuss later, this has implications for the appropriate delivery of outputs of those working at level II in particular. Although this is only a thumbnail sketch of the relationship between individuals at levels IV, III and II, we can begin to see that conflict is a part of the cooperation necessary between individuals who construct and solve problems in quite distinct ways.

6.5.2 Level III: System Design

Our description of concept design was concerned with the relationships between individuals within a single design organization. However, it is rare for one design practice to be able to offer all the specialist aspects of design

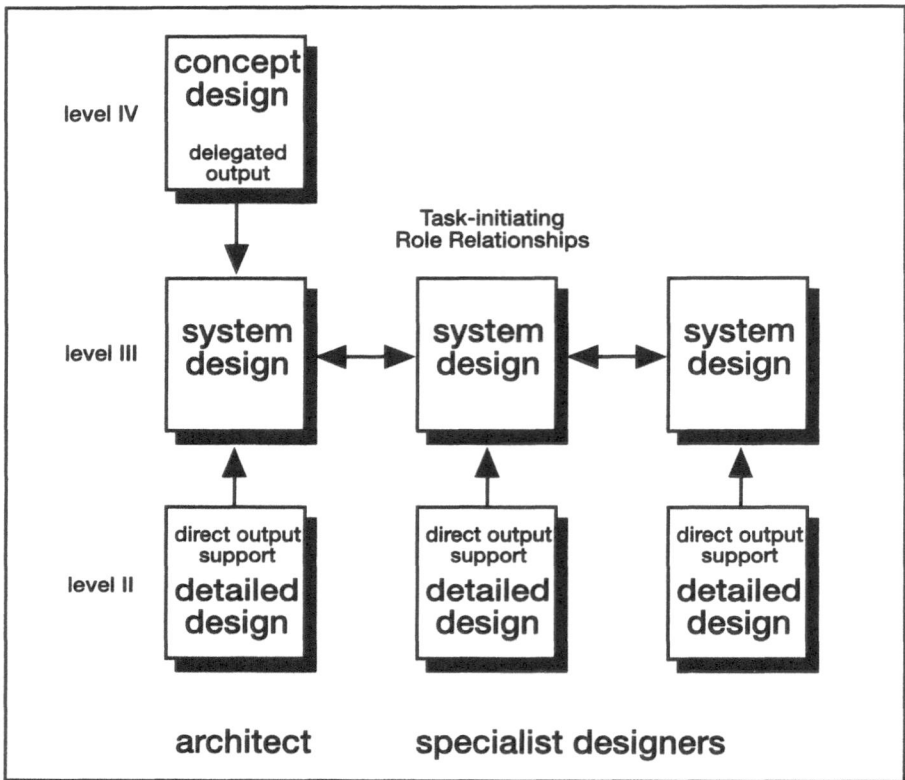

Fig. 6.2. Task-initiating role relationships between level III system designers.

required for a modern construction project. Instead it is broken down into a variety of different systems: plumbing, HVAC, electrical, lifts, structural design, and cladding, for example. Successful construction design requires the integration of these contributions from system designers in participating organizations in a way that works both during construction and in the completed product.

The various level III individuals working on system design work effectively together in what might be termed "task initiating role relationships". This means that each individual is accountable to their own manager for ensuring that the needs of their organization's system are taken into account, by attempting to persuade the others of their requirements. It is essentially a process of give and take to ensure that all systems work, and that they work together, for the good of the overall building.

Fig. 6.2 shows the "task initiating role relationships" between level III individuals who are "delegated output" from level IV, and who each rely on direct output support from level II detailed designers. Fig. 6.3 shows a schematic of the relationships at this level between individuals at level III.

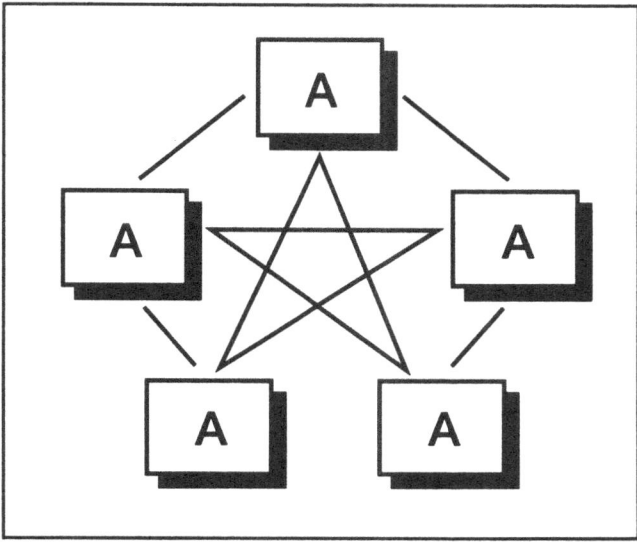

Fig. 6.3. Schematic diagram of task-initiating role relationships between level III system designers in participating organizations.

Successful cooperative work at level III is important to the whole project. However, the importance of this work is often overlooked, and tasks may be decomposed, assigned and reviewed on either side of this level. This means that within a design practice, relationships between individuals (at levels IV and II) cannot develop because they are, in terms of levels, too far apart from each other.

Relationships in level III system design also cross both level and corporate boundaries simultaneously. This may lead to serious problems, since team members are not only contributing quite distinct specialisms, but are also looking at the world and the work they have to do in completely different ways. Cooperation is successful when all firms cooperate at level III to ensure that the various systems that each contributor is providing will integrate together in a way that does not compromise the working or installation of any one system.

Additionally, it may be the case that if an individual of an inappropriate level of capability is assigned to this work it can have quite damaging implications: if an individual of level IV capability is involved they will tend to have too much influence, and the real concerns and needs of other contributors may be overlooked; equally, if an individual of level II is involved, they will tend to feel out of their depth, looking to the other members of the team for direction and management, and will expect to be told what information is required of them for each meeting, rather than taking the initiative.

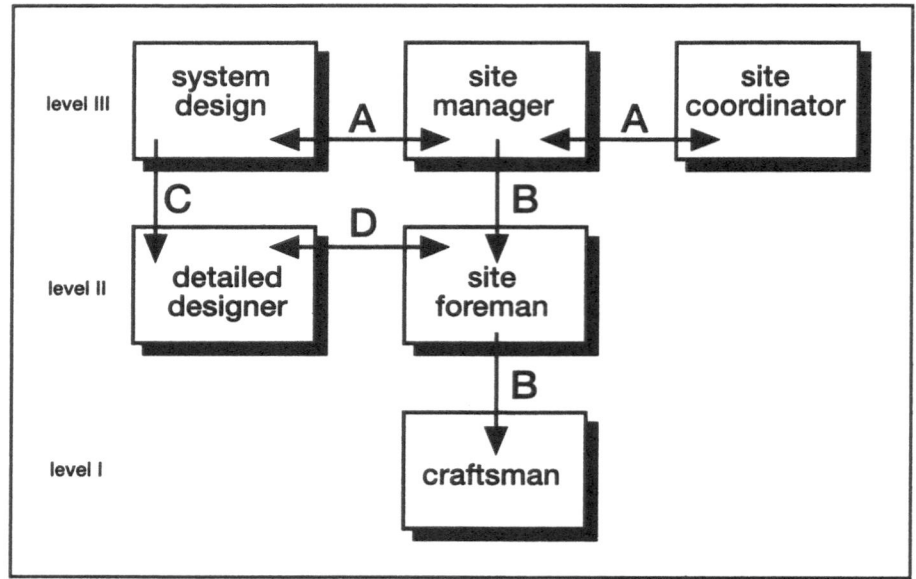

Fig. 6.4. Relationships involved in level II detailed design work.

6.5.3 Level II: Detailed Design

Work at this level produces drawings that can be used by constructors to produce a three-dimensional product. There are essentially four types of relationship involved here, as shown in Fig. 6.4.

Relationship A exists between designers and constructors and is concerned with meeting production targets. There is a requirement to balance the production constraints of time and cost of the solution with that considered best from a design perspective. The site manager and site coordinator interact with the system designer to ensure the delegation of work to produce detailed working drawings at the appropriate time from the detailed designer.

Relationship C is that of delegation downwards from the system designer to the detailed designer. This, of course, is dependent on the effectiveness of relationship A between system designer, site manager and site coordinator.

Relationship B is the delegation downwards characteristic of production hierarchies. The results of the cooperation between those at level III and those at level II (relationship D) are fed into the work of those people actually producing the building – the craftsmen working at level I.

Conflict exists here due to the boundary between a specialist hierarchy and a managerial hierarchy. A managerial hierarchy is founded on the assumption that work is delegated and delivered through the bottom of organizations; design organizations on the other hand – who tend to be more aware of their output at higher levels (at level IV concept design) – may not recognize that at this stage they are required to manage the work of their organizations by allocating increasingly simple tasks downwards. What may happen here is that the working drawings that are produced by the detailed designer at level II may be more geared to the needs of senior managers than those of the construction personnel.

6.5.4 Conflict in Construction Design: Summary

Conflict between individuals working in construction design is rooted in the relationships between individuals working at various levels, and in the nature of individuals' approaches to work. Patterns of accountability and authority in individuals' relationships can both support effective cooperative working, and lead to conflict due to the product-orientated nature of construction projects and the contractual relationship between participants. Effective output at the highest level of work, level IV concept design, relies on support from lower levels, but its specialism leads to management responsibilities being overlooked. Level III, system design, is important in the integration of systems in the final product, but if all participants are not of level III capability or if the relationships are not maintained effectively, conflict can arise. At the lowest level, detailed design, a number of complex relationships need to be maintained to ensure that the work of the detailed designer at level II is appropriate to the needs of various individuals across organizations.

6.6 Implications for the Design of Technology for Cooperative Working

A number of specific implications for the design of technology to support cooperative working may be drawn from this brief examination of construction design. The recommendations are based upon specific issues considered in the example above and also on the ways in which the concept of "level of work" can contribute to the design of CSCW systems. We are currently exploring these issues further in empirical studies of requirements for collaborative technology in a large information technology (IT) manufacturer.

6.6.1 Examine the Nature of "Work"

First, we see a need to gain an understanding of "work", and not only of "cooperation", and the focus on conflict in this chapter has helped us to approach this. An understanding of work can help us to design systems that provide support for the work involved in producing organizational output, and possibly bring about organizational change. Thus, one general recommendation we can make is not to attempt to deny or combat conflict, but to recognize its involvement in organizational output. At the same time, conflict should not be topicalized, since it may be the case that there is no work that is not inherently both conflictual and cooperative. What we can recognize, however, is the nature and effects of difference: conflicting "subjective realities" must be realized as an inescapable part of individuals' approach to work. It is clear that there is a requirement for detailed domain analysis to assess the nature both of the activities and tasks that are undertaken, and the capabilities of the individuals to perform them and interact with other individuals. We are pursuing this issue through the design of computer-based tools to profile levels of capability for specialist design work.

6.6.2 Use Levels of Capability to Design Support for Working Relationships

We can make a number of specific recommendations drawing on our example:

1. Provide routes for direct output support: technology for cooperative working, especially at level IV, should allow the integration of direct outputs. This may involve explicit support for scheduling, shared concept spaces, shared editing (Dykstra and Carasik 1991; Greif et al. 1986; Lewis and Hodges 1988; Olsen et al. 1990; Opper 1988), shared-workspace tools (Knister and Prakash 1990; Minneman and Bly 1991) and support for decision making (Conklin and Begeman 1988; Poole et al. 1988). It is clear that, for example, systems for document routing (Karbe et al. 1990) can be usefully enhanced by embodying knowledge about the nature of levels of work and the need to facilitate direct output support between levels.

2. Mediate conflicting requirements by supporting task initiating role relationships: at level III in particular, the example indicates the need to design systems that allow participants to view the state of the whole project and work explicitly with conflicting requirements. This may involve the use of "intelligent agents" (Gibbs 1989) which mediate between individuals at level III from different specialisms, providing contextual help where appropriate, or providing support for group design and planning (Bødker et al. 1988; Bødker and Gronbaek 1991; Tang and Leifer 1988).

3. Manage the interface between conflicting hierarchies by supporting and maintaining effective relationships: the discussion of level II detailed design suggested that work at this level requires effective relationships to exist. Here it must be ensured that information is routed appropriately between

organizations, functions and individuals working at different levels. This may involve support for both informal interaction within and between participant organizations on a project, trading on knowledge about the level at which individuals are working and the outputs they produce.

6.7 Conclusion: Models of Organizations, the Nature of Work and Enhanceable Systems

The concept of "level", and the relationships between levels are, we suggest, enduring features of organizational work. Organizational output, however, will inevitably change over time. We suggest that the focus in the design of systems should be on the provision of enhanceable systems that can be modified to take account of changing organizational output.

Technological imperatives in CSCW have led to a less than close attention to the organizational requirements for technology to support cooperative working. The focus of this chapter, in line with a European emphasis on "work-oriented design" (Bødker 1991; Ehn 1988), is thus an attempt to complement applications development. Nevertheless it is clear that any "model" of an organization is only a partial story – illustrated by the vast number of diverse theories and models of organizations that have been proposed this century (see Jirotka and Gilbert 1990a; 1990b). One explanation is that all such models and theories of organizations are merely systematizations of individuals' tacit knowledge about how to behave inside organizations. The argument is that a model or theory of an organization, when it is articulated, is used as a resource for the member of the organization to explain, justify, rationalize, and understand their own and others' actions in an organizational context. Thus the range of models and theories of organizations – as structure, network, organism, information processor, coalition or culture – are only partial accounts of certain aspects of "doing work in an organization".

The implications for CSCW design are clear: to base a system directly on one such model would not provide support for the range of activities characteristic of organizational life and work. For example "coordination systems" (Ellis et al. 1991; Karbe et al. 1990) – whether form-orientated, procedure-orientated or conversation-orientated – are all based on the "organization as network" model, and have been found to be less than effective, since they assume a static and inflexible network structure, even with workplace involvement and participatory design (Ehn 1988).

For some (Jirotka and Gilbert 1990b), the alternative is explicitly to adopt an ethnomethodological stance and suggest that what should be both studied and modelled is how members of organizations view organizations, and use the concept of "organization" as a scheme of interpretation. The design imperative here is to support the "skills and craft" in work in organizations and provide flexible and adaptable systems to support the variety of activities and practices that characterize organizational work. The media space can be seen as one device that supports skills and craft through a recognition that work is composed of variegated activities, not all of which are focused collaboration.

The injunction to support skills and craft is, however, both vague and, it seems to us, possibly misguided. The essence of skills and craft is that they change over time – are refined, developed and modified in relation to organizational contexts and demands. The sorts of recommendations we have made using the concept of "level of work" from SST, however, we see as persistent features of the work involved in producing organizational output and which underlie skills and craft.

We feel that only by arriving at an adequate description of work, using frameworks such as SST, can we design systems appropriately to support cooperative working and the conflict inherent within it.

Chapter 7

Going Off the Rails: Understanding Conflict in Practice

P.T. Hughes

7.1 Introduction

This chapter presents an empirical information systems design perspective on the issues and requirements of machine support for human cooperation and conflict in real-time conferencing systems. The distinction between *environment* and (embedded) *application* is used. By "environment", I mean the set of services available to all applications in the system, primarily concerned with communication between applications, and between applications and their users.

Our domain of interest, in technological terms is in non face-to-face, synchronous shared window conferencing. In more user-orientated terms one translation of this is "machine mediated meetings". The main objective of this is to provide a naturalistic cooperation *environment* for arbitrary numbers of computer users, in which they can share embedded applications (word processors and spreadsheets spring to mind). So, at this stage of our work, we are not primarily concerned with specific applications.

This work has been carried out at BNR Europe as part of the EuroCoOp project (ESPRIT 5303), and has proved to be a very fruitful source of insight on cooperation *and* conflict, together with a better understanding of the role of achievement, or "articulation work" in cooperation.

The results are leading us to rethink some of the accepted "baseline" concepts in CSCW; for example, in the so-called "floor control" of meetings and in the usefulness and applicability of the "what you see is what I see" (WYSIWIS) abstraction (Stefik et al. 1986).

We have begun our investigations by trying to understand and support small (two to four people), *ad hoc*, informal meetings: the very sort of *casual* encounters that people have many times a day as they go about their work, especially in an organizational context. We aim to allow them to do this comfortably and repeatably even though they may be separated by a continent or an ocean. This approach is in contrast to supporting *formal* meetings, which are explicitly (and sometimes laboriously) set up, and in which some interaction policy is observed and enforced by the participants; for example, the standard Rules of Order, with clearly identified and stable roles being assigned and enacted.

The chapter is organized in the following way. First, I take a brief look at exactly what we mean when we use the terms "cooperation" and "conflict". I will then try to illustrate these ideas by reference to our experiments in which subjects make use of a prototype synchronous shared window system. Finally, I shall outline some emerging questions and requirements for the design of such conferencing systems, and some potential future work in this direction.

7.2 Perspective on Cooperation and Conflict

Upon looking up the words "conflict" and "cooperation" in a dictionary (Macdonald 1981), I find the following words used in the definitions:

Conflict:
Violent collision
Struggle, contest, battle
Fight, contend, oppose, clash, contradiction
Cooperation:
Working together
Joint operation

The definitions are couched in behavioural language. It is probably in these terms that the concepts are usually thought of or expressed. However, in the CSCW area, this usage is not only metaphorical, but also, I think, fails to capture some important characteristics of cooperation and conflict.

In behavioural terms, both "cooperation" and "conflict" require some level of engagement by the participants. This is obvious in "cooperation", but more subtle in "conflict" as defined above. For example, someone running away from a fight – refusing to engage in conflict – is behaving, in some sense, *uncooperatively*. Thus "conflict" has cooperative overtones. Of course, the distinction is not primarily one of behaviour in the discourse situation, but of reference. People also engage in conflict when they strive towards different and mutually exclusive goals. This is my definition of "conflict", and the word will be used with this sense from now on.

Such conflict of goals is not to be regarded as aberrational – to be avoided or diffused – but *expected*. This is because people are intelligent, knowledgeable and independent social agents going about their business in the real world. Conflict is therefore *inevitable*, and design effort should not be directed towards suppressing conflict, but towards facilitating its resolution. The occurrence of *unintentional* conflict represents some form of breakdown or failure of communication or interpretation. Avoidance of this unintentional conflict is a major aspect of CSCW system design, and is the focus of this chapter.

Conflicting behaviour is deliberately used by people in conversation, for example, to stress a point or to gain attention. My view is that, in the area of social interaction (and hence CSCW), everything which is not necessarily impossible is, and should be, possible. There are no impossibilities; only the social consequences of social actions. I interpret this in system requirements terms to be support for social action and feedback – allowing for interpretation and consequence – in the particular usage situation.

The CSCW systems designers' job is therefore not to suppress conflict (which may be a necessary ingredient in the users' current social situation; totally unforeseen and unforeseeable by the designers), but to facilitate and amplify social action within the constraints of the technology.

7.3 Conflict in Practice

Having outlined some rather general features of what I consider to be good conferencing systems design, I want to consider some particular CSCW design questions that are concerned with the foundational concept of shared material. The particular shared "material" I want to focus on is the appearance or view of an application employed in a multi-user context.

At BNR Europe, we have been conducting a programme of user-centred and user-involved design trials in the area of real-time synchronous conferencing and have gained direct, useful experience of the issues surrounding shared application views. This has been achieved through a series of trials, which have been reported elsewhere (Hughes et al. 1991).

One of our aims was to explore the breakdown space of a real system intended to operate in a shared information text space and support the social interaction of users. Our first series of trials were concerned with subjects' moment-to-moment coordination of their actions on shared text documents, in which we used a modified co-discovery learning technique. In doing this, we deliberately gave the subjects a system that we knew would break down in the area of real-time information sharing. We observed a good deal of intentional conflict (in the task-related discussion) and unintentional conflict (in the subjects' use of the system). We are

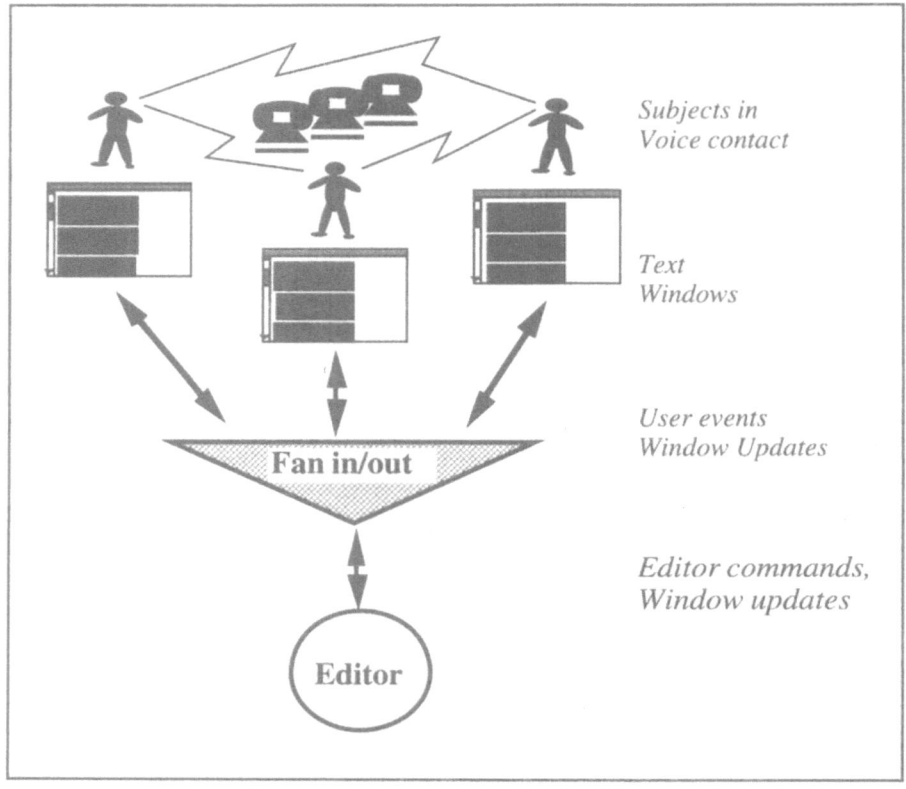

Fig. 7.1. Conceptual experimental setup.

currently investigating the causes of this unintentional conflict and how these might be removed.

Fig. 7.1 illustrates the experimental set-up. A detailed description of this and the analysis procedures (and examples of subjects' talk) can be found in Morris (1991). Groups of two or four subjects had common access to a text editor by means of a software fan in/out component which channelled user commands into the editor, and broadcast editor output to each connected user window. Hence, a strict window-based, as opposed to full screen-based, WYSIWIS was enforced by the system. In addition, all the subjects were able to hear and speak to each other by means of a telephone conference link, supported by the local private automatic branch exchange (PABX). It also important to note that the fan in/out did not treat any subject's input or output differently from any other subject's input and output; there was no "floor control" built into the system.

We conducted five two-party sessions and five four-party sessions with this set-up, employing twenty subjects (eighteen male and two female) in total. This meant that each person took part in one four-party session and one two-party session. Each session's task was drawn from a repertoire of four ranking tasks. We ensured that (i) the sessions in which any particular person participated were not consecutive, and (ii) every subject had a different task in each of their sessions.

At the start of each session, each workstation screen contained two windows, one containing the text describing the task and its associated information, and one blank window. Subjects were told they would be participating in a "group communication" experiment, and were not explicitly told that these windows obeyed strict WYSIWIS – and were thus essentially common "property" of *all* the participants. Naturally enough, most subjects initially assumed that what they saw and did was "private" in that the others did not see or have access to this information. The discussion below is based on a comparison between the data from the ten sessions carried out under the same experimental conditions. We did not conduct "control" sessions where, for example, the subjects were explicitly trained in the behaviour of the system before attempting the task. In retrospect, this was an omission, but one which, I believe, does not invalidate the discussion in this paper.

Subjects usually scrolled the document out of curiosity very early in the sessions. This immediately gave rise to *unintentional* conflict, because some would be reading while others were scrolling. When this occurred, the subjects commented about it to each other over the telephone link. To explain this apparently strange behaviour of the system, various hypotheses were put forward by the subjects, such as:

- The system automatically scrolls all windows either continuously or from time-to-time, rather like a "paternoster" lift system

- One of the experimenters was arbitrarily scrolling the windows

- Anyone could manipulate the windows, and everyone could see the results of this

As subjects attempted to verify the third hypothesis, they would usually decide that no one should touch anything for a while. However, this strategy was subverted by buffering and delays inherent in the trial system. While subjects checked verbally that no one was doing anything, the system would still be processing buffered events from the previous chaotic period, for example causing the windows to scroll. Since a large number of events had normally built up by the time the subjects decided to try out this test, the time taken by the system to process them all was several minutes. In most cases, the subjects did not wait this long before concluding that the shared window hypothesis was probably incorrect.

However, this exercise had the effect of flushing most of the accumulated events, resulting in the success of this test if it were conducted a second time. This time the apparent settling time was within the time users were prepared to wait (a few seconds).

When the system had settled down, usually someone would be asked to scroll the window, and the others were asked what they could see. This would usually verify the third hypothesis. Eventually, most sessions came to the conclusion that the windows were common property; after this, the remainder of the session duration involved much *less* talk about the *system*, and much *more* talk about the *task in hand*.

The windows were now treated as public property – usually anyone manipulating a window would first seek approval for this from the others (using the voice link). In this way, using voice coordination alone, the subjects managed their common access to the windows apparently very comfortably, and very little unintentional conflict was observed. The common (WYSIWIS) windows had become a shared window.

7.4 Going off the Rails: Requirements and Questions

This section attempts to do two things:

1. Summarize some abstract (for want of a better word) "requirements" on the avoidance of "going off the rails", i.e. cooperation breaking down through unintentional conflict.

2. Instead of attempting to present "correct" answers, ask some of the correct unanswered questions about supporting cooperative work.

7.4.1 General Requirements

Focusing on the "conflict" aspects of cooperative work, I believe that support in this area should be for:

- The avoidance of unintentional conflict
- Situated (and unforeseen) deliberate use of conflict
- Resolution of conflict

Whatever the exact concrete means of support chosen, it must:

- Be appropriate to the situation and task focus of the user domain
- Be timely
- Provide necessary and sufficient information so as to maintain cooperation through mutual awareness, and effect its continuous repair

Cooperative mutual awareness is transparent in real-world situations, because most people, from childhood, have become highly skilled in interacting with each other. In machine-mediated cooperative working, the requirements for this mutual awareness have not been explicitly recognized in the past, but yet form the prerequisite for conferencing systems' functionality.

7.4.2 Coordination of Views and Actions

The sharing of an application in the example in the previous section was achieved only by a certain amount of effort on the part of the subjects. Even when in this sharing mode, the subjects continued not only to coordinate their actions using the voice link, but also their views of the application as well.

The fact that the subjects persistently cross-checked what each other could see (for example where the cursor was, which part of the document was displayed and so on) may be due to one or a mixture of the following reasons:

1. Subjects did not trust the experimental system after their initial difficulties.

2. Residual delays in the experimental system operation meant that cross-checking was still necessary.

3. Socially competent behaviour requires that individuals maintain an accurate, up-to-date knowledge of what others are doing and what they have seen and heard.

Point 3 is a very interesting possibility, and we intend to investigate this further.

Thus, we have a distinction between "technological WYSIWIS" – identical behaviour of some object being displayed on several screens simultaneously – and "social WYSIWIS" - the common, aligned perception of an object *as a single entity* by a group of people. We now have to discover what achievements and re-achievements are necessary to obtain social WYSIWIS from a baseline of technological WYSIWIS; and, more radically, whether technological WYSIWIS is the ideal baseline for this.

Fig. 7.2 illustrates the interplay of these concerns. A prerequisite for cooperation is mutual awareness, which is achieved through mutual knowledge of what people are doing and what they perceive (see and hear, and so on). This knowledge shapes, and is shaped by, how people coordinate what they do and what they perceive.

I postulate that as long as mutual awareness is maintained, users can coordinate their actions (e.g. turn-taking) over shared material without explicit system intervention in the form of embedded protocols for "floor control". Stated another way, the presence of such embedded protocols is characteristic of CSCW systems that do not recognize or support the need for mutual awareness.

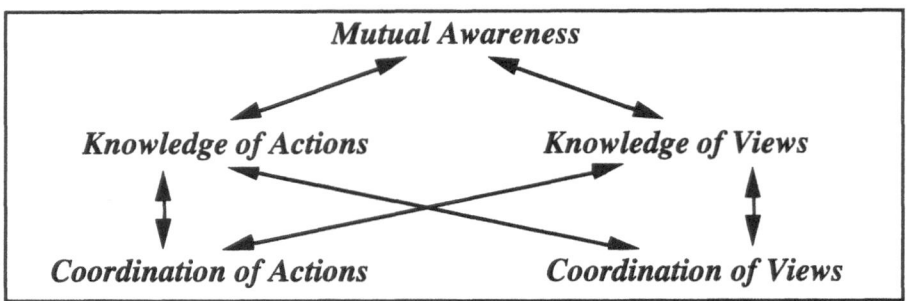

Fig. 7.2. Illustration of the interplay of concerns in supporting cooperation.

7.4.3 Further Questions and Observations

Having outlined the above general requirements, the important questions follow:

1. What degree of system assistance is required to support mutual awareness?
2. What form should any system assistance take?
3. How much information should the system give to users?
4. How much should users have to find out for themselves?

Answers to questions 1 and 2 have to strike an appropriate balance between how much users should be left to achieve for themselves, and how much the system should do for users.

An important feature of this knowledge seems to be that it is achieved and constantly repaired in human interaction, not only explicitly but also implicitly. This means that information in a conferencing system must be presented in ways reflecting this; for example, through direct presentation (which is most commonly used at present), and through "out of the corner of an eye" access – peripherally presented and accessed information (which has received less attention!).

In addition, there are also important questions concerning the best type and mix of media (for example, video) to be used in providing this information. I believe that the on-screen video that has been used in some CSCW systems to date has been more effective in elaborating technology than in enhancing cooperation.

7.4.3.1 Shared Framework

Many previous systems have also addressed the issues of a suitable cooperation framework, or environment, by providing some intuitive metaphors upon which to base system usage; for example, the "Rooms" (Cook et al. 1990) and other metaphors (Stefik et al. 1987). In my view, these are of superficial utility in addressing the issues of maintaining mutual awareness of users. What I believe is needed is a more constructional approach on the part of the users – a "do it yourself" metaphor.

Hence, the problem is not to design better, more usable metaphors for cooperative work systems, but how to provide end-user tools to allow users to construct, and reconstruct, locally meaningful shared frames of reference in which to embed their work. For example, a simple palette of shared objects (a line, a text label) that can acquire significance for the particular users in their particular situation.

7.4.3.2 Worst Case Design

Our experiences with our experimental system have taught us that successful design in conferencing systems (and CSCW systems in general) must take account of real-world problems and constraints inherent in the technology, such as delays, and buffering and queuing effects. At present, the best way of achieving this is still a research topic.

7.5 Summary and Future Work

The emerging picture of support for synchronous shared screen conferencing environments, in my view, is more about user communication and coordination of their views and knowledge than about explicit coordination of their action ("floor control"). Thus, in this area, the business opportunities for telecommunications companies are as rich as those for computer companies – if not more so!

Apart from adding to the embedded application functionality in our prototype system, to enable exploration of a richer information space, we plan to investigate systematically the above issues and questions. We will continue to rely on the methodology of user-involved experimentation to this end, as we believe this approach, which has proved so fruitful in the past, will become an even more powerful tool for CSCW systems design in the future.

Acknowledgements. This paper could not have been written without the efforts of my colleagues, Michele Morris and Tony Plant, on the EuroCoOp project. I am grateful to Michele Morris for a discussion on the types of conflict we encountered in our experiments. All rights reserved. Northern Telecom 1991.

The Computer Won't Let Me: Cooperation, Conflict and the Ownership of Information

C. Condon

8.1 Theme

This chapter aims to show that attempts to use computer-supported cooperative work (CSCW) systems to resolve interpersonal conflict will only translate it into conflict between the user and the computer system. Interpersonal conflict can sometimes be productive; human–computer conflict just leads to a frustrated cry: "The computer won't let me".

8.2 Background

My interest in CSCW comes from the convergence of four earlier project mainly conducted by BICC in association with BIBA:

- Human-centred computer integrated manufacturing (CIM)
- Experiments with video on the shop floor
- Development of a HyperCard based management information system
- Development of a distributed HyperCard based local accounts system

The most important of these was human-centred CIM, project 1217 in the European ESPRIT programme, extensively described by a collection of papers in Rosenbrock (1989). The project was based on a philosophy of manufacturing proposed by Cooley (1987), which concerns itself with the effects of automation on people in manufacturing. The ultimate aim of CIM is often seen as computer controlled manufacturing, in which people are not needed. In fact, people are almost always needed, but this attitude relegates them to a secondary role, supporting the CIM system – they come to be seen as unreliable elements of an otherwise reliable machine, to be removed if possible.

The idea behind human-centred CIM is to reverse this priority, placing people first and using information technology (IT) to support them. Manufacturing is seen as a human activity: the machines are there to support people in what they need to achieve. In the ESPRIT project, BICC's contribution, described in Hancke and Hamlin (1988) and Hamlin (1989), is a local interactive work scheduler allowing each manufacturing cell to control the planning and scheduling of its own work. The product, ACiT, is now sold by a spin-off company, Human Centred Systems. Besides empowering the local factory floor workers, this approach actually improves the effectiveness of the manufacturing process: schedules are adaptable, able to fit in with locally understood constraints and capabilities.

The human-centred approach to manufacturing, the hypertext approach to system structure, object-oriented communications and an understanding of the value of video in manufacturing came together in the creation of MILAN (multimedia integrated local area network). MILAN was developed as part of RACE project R1039, distributed international manufacturing using networks (DIMUN), as a demonstrator for the capabilities of future broadband communications. It has since been used in earnest and has been successfully implemented (despite its name) over long distance digital links.

8.3 Taxonomy

I realize that there are probably already too many CSCW taxonomies, but would still like to suggest another one – the "political" categorizing of systems. Most CSCW systems (and many other multi-user systems) could be placed into one of three categories: the fascist, the communist and the anarchist. The "fascist" approach is typified by ICL's desktop conferencing system, in which one chairperson is always in control, having the right to decide who can use the keyboard at any one time (see Fig. 8.1).

The second form, the "communist" system, places the system in control (see Fig. 8.2). Although it can only reflect the activities of the other users, the system becomes the ultimate authority. This category includes simple file locking techniques in which the system will maintain data integrity by refusing to allow a user to update a file at an unsuitable moment, through to complex meeting room support systems with facilities for computer controlled voting procedures, consolidation of joint documents and so on.

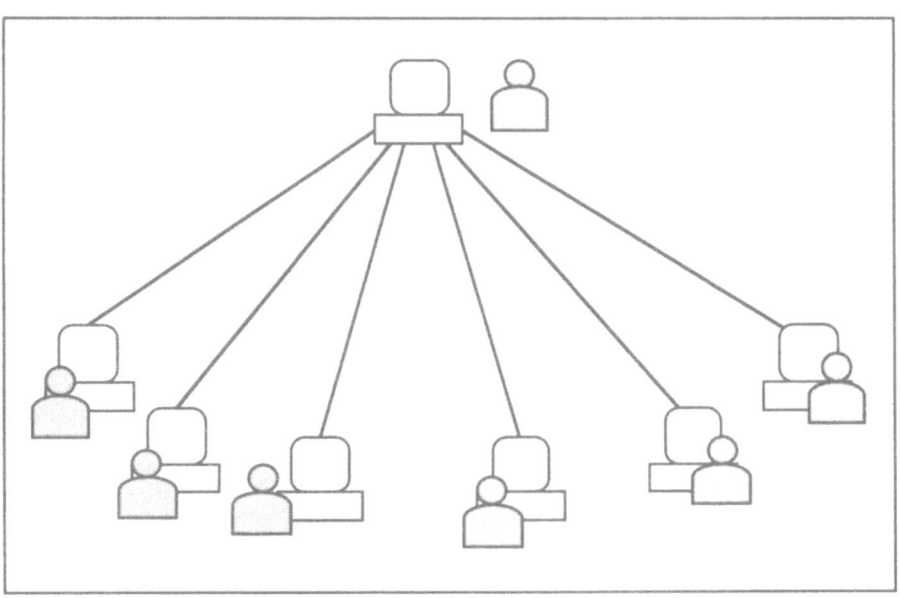

Fig. 8.1. "Fascist" CSCW controlled by the chairperson.

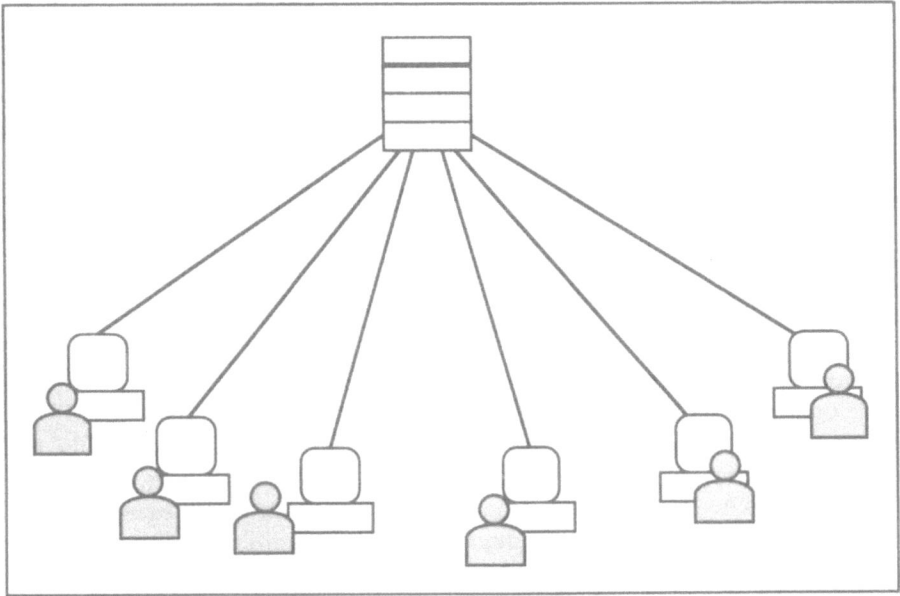

Fig. 8.2. "Communist" CSCW controlled by the computer system.

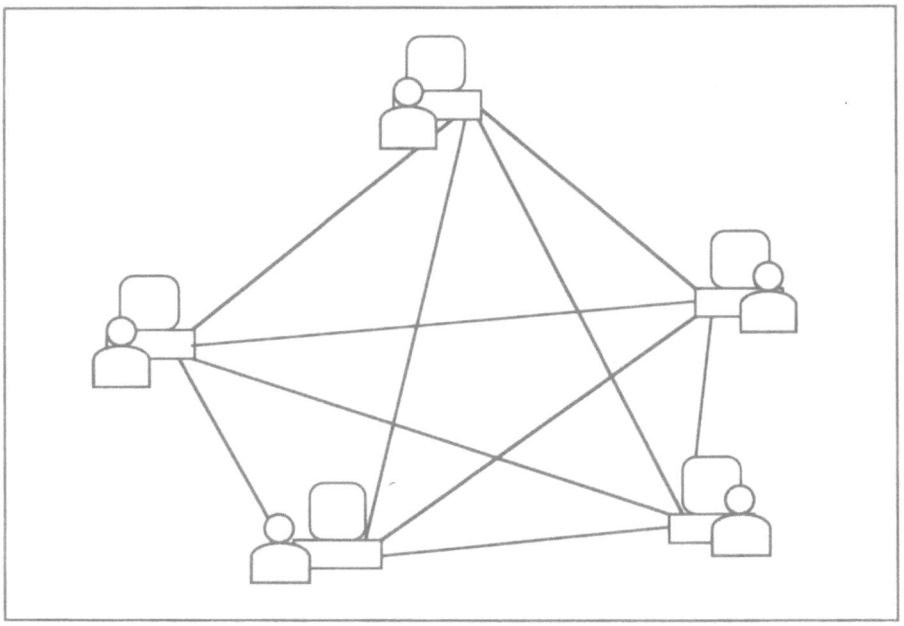

Fig. 8.3. "Anarchist" CSCW: no control.

The final category is usually known as "free-for-all"; in political terms, anarchy (see Fig. 8.3).

I propose that an anarchist approach is the only viable model for the design of CSCW systems. The movement from the mainframe to the personal computer has meant that control has moved from the organization to the individual. Once empowered, people will tend to reject central control. The CSCW systems that we build must therefore co-exist with existing personal computers, building on and integrating with their existing functionality.

8.4 Ownership of Information

Mainframe and microcomputers have evolved along two separate tracks – the corporate and the personal. CSCW might seem like a convergence of these two (like the recent announcement of a joint venture by IBM and Apple), but most existing systems start from one viewpoint or the other. It is worth looking at this distinction in terms of information ownership, as I believe this to be at the heart of many of CSCW's problems.

Corporate information belongs to the organization. Data is highly structured and is generally accessed through standard screens, protected by extensive data input vetting to ensure that only the "correct" data gets into

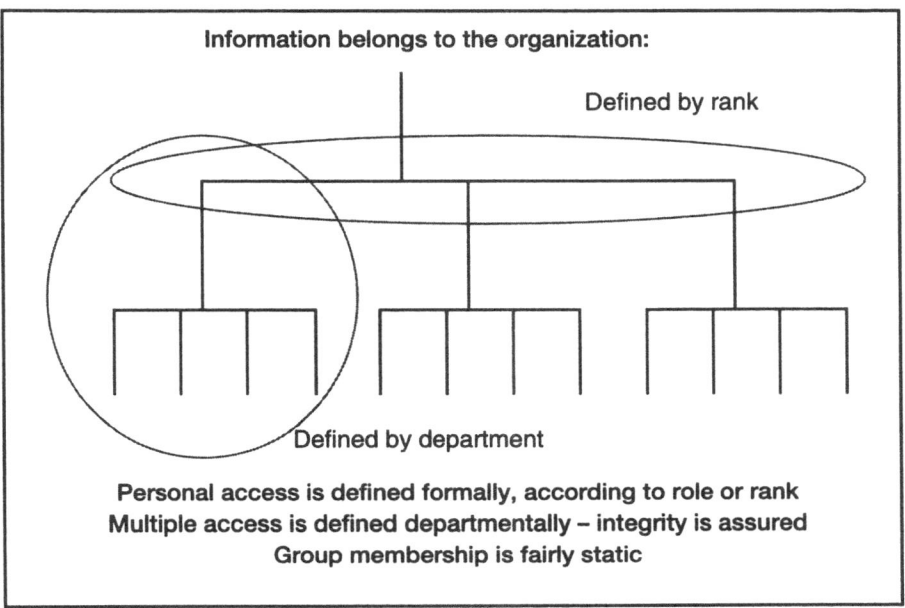

Fig. 8.4. Corporate information.

Information belongs to the individual
Personal access is defined informally, personally
Multiple access is defined informally, by the individual

Fig. 8.5. Personal information.

the system. Data integrity is established through techniques such as normalization that are applied to the design of the database and maintained by the database management system (see Fig. 8.4).

By contrast, information held on a personal computer is personal. Except when an application has been externally designed to integrate with the corporate systems, we can create, amend or delete almost anything we like. File organization and file names are personally decided and might be meaningless to others. Although the information might be structured, this structure is not externally imposed and is often only of significance to its creator (see Fig. 8.5).

What, then, of the ownership of information in CSCW systems? Some current systems like Philips Maestro and Lotus Notes are aimed at meeting specific corporate needs and support a corporate view of data, whereas simple applications like Timbuktu and pcAnywhere (and many office automation systems) ignore the content of the information. More sophisti-

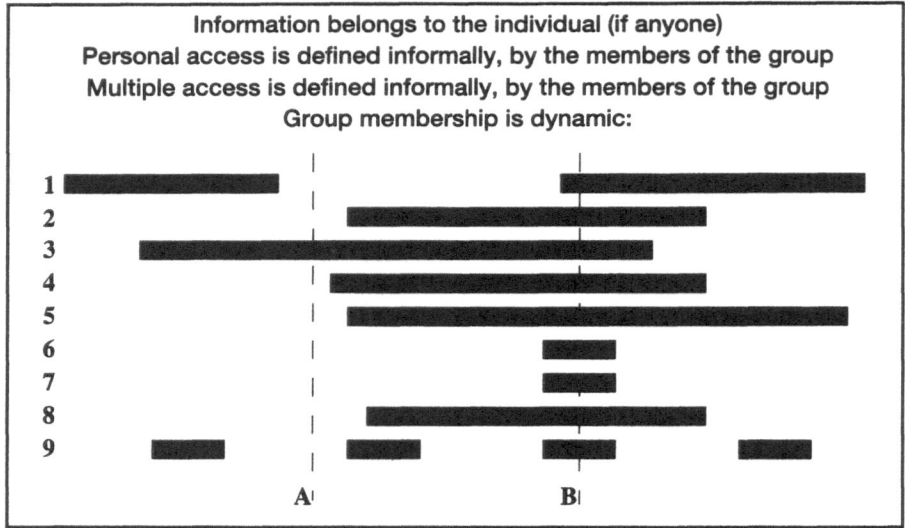

Fig. 8.6. Group information. In the example, the group at point A is just one person, whereas by B nine people are temporarily involved. No one person is continually present to maintain continuity. (Although it is likely that responsibility for a specific role or function might be handed from person to person, this cannot be relied on.) This is typical of the way in which groups break up, form and reform when carrying out innovative or speculative work.

cated systems introduce the concept of group ownership of information. This is usually implemented with some kind of hierarchy (see Fig. 8.6).

Advanced communications facilities, both formal and informal, can combine to make physical boundaries irrelevant. In consequence, there is no need to keep work groups static. They can change continually, communicating with each other, transferring information, controlling remote equipment, accessing remote information and working cooperatively on shared information.

8.5 Consequences for CSCW Design

Although the view outlined above might seem overly simplistic, it highlights the main problem of groupware from the point of view of the system designer – the lack of a clear owner. In fact, group information already exists, in the personal computing area and in electronic mail, as people pass information among themselves, but it lacks both control and coordination. Many workers have assumed that CSCW requires a typical database approach. Greif and Sarin (1986) show an early example of this approach, though they had to adapt it: "Rather than treating all integrity constraints as equal and always inviolate, different users can be allowed to violate particular constraints". Can we reconcile the freedom of the personal system with the integrity of the corporate system: is it possible to have coordination without control?

Some answers may lie in the way we design and implement software, but the problem itself is a human one. We must have a comprehensive view of the way that individuals, groups and organizations "own" information: how it can be owned, what ownership means in that context and, most importantly, who owns it. I believe this is one of the most critical areas for the CSCW systems designer. The types of cooperation and conflict we must deal with concern issues such as the cooperative ownership of a group document, or the potential conflict when I attempt to change "your" document. What happens (as in our system) where a document has a multiple existence?

One simple way to decrease the likelihood of conflict comes through the adoption of object-oriented design. The chances of two people attempting to change the same object at the same time are small; the chances of them changing the same attribute of the same object are even smaller. By working with objects that are as small and simple as possible, we can decrease the potential for conflict within the system still further. This does not mean that conflict does not exist: two people might still argue about their joint product, but the system communicates their interaction rather than attempting to mediate. This principle lies behind a system we have built at BICC MILAN (multimedia integrated local area network). The system is more fully described elsewhere (Condon 1990), so I will give only a brief overview here.

8.6 The MILAN System

The desktop metaphor popularized on the Apple Macintosh, and now a *de facto* standard for office applications, works well in the two-dimensional world of office paperwork. However it is not sufficiently powerful for the three-dimensional world of manufacturing. Although aware of the dangers of poor metaphors described in Carroll and Thomas (1982), we finally adopted a "meeting room" metaphor (see Fig. 8.7). Other groups who are addressing multimedia computing and communications issues have adopted similar approaches under such names as Hyper Rooms or Virtual Rooms, for example Xerox's 3-D Rooms (Clarkson 1991).

Once entered, the room includes a live video window showing the people present in the room and also lists their names. There are also a number of objects in the room, such as the copier, the fax and the waste-paper basket, to which documents can be dragged. Some objects and areas are more specialized. The first of these is the door, which is used to leave the room. Three other areas define forms of ownership of the information in the system:

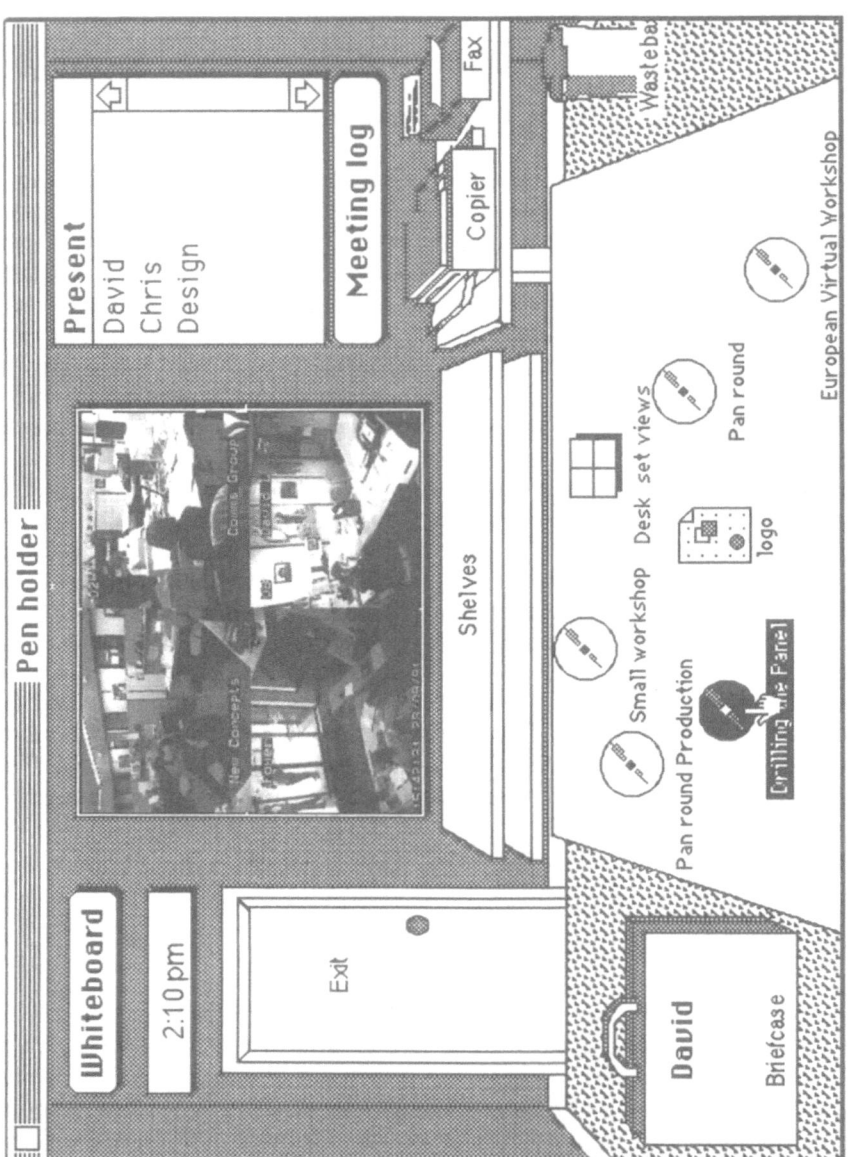

Fig. 8.7. A meeting room.

- *The briefcase.* All information in the briefcase is *private* to one individual
- *The table.* The table contains *public* information, which can be "picked up" and copied by any user
- *The wall.* This represents *shared* information, fully accessible by all users

A room represents a work-space for a group of people. Each room is different, but any given room is the same for those who enter it. The integrity of this might break down, as described below, but can always be restored by one user copying the room from another's machine. The one exception to this is the briefcase. Each user has their own personal briefcase which they "carry" into every room. The briefcase duplicates the functionality of the Macintosh desktop and all information in it is private and belongs to that individual.

Although the information in the briefcase is private, a user can choose to make something public by dragging it from their briefcase onto the table top. The icon then appears on all of the users' screens. The file itself is not copied, remaining on the local machine until another user chooses to drag it to their briefcase. This generates a standard file dialogue, allowing that user to copy the file to their machine. The new copy then belongs to that user – there is no ownership conflict.

The wall contains shared information. Some is simply information generated by the system, such as the time or the list of people present. The meeting log is a collection of timed and attributed comments made by the various participants during the meeting. As none of these examples can be edited, there is no room for conflict, though the log can be used to express simple forms of conflict:

15:13 Chris: Next meeting on 13th Decembeer

15:14 David: Only if the meeting with Smith can be postponed

In this case, the very nature of a meeting log demands high integrity: it is a record of a meeting and must not be falsified. This means, for example, that Chris cannot even correct the mis-typing of "December".

Two other areas of the wall do, however, provide very good examples of the potential for conflict. The way in which MILAN copes with interpersonal conflict in these areas – the whiteboard and the video window – are discussed in Sections 8.7 and 8.8.

8.7 Task Conflict in the Whiteboard

The main example of fully interactive CSCW software in MILAN is the shared whiteboard. This supports simple sketching facilities, with the facility to import drawings from standard computer aided design (CAD) systems. Meeting members can operate on the whiteboard at the same time,

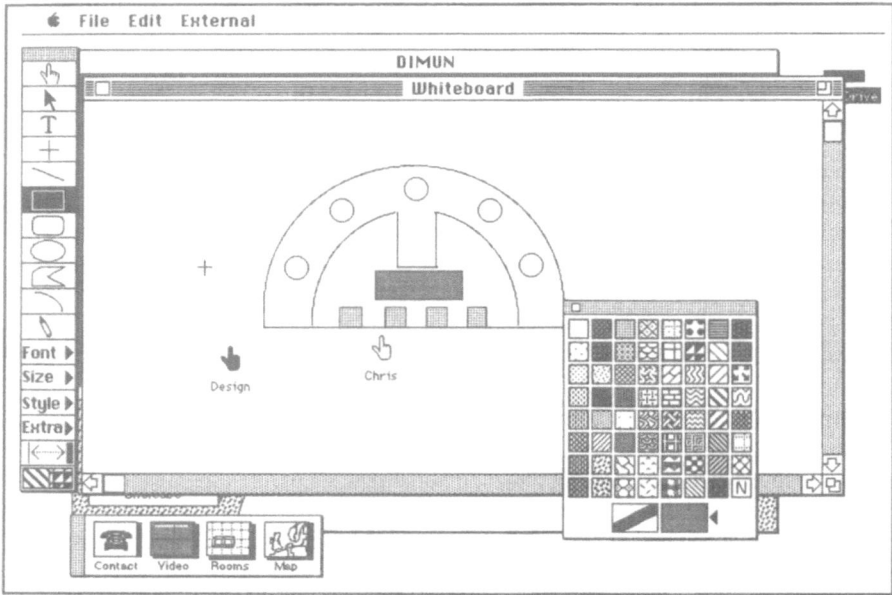

Fig. 8.8. The shared whiteboard.

with each change being broadcast to all current participants. Each person also has a pointer, which is shown on all the screens (see Fig. 8.8).

The most serious potential for conflict comes when two people attempt to change the same object at the same time. Change does not take place simultaneously – a problem that is exaggerated by our decision not to broadcast an action until it is complete. The conventional approach to this problem is to ensure the integrity of the data by a two-stage update: lock first, then update. We could easily implement this by locking an object when it is selected, but this would hinder compatible changes. For example, the pattern of an object and its shape are separate attributes and can be changed independently (see Fig. 8.9). Conflict will therefore only occur where two people make incompatible changes to the same attribute, for example the position of the object (see Fig. 8.10). We deal with this simply by communicating each person's action to the other's screen (see Fig. 8.11).

Each user now understands that the conflict exists and everyone can work together to solve it. Attempts by the computer system to hide the conflict or to impose a solution could not work, as the computer does not have access to the reasons for the users' actions. In the highly unlikely event of three or more incompatible changes at the same time, each user sees one of the others' changes.

The greatest problem with this solution occurs if the conflict is not resolved and two copies of the whiteboard remain different. Although this might seem anathema to a traditional systems analyst – the loss of data

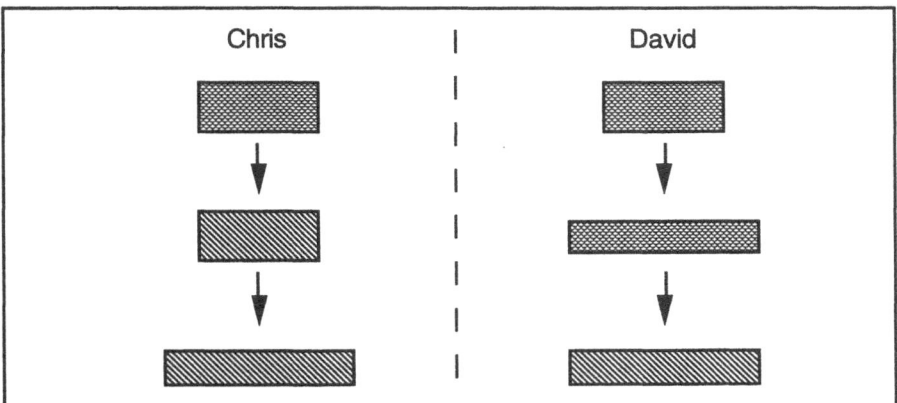

Fig. 8.9. The pattern of an object and its shape are separate attributes, and may be changed independently.

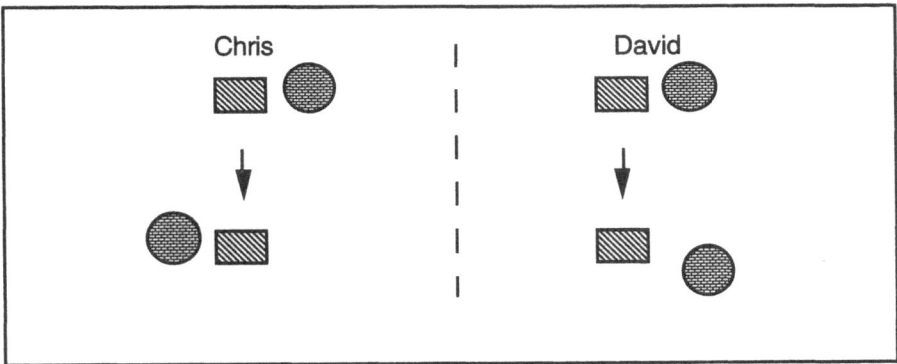

Fig. 8.10. Conflict occurs when two people make incompatible changes to the same object.

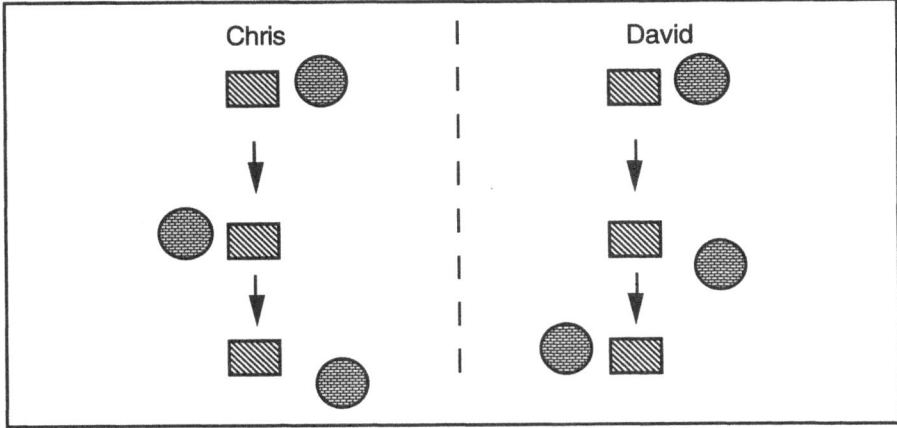

Fig. 8.11. Each person's action is communicated to the other's screen.

integrity – it represents the most honest representation of the group's decision. An option exists to copy another user's whiteboard to replace one's own, ensuring total integrity, but in practice, the participants will usually resolve the problem immediately through discussion over the multimedia communications channels. The moment one participant makes an unambiguous change, all other whiteboards are brought into line.

8.8 Ownership Conflict in the Video Views

The cellular structure of the enterprise is reflected in the distributed control of peripherals. Each shared peripheral is connected to the workstation owned by the person with the greatest interest or need for it. For instance, video discs are installed with the person who is the most likely to need them. However others can control these peripherals from anywhere on the network. The most interesting of these peripherals is the Uniplex multiview unit from Dedicated Micros, which controls the video views shown to the users.

Video windows must be handled in a fundamentally different way from text windows. We can read text comfortably only over a small range of character sizes. When we want to display many text windows we do not change the scale but put titles at the top and then overlap the windows with the titles showing, just as we do with sheets of paper on the desk. Video images can be recognized over a wide range of sizes but their key elements are usually in the centre of the frame. It is impractical to overlap them but realistic to "tile" them, i.e. reduce their size so that they can fit together as a matrix.

The Uniplex presents up to 16 views under computer control in a wide variety of tiled window layouts. Although it does not give an unlimited number of channels or complete freedom of layout it has sufficient flexibility to prototype the way in which a large number of video images can be handled on the screen (see Fig. 8.12).

The issue of video in MILAN is discussed in more detail by Leevers (1991). Here, I simply want to consider the "ownership" of a video view. One way of looking at this is to say that a view should belong to the person

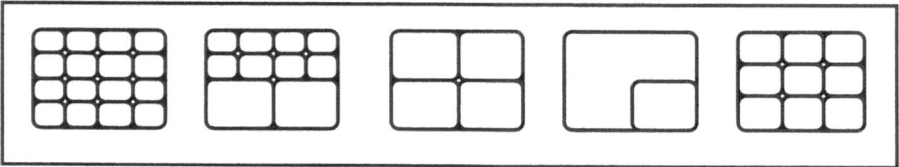

Fig. 8.12. Examples of Uniplex multiview layouts.

shown in that view, but many of our views are not of people but of objects of common interest. In use, cameras were also pulled back, showing an entire room rather than an individual's head and shoulders. Other cameras migrated to "public" areas such as reception or the coffee machine, and we gradually formed the concept of the "electronic open plan", uniting geographically distributed people as if they were working in a single open plan office. Each of these people sees the same group of views – what you see is what I see (WYSIWYS).

In these circumstances, it seemed best to allow people to take control of a particular view. This means, for example, that one person might control the upper left view, another the bottom right, with dialogue boxes used to hand over control. Although it seemed fair, we found that in practice people were confused and frustrated by the delays introduced. Our final version removed all controls. Now, any user can change the layout in use or can drag a picture (a snapshot of the view from that camera) from the selection on the right into any of the positions shown. Of course conflict occurs but, as with the whiteboard, the system is merely reflecting the conflicting views of the participants. As with the whiteboard, the conflict can be discussed and resolved by those taking part (see Fig. 8.13).

A more intrusive example of this difficulty lies with the control of the video recorder, which can also be controlled by anyone on the network. Currently, if anyone chooses the "record" option a new menu, "On the record", appears on everyone's machine (see Fig. 8.14). This new menu has only one option – "Stop" – which, due to the mechanical nature of the recorder, will allow anyone to stop the recording before it has even started. With the introduction of video compression techniques, such as Apple's QuickTime, we hope to go one step further, automatically recording the

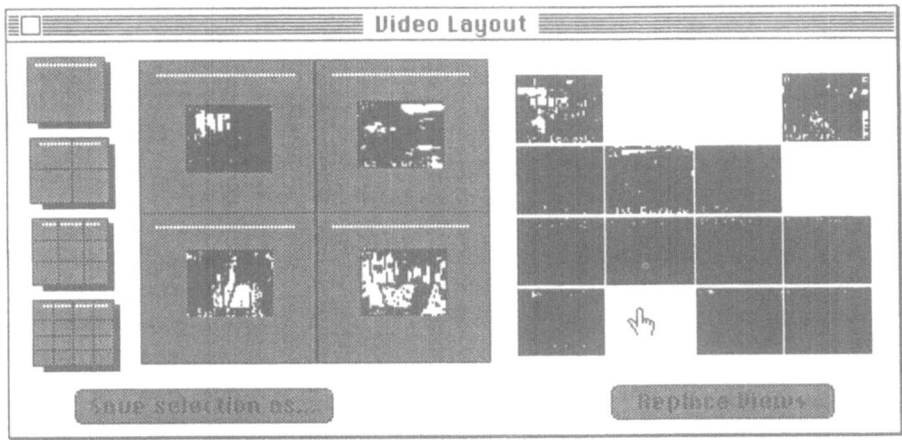

Fig. 8.13. The video layout control window.

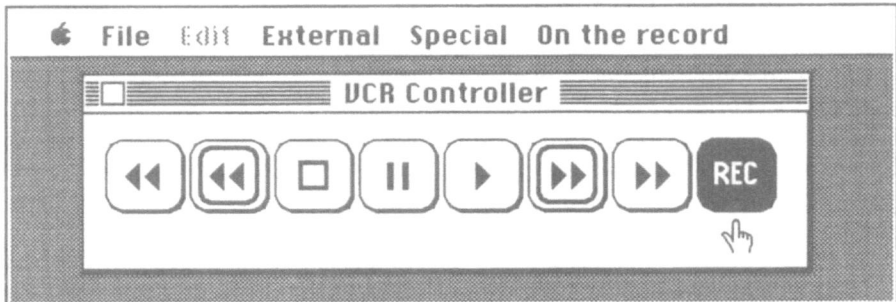

Fig. 8.14. The VCR controller.

most recent five minutes of a meeting to hard disc, continually overwriting it unless an explicit request is made to keep it.

8.9 Conclusions

We do not believe that our understanding of CSCW, or that of other researchers, has yet reached the level of sophistication at which we could dare to use it to "improve" human interaction. All we can do, at best, is to provide users with a few tools which give them the freedom to add to the group interaction, not subtract from it, to communicate interpersonal conflict, not resolve or prevent it. Users must be able to use the group system in exactly the way that they use personal computers. The idea of someone else taking away your control of your own keyboard or denying you access to a document you were in the middle of working on is not acceptable.

It might be seen as a problem that a normal meeting can result in each participant coming away with a different conclusion. We can design explicit tools to assist this, but they must not be mandatory. One example is the kind of audit trail which is often included with multi-user software. Multiple versions of a document can co-exist, but each copy contains a history of all changes made to it. Rather than the computer system imposing limits to maintain data integrity, users are now free to consolidate the changes if they wish.

The ideal would be to design systems where the interface is so transparent that we are truly aware of the other users and unaware of the computer (except when we explicitly call it in to carry out a task). Unfortunately, if we are ever to achieve this, the system must also be capable of reflecting all aspects of human conflict and cooperation. This means overthrowing one of the most sacred cows of software design: data integrity.

In some areas of work, such as software development, data integrity is accepted as necessary by the users and formal constraints are placed on interaction (version control and so on), and there is no reason to suppose that similar constraints should not be applicable in CSCW. But these constraints must be chosen by the users as applicable to their problem, not instituted to solve systems problems.

This issue is discussed in a paper on reflexive CSCW by Thimbleby et al. (1990). In talking about the ways in which CSCW techniques can support the individual user, they also strongly make the point that such systems must be non-intrusive. They note the "limitations of invasive, normative interfaces" in CSCW and suggest that their idea for Reflexive CSCW "is more rooted in practical reality because it can be built around the user's present environment, using his regular file space (or whatever) as a base; rather than being a `project organizer' that expects him to re-orient his way of working to suit the new tool". Although this looks at a narrow area of CSCW, the principles behind it must lie at the heart of all CSCW systems. Although we like to think of CSCW systems as a new area, they will inevitably be seen by the user as an extension of existing personal computing facilities and must never, under any circumstances, reduce the effectiveness of the existing facilities.

Many previous researchers have seen the potential for advanced communications to break down organizations, allowing *ad hoc* grouping rather than rigid departmental structures. Of course, the users (or their managers) may choose to ignore this potential and use the systems to create more authoritarian structures. For example, the Empirica study of teleworking (Huws et al. 1990) point out that such predictions were made by most proponents of teleworking, whereas "the largest telework organization we are aware of, the FI group, has a hierarchical structure, with seven tiers of management". All we can do is to attempt to design CSCW systems that allow the greatest freedom to the users, making sure they have the freedom to create the kinds of organizations they need.

References

Anderson JR, Boyle F, Corbett AT and Lewis MW (1990) Cognitive modelling and intelligent tutoring systems. Artificial Intelligence 42: 7–49

Appelt D and Kornfield A (1987) A computational model of referring. In: Proceedings of the Tenth International Joint Conference on Artificial Intelligence, Milan. Morgan Kaufman, San Mateo, CA, pp 640–647

Aries E (1976) Interaction patterns and themes of male, female, and mixed groups. Small Group Behavior 7: 7–18

Axelrod R (1984) The Evolution of Co-operation. Basic Books, New York

Baker PM (1981) The division of labor interdependence, isolation, and cohesion in small groups. Small Group Behavior 12(1): 93–106

Bales RF (1950) Interaction Process Analysis. University of Chicago Press, Chicago, IL

Bales RF and Borgatta EF (1955) Size of group as a factor in the interaction profile. In: Hare AP, Borgatta EF and Bales RF (ed.) Small Groups: Studies in Social Interaction. Knopf, New York.

Bannon L and Schmidt K (1989) CSCW: four characters in search of a context. In: Proceedings of the First European Conference on Computer Supported Cooperative Work (EC-CSCW '89), Gatwick, 13–15 September, pp 358–372

Bannon L, Bjorn-Andersen N and Due-Thompson B (1988) Computer support for cooperative work: an appraisal and critique. In: Proceedings, Eurinfo-88: Information Systems for Organizational Effectiveness. North-Holland, Amsterdam

Bartos OJ (1970) Determinants and consequences of toughness. In: Swingle P (ed) The Structure of Conflict. Academic Press, New York

Bass BM (1980) Team productivity and individual member competence. Small Group Behavior 11(4): 431–504

Baxter LA (1982) Conflict management: an episodic approach. Small Group Behavior 13(1): 23–42

Becker HS (1960) Notes on the concept of commitment. American Journal of Sociology 66: 32–40

Becker HS (1967) Whose side are we on? Social Problems 14: 239–247

Becker HS (1982) Art Worlds. University of California Press, Berkeley

Bell J and Hardiman RJ (1989) The third role – the naturalistic knowledge engineer. In: Diaper D (ed) Knowledge Elicitation: Principles, Techniques and Applications. Ellis Horwood, Chichester

Bentley A (1926) Relativity in Man and Society. GP Putnam, New York

Bion W (1961) Experiences with groups. Tavistock Publications, London

Blake RR and Mouton JS (1962) The intergroup dynamics of win–lose conflict and problems solving collaboration in union–management relations. In: Sherif M (ed) Intergroup Relations and Leadership. Wiley, New York

Blake RR, Shepard HA and Mouton JS (1964) Managing Intergroup Conflict in Industry. Gulf, Houston

Blaye A (1988) Peer interaction in solving binary matrix problems: possible mechanisms causing individual progress. In: Mandle H, De Corte E, Bennet N and Friedrich HP (ed) Learning and Instruction: European Research in an International Context. Pergamon Press, Oxford

Bly S (1988) A use of drawing surfaces in different collaborative settings. In: Proceedings of the Conference on Computer Supported Cooperative Work (CSCW-88), Portland, OR, September. ACM, New York, pp 250–257

Bødker S (1990) Activity theory as a challenge to systems design. In: Proceedings of ISRA-90, The Information Systems Research Arena of the 90's, Copenhagen, 14–16 December 1990

Bødker S (1991) Through the Interface. Lawrence Earlbaum, Hillsdale, NJ

Bødker S and Gronbaek K (1991) Cooperative prototyping – users and designers in mutual activity. International Journal of Man–Machine Studies 34(3)

Bødker S, Knudson JL, Kyng M, Ehn P and Madsen KH (1988) Computer Support for cooperative design. In: Proceedings of the Conference on Computer Supported Cooperative Work (CSCW-88), Portland, OR, September. ACM, New York, pp 377–395

Boland R (1989) Metaphorical traps in developing information systems for human progress. In Klein HK and Kumar K (ed) Systems Development for Human Progress. Elsevier, Amsterdam

Borning A and Travers M (1991) Two approaches to casual interaction over computer and video networks. In: Robertson S, Olson G and Olson J (ed) Proceedings of the Human Factors in Computing Systems Conference, CHI-91, New Orleans. ACM, New York

Bowers J and Churcher J (1988) Local and global structuring of computer mediated communication: developing linguistic perspectives on CSCW in COSMOS. In: Proceedings of the Conference on Computer Supported Cooperative Work (CSCW-88), Portland, OR, September. ACM, New York, pp 125–139

Bowker G and Star SL (1991) Situations vs. standards in long-term, wide-scale decision-making: the case of the international classification of diseases. In: Proceedings of the 24th Hawaiian International Conference on Systems Sciences, vol IV. IEEE Computer Society Press, Washington, DC, pp 73–81

Brehmer B (1976) Social judgement theory and the analysis of interpersonal conflict. Psychological Bulletin 83(6): 985–1003

Brehmer B and Hammond KR (1977) Cognitive factors in interpersonal conflict. In: Druckman D (ed) Negotiations: Social-Psychological Perspectives. Sage, Beverly Hills, CA

Brooks FP (1975) The Mythical Man-Month: Essays on Software Engineering. Addison-Wesley, Reading, MA

Brown BR (1968) The effects of the need to save face on interpersonal bargaining. Journal of Experimental Social Psychology 4: 107–122

Brown BR (1977) Face-saving and face-restoration in negotiations. In: Druckman D (ed) Negotiations: Social-Psychological Perspectives. Sage, Beverly Hills, CA

Brown W and Jaques E (1965) Glacier Project Papers. Heinemann, London

Callon M and Law J (1982) On interests and their transformation: enrolment and counter-enrolment. Social Studies of Science 12: 615–625

Carberry MS (1988) Modelling the user's plans and goals. Computational Linguistics 14(3): 23–37

Carroll JM and Thomas JC (1982) Metaphor and the cognitive representation of computing systems. IEEE Transactions on Systems, Man and Cybernetics 12(2): 107–116

Carron AV (1982) Cohesiveness in sport groups: implications and considerations. Journal of Sport Psychology 4: 123–138

Chalfonte BL, Fish RS and Kraut RE (1991) Expressive richness: a comparison of speech and text as media for revision. In: Robertson S, Olson G and Olson J (ed) Proceedings of the Human Factors in Computing Systems Conference, CHI-91, New Orleans. ACM, New York, pp 21–26

Chandràsekaran B (1981) Natural and social system metaphors for distributed problem solving: introduction to the issue. IEEE Transactions on Systems, Man and Cybernetics 11(1): 1–5

Chase S (1951) Roads to Agreement. Harper, New York

Ciborra C and Olson MH (1988) Encountering electronic work groups: a transaction costs perspective. In: Proceedings of the Conference on Computer Supported Cooperative Work (CSCW-88), Portland, OR, September. ACM, New York, pp 94–101

Cissna KN (1984) Phases in group development: the negative evidence. Small Group Behavior 15(1): 3–32

Clark HH and Brennan SE (1991) Grounding in communication. In: Resnick LB, Levine JM and Teasley SD (ed) Perspectives on Socially Shared Cognition. American Psychological Association, Washington, DC, pp 127–149

Clarkson MA (1991) An easier interface. Byte 16, February

Clegg C (1988) Appropriate technology for humans and organizations. Applied Ergonomics 19(1): 25–34

Cohen M and Ludwig LF (1991) Multidimensional audio window management. International Journal of Man–Machine Studies 34(3): 319–336

Collaros PA and Anderson LR (1969) Effect of perceived expertness upon creativity of members of brainstorming groups. Journal of Applied Psychology 53(2): 159–163

Collins HM (1990) Artificial Experts: Social Knowledge and Intelligent Machines. MIT Press, Cambridge, MA

Condon C (1990) Networked cooperative work: usability issues of MILAN. In: Proceedings Telematics-90, University of Bremen

Conklin J and Begeman ML (1988) gIBIS: a hypertext tool for exploratory policy discussion. In: Proceedings of the Conference on Computer Supported Cooperative Work (CSCW-88), Portland, OR, September. ACM, New York, pp 140–152. Also published as MCC Technical Report STP-082-88

Cook S, Birch G, Murphy A and Woolsey J (1990) Modelling groupware in the electronic office. International Journal of Man–Machine Studies 34: 369– 393

Cooley M (1987) Architect or Bee? The Human Price of Technology, 2nd edn. Hogarth Press, London

Corsaro WA and Rizzo TA (1990) Disputes in the peer culture of American and Italian nursery-school children. In: Grimshaw AD (ed) Conflict Talk: Socio-linguistic Investigations of Arguments in Conversations. Cambridge University Press, Cambridge

Coser LA (1956) The Functions of Social Conflict. Routledge and Kegan Paul, London

Crott HW, Kayser E and Lamm H (1980) The effects of information exchange and communication in an asymmetrical negotiation situation. European Journal of Social Psychology 10: 149–163

CSMIL (1991) ShrEdit 1.2, a shared editor for the Apple Macintosh: user's guide and technical description. Cognitive Science and Machine Intelligence Laboratory, University of Michigan

Curtis B, Krasner H and Iscoe N (1988) A field study of the software design process for large systems. Communications of the ACM 31(11)

Dahrendorf R (1959) Class and Class Conflict in Industrial Society. Routledge and Kegan Paul, London

Daves WF and Holland CL (1989) The structure of conflict behaviour of managers assessed with self- and subordinate ratings. Human Relations 42(8): 741–756

de Saussure F (1916) Course in General Linguistics. Fontana, London (edited by J Culler, 1974)

de Bono E (1985) Conflicts: A Better Way to Resolve Them. Penguin, Harmondsworth

Delisle NM and Schwartz MD (1987) Contexts – a partitioning concept for hypertext. ACM Transactions on Office Information Systems 5(2): 168–186

DeStephen RS and Hirokawa RY (1988) Small group consensus: stability of group support of the decision, task process, and group relationships. Small Group Behavior 19(2): 227–329

Deutsch M (1969) Conflicts: productive and destructive. Journal of Social Issues 25(1): 7–41

Deutsch M (1973) The Resolution of Conflict: Constructive and Destructive Processes. Yale University Press, New Haven

Dewey J (1920) Reconstruction in Philosophy. Henry Holt, New York

Di Sessa AA (1986) Models of computation. In: Norman DA and Draper SW (ed) User Centred System Design: New Perspectives in Human Computer Interaction. Lawrence Earlbaum, Hillsdale, NJ

Dietz JLG and Widdershoven GAM (1991) Speech acts or communicative action? In: Bannon L, Robinson M and Schmidt K (ed) Proceedings of the Second European Conference on CSCW (EC-CSCW '91). Kluwer, Dordrecht, pp 235–248

Doise W (1990) The development of individual competencies through social interaction. In: Foot HC, Morgan MJ and Shute RH (ed) Children Helping Children. Wiley, Chichester

Doise W and Mugny G 984) The Social Development of the Intellect. Pergamon Press, London

Doise W, Mugny G and Perret-Clermont A-N (1975) Social interaction and the development of cognitive operations. European Journal of Social Psychology 5(3): 367–383

Downs E, Clare P and Coe I (1988) SSADM Application and Context. Prentice- Hall, New York

Drucker P (1968) The Practice of Management. Pan, London

Druckman D, Rozelle R and Zechmeister K (1977) Conflict of interest and value dissensus: two perspectives. In Druckman D (ed) Negotiations: Social-Psychological Perspectives, Sage, Beverly Hills, CA

Durfee EH and Lesser VR (1987) Using partial global plans to coordinate distributed problem solvers. In: Proceedings of the Tenth International Joint Conference on Artificial Intelligence, Milan, August. Morgan Kaufman, San Mateo, CA, pp 875–882

Dykstra EA and Carasik RP (1991) Structure and support in cooperative environments – the Amsterdam conversation environment. International Journal of Man–Machine Studies 34(3) 419–434

Dyson JW, Godwin PH and Hazlewood LA (1976) Group composition, leadership orientation, and decisional outcomes. Small Group Behavior 7(1): 114–128

Easterbrook SM (1991) Handling conflict between domain descriptions with computer-supported negotiation. Knowledge Acquisition 3(4): 255–289

Edney JJ and Bell PA (1984) Sharing scarce resources: group-outcome orientation, external disaster, and stealing in a simulated commons. Small Group Behavior 15(1) 87–108

Ehn P (1988) Work-oriented design of computer artifacts. Lawrence Earlbaum, Hillsdale, NJ

Ehrlich SF (1987) Strategies for encouraging successful adoption of office communications systems. ACT Transactions on Office Information Systems 5(4): 340–357

Elias FG, Johnson ME and Fortman JB (1989) Task focused self disclosure: effects on group cohesiveness, commitment to task, and productivity. Small Group Behavior 20(1): 87–96

Ellis CA, Gibbs SJ and Rein GL (1990) Design and use of a group editor. In: Cockton G (ed) Proceedings of the IFIP Engineering for Human–Computer Interaction Conference. North-Holland, Amsterdam, pp 13–25. Also published as MCC Technical Report STP-263-88

Ellis CA, Gibbs SJ and Rein GL (1991) Groupware: some issues and experiences. Communications of the ACM 34(1): 39–58. Also published as MCC Technical Report STP-414-88

Ellis DG and McAllister L (1980) Relational control sequences in sex-typed and androgynous groups. Western Journal of Speech Communication 44: 35–49

Engelbart D (1984) Authorship provisions in AUGMENT. In: Proceedings of the IEEE Compcon Conference. Reprinted in Greif I (ed) (1988) Computer-Supported Cooperative Work: A Book of Readings. Morgan Kaufmann, San Mateo, CA, pp 107–126

Engestrom Y and Engestrom R (1988) Computerized medical records, production pressure and compartmentalization in the work activity of health centre physicians. In: Proceedings of the Conference on Computer Supported Cooperative Work (CSCW-88), Portland, OR, September. ACM, New York, pp 65– 84

Eskilson A and Wiley MG (1976) Sex composition and leadership in small groups. Sociometry 39: 183–194

Evans NJ and Jarvis PA (1980) Group cohesion: a review and re-evaluation. Small Group Behavior 11(4): 359–370

Eveland J and Bikson T (1988) Work group structures and computer support: a field experiment. In: Proceedings of the Conference on Computer Supported Cooperative Work (CSCW-88), Portland, OR, September. ACM, New York, pp 324–343

Falk G (1981) Unanimity versus majority rule in problem-solving groups: a challenge to the superiority of unanimity. Small Group Behavior 12(4): 379–399

Farallon (1988) Timbuktu user's guide. Farallon Computing Inc, Berkeley, CA

Feigenbaum E and McCorduck P (1984) The Fifth Generation. Penguin, Harmondsworth

Fink CF (1968) Some conceptual difficulties in the theory of social conflict. Journal of Conflict Resolution 12: 412-460

Fish RS, Kraut RE and Chalfonte BL (1990) The Videowindow system in informal communications. In: Proceedings of the Conference on Computer Supported Cooperative Work (CSCW-90), Los Angeles, CA, 7–10 October. ACM, New York, pp 1–11

Fisher R and Ury W (1981) Getting to Yes: Negotiating Agreement Without Giving In. Hutchinson, London

Flood RL and Jackson MC (1991) Creative Problem Solving. Wiley, Chichester

Folger JP and Poole MS (1984) Working Through Conflict: A Communication Perspective. Scott Foresman, Glenview, IL

Ford DL, Nemiroff PM and Pasmore WA (1977) Group decision-making performance as influenced by group tradition. Small Group Behavior 8(2): 223–228

Franz CR and Robey D (1984) An investigation of user-led system design: rational and political perspectives. Communications of the ACM 27: 1202–1209

Fujimura J (1988) The molecular biological bandwagon in cancer research: where social worlds meet. Social Problems 35: 261–83

Garfinkel D, Gust P, Lemon M and Lowder S (1989) The SharedX multi-user interface user's guide, version 2.0. Research report STL-TM-89-07, Hewlett-Packard Laboratories, Palo Alto, CA

Garfinkel H (1967) Studies in Ethnomethodology. Prentice-Hall, Englewood Cliffs, NJ

Gasser L (1986) The integration of computing and routine work. ACM Transactions on Office Information Systems 4: 205–225

Gasser L, Braganza C and Herman N (1986) MACE: a flexible testbed for distributed AI research. Technical Report CRI 87-01, Computer Research Institute, University of Southern California

Gaver W (1991) Working together in media space: CSCW research at EuroPARC. In: Proceedings of the Seminar on Computer Supported Cooperative Work – The Multimedia and Networking Paradigm, July 1991, Brunel University, UK, Unicom Seminars Ltd

Gemmill G (1986) The mythology of the leader in small groups. Small Group Behavior 17(1): 41–50

Gemmill G (1989) The dynamics of scapegoating in small groups. Small Group Behavior 20(4) 406–418

Gemmill G and Wynkoop C (1991) The psychodynamics of small group transformation. Small Group Research 22(1): 4–23

Gemmill G and Kraus G (1988) Dynamics of covert role analysis: small groups. Small Group Behavior 19: 299–311

Gero A (1985) Conflict avoidance in consensual decision processes. Small Group Behavior 16(4): 487–499

Gersick CJG (1988) Time and transition in work teams: towards a new model of group development. Academy of Management Journal 31: 9–41

Gersick CJG (1989) Marking time: predictable transitions in task groups. Academy of Management Journal 32: 274–309

Gersick CJG (1991) Revolutionary change theories: a multilevel exploration of the punctuated equilibrium paradigm. Academy of Management Review 16: 10–36

Gerson E and Star SL (1986) Analyzing due process in the workplace. ACM Transactions on Office Information Systems 4: 257–270

Gibb JR (1954) Factors producing defensive behavior within groups. Annual technical report of the Human Relations Laboratory, University of Colorado, Boulder, CO

Gibbs S (1989) LISA and extensible groupware toolkit. In: Proceedings of the Human Factors in Computing Systems Conference, CHI-89, Austin, TX. ACM, New York

Glachan M and Light P (1982) Peer interaction and learning: can two wrongs make a right? In Butterworth G and Light P (ed) Social Cognition Studies of the Development of Understanding. Harvester Press, Brighton

Goodlet JS (1988) The development of an issue-based information system for supporting design. Cognitive Science Research Paper 144, School of Cognitive and Computing Sciences, University of Sussex

Greenberg S (1991) An annotated bibliography of computer-supported cooperative work. In Greenberg S (ed) Computer-supported Cooperative Work and Groupware. Academic Press, London

Greenberg S (1991) Computer-supported cooperative work and groupware – an introduction. International Journal of Man–Machine Studies 34(2)

Greif I and Sarin S (1986) Data sharing in group work. In: Peterson D (ed) Proceedings of the Conference on Computer Supported Cooperative Work (CSCW-86), Austin, TX. ACM, New York

Greif I (ed) (1988) Computer-Supported Cooperative Work: A Book of Readings. Morgan Kaufmann, San Mateo, CA

Greif I, Seliger R and Weihl W (1986) Atomic data abstractions in a distributed collaborative editing system. In: Proceedings of the 5th Annual Symposium on Principles of Programming Languages. ACM, New York

Grimshaw AD (1990) Conflict Talk: Socio-linguistic Investigations of Arguments in Conversations. Cambridge University Press, Cambridge

Gross N, McEachern AW and Mason WS (1958) Role conflict and its resolution. In: Thomas EJ (ed) Role Theory: Concepts and Research. Wiley, Chichester

Grosz BJ (1977) The representation and use of focus in a system for understanding dialogues. In: Proceedings of the Fifth International Joint Conference on Artificial Intelligence. Morgan Kaufman, San Mateo, CA

Grosz BJ (1978) Discourse analysis. In: Walker D (ed) Understanding Spoken Language. Elsevier/North-Holland, New York, pp 235–268

Grosz BJ (1981) Focussing and description in natural language dialogues. In: Joshi AK, Sag I and Webber B (ed) Elements of Discourse. Cambridge University Press, Cambridge

Grosz BJ and Sidner C (1986) Attention, intentions and the structure of discourse. Computational Linguistics 12(3): 175–204

Grudin J (1991) Obstacles to user involvement in software product development, with implications for CSCW. International Journal of Man–Machine Studies 34(3)

Gulliver PH (1979) Disputes and Negotiations. Academic Press, New York

Hagen BH and Burch G (1985) The relationship of group process and group task accomplishment to group member satisfaction. Small Group Behavior 16(2): 211–233

Hall J (1971) Decisions, decisions, decisions. Psychology Today 5: 51–54, 86–87

Hall S (1982) Conformity, consensus and conflict. In: Social Sciences: A Foundation Course, Block 5, Unit 21. Open University Press, Milton Keynes

Hamlin M (1989) Human-centred CIM. Professional Engineering, April

Hancke T and Hamlin M (1988) Evaluation of the human-system interface of a production island in a human centred CIM system. Deliverable R26, ESPRIT 1217, Human Centred Systems, Maylands Avenue, Hemel Hempstead HP2 4SJ, UK

Hare AP and Naveh D (1985) Creative problem solving, Camp David summit 1978. Small Group Behavior 16(2): 123–138

Heath C and Luff P (1991) Disembodied conduct communication through video in a multi-media office environment. In: Robertson S, Olson G and Olson J (ed) Proceedings of the Human Factors in Computing Systems Conference, CHI- 91, New Orleans. ACM, New York, pp 99–103

Hellriegel D, Slocum JW and Woodman RW (1989) Organizational Behaviour (5th edn). West Publishing Company, St Paul

Hermann MG and Kogan N (1977) Effects of negotiators' personalities on negotiating behaviour. In: Druckman D (ed) Negotiations: Social-Psychological Perspectives. Sage, Beverly Hills, CA

Hewitt C (1985) The challenge of open systems. Byte 10: 223–242

Hewitt C (1986) Offices are open systems. ACM Transactions on Office Information Systems 4: 271–287

Hewitt C and DeJong P (1984) Open systems. In: Brodie ML, Mylopoulous J and Schmidt JW (ed) On Conceptual Modeling. Springer-Verlag, New York, pp 147–164

Hewstone M and Brown R (1986) Contact is not enough: an intergroup perspective on the "contact hypothesis". In: Hewstone M and Brown R (ed), Contact and Conflict in Intergroup Encounters. Blackwell, Oxford

Hirschheim RA, Klein H and Newman M (1987) A social action perspective of information systems development. In: DeGross J and Kriebel C (ed) Proceedings of the 8th ICIS conference. ACM, New York, pp 45–56

Hirschhorn L (1988) The Workplace Within: Psychodynamics of Organizational Life. MIT Press, Cambridge, MA

Hofstede G (1980) Culture's Consequences: International Differences in Work-Related Values, Sage, Beverly Hills, CA

Homans G (1950) The Human Group. Harcourt, Brace/World, New York

Howell JP, Dorfman PW and Kerr S (1986) Moderating variables in leadership research. Academy of Management Review 11: 88–102

Huczynski A and Buchanan D (1991) Organizational Behaviour (2nd edn). Prentice-Hall, London

Hughes EC (1971) The Sociological Eye. Aldine, Chicago, IL

Hughes PT, Plant TA, Morris ME and Seel NR (1991) Collaboration media: the problem of design by use and the use of design. In: Proceedings of the Seminar on Computer Supported Cooperative Work – The Multimedia and Networking Paradigm, July 1991, Brunel University, UK, Unicom Seminars Ltd

Huhns MN (ed) (1987) Distributed Artifical Intelligence. Morgan Kaufmann, Los Altos, CA

Hutchison CS and Rosenberg D (1992) The organization of organizations: a holistic perspective, AI Group Technical Report 92-2, Kingston Polytechnic, UK

Huws U, Korte WB and Robinson S (1990) Telework: Towards the Elusive Office. Wiley, Chichester

Ishii H (1990) TeamWorkstation: towards a seamless shared space. In: Proceedings of the

Conference on Computer Supported Cooperative Work (CSCW-90), Los Angeles, CA, 7–10 October. ACM, New York, pp 13–26

Ives B and Olson MH (1984) User involvement and MIS success: a review of the research. Management Science 30: 586–603

Jamieson DW and Thomas KW (1974) Power and conflict in student–teacher relationships. Journal of Applied Behavioral Science 10: 321–336

Janis IL (1972) Victims of Group-Think: A Psychological Study of Foreign-Policy Decisions and Fiascoes. Houghton Mifflin, Boston, MA

Jaques E (1976) A General Theory of Bureaucracy. Heinemann, London

Jaques E (1989) Requisite Organization. Cason Hall, New York

Jessup LM, Connolly T and Tansik DA (1990) Toward a theory of automated group work: the de-individuating effects of anonymity. Small Group Research 21(3) 333–348

Jirotka M and Gilbert GN (1990a) 100 & 31 flavours of organizations, Social and Computer Sciences Research Group, University of Surrey

Jirotka M and Gilbert GN (1990b) On the social organization of organizations, Social and Computer Sciences Research Group, University of Surrey

Johnson NE, Tomlinson CM and Johnson L (1990) Second generation expert systems and knowledge elicitation. International Journal of Systems Research and Information Science 4: 87–99

Johnson NE, Tomlinson CM and Johnson L (1992) Validating knowledge within knowledge elicitation. International Journal of Systems Research and Information Science (in press)

Joiner R (1991) The negotiation of dialogue focus: implications for the design of computer supported cooperative learning environments. In: Bowers J and Benford S (ed) Studies in Computer Supported Cooperative Work: Theory, Practice and Design. North-Holland, Oxford

Jones RE and White CS (1985) Relationships among personality, conflict resolution styles, and task effectiveness. Group and Organization Studies 10(2): 152–167

Karbe B, Ramsperger N and Weiss P (1990) Support of cooperative work by electronic circulation folders. In: Proceedings of the Conference on Office Automation Systems, Cambridge, MA

Katz GM (1982) Previous conformity, status, and the rejection of the deviant. Small Group Behavior 13(3): 403–414

Keeney RL and Raiffa H (1976) Decisions with Multiple Objectives: Preferences and Value Tradeoffs. Wiley, New York

Kelly JR, Futoran GC and McGrath JE (1990) Capacity and capability: seven studies of entrainment of task performance rates. Small Group Research 21(3): 283–314

Kiesler S, Siegel J and McGuire TW (1984) Social psychological aspects of computer-mediated communication. American Psychologist 39(10): 1123–1134

Kilmann RH, Saxton MJ and Serpa R (1985) Gaining Control of the Corporate Culture. Jossey-Bass, San Francisco

Kimberly JC (1987) Instrumental and expressive structures in groups in organizational settings. Small Group Behavior 17(4) 395–406

King J and Star SL (1990) Conceptual foundations for the development of organizational decision support systems. In: Proceedings of the 23rd Hawaiian International Conference on Systems Sciences, vol III. IEEE Computer Society Press, Washington, DC, pp 143-151

Klein M (1991) Supporting conflict resolution in cooperative design systems. IEEE Transactions on Systems, Man and Cybernetics 21(6)

Kling R and Iacono S (1984) The control of information systems development after implementation. Communications of the ACM 27: 1218–1226

Kling R and Scacchi W (1982) The web of computing: computing technology as social organization. Advances in Computers 21: 3-78

Knister M and Prakash A (1990) DistEdit: a distributed toolkit for supporting multiple group editors. In: Proceedings of the Conference on Computer Supported Cooperative Work (CSCW-90), Los Angeles, CA, 7–10 October. ACM, New York

Kozan MK (1989) Cultural influences on styles of handling interpersonal conflicts: comparisons among Jordanian, Turkish and U.S. Managers. Human Relations 42(9): 787–799

Kraut RE, Edigo C and Galegher J (1988) Patterns of contact and communication on scientific collaboration. In: Proceedings of the Conference on Computer Supported Cooperative Work (CSCW-88), Portland, OR, September. ACM, New York, pp 1–12

Kuhn T (1970) The Structure of the Scientific Revolutions. University of Chicago Press, Chicago, IL

Kunz W and Rittel H (1970) Issues as elements of information systems. Technical Report S-78-2, Institut fur Grundlagen der Planung i.A., Universitat Stuttgart, Keplerstrasse 11, 7000 Stuttgart 1, Germany

Kuutti K (1990) Activity theory and its application to information systems research and development. In: Proceedings of ISRA-90, The Information Systems Research Arena of the 90's, 14–16 December 1990, Copenhagen

Lane IM, Matthews RC, Chaney CM, Effmeyer RC, Reber RA and Teddlie CB (1982) Making the goals of acceptance and quality explicit effects on Group decisions. Small Group Behavior 13(4): 542-554

Latour B (1987) Science in Action. Harvard University Press, Cambridge, MA

Latour B and Woolgar S (1979) Laboratory Life. Sage, Beverly Hills, CA

Law J (1987) Technology, closure and heterogeneous engineering: the case of the Portuguese expansion. In: Bijker W, Pinch T and Hughes PT (ed) The Social Construction of Technological Systems. MIT Press, Cambridge, MA, pp 111–134

Lea M and Spears R (1991) Computer-mediated communication, de-individuation and group decision-making. International Journal of Man–Machine Studies 34: 283–301

Leevers D (1991) Multimedia communications in DIMUN. In: Proceedings Teleconference Europe-91, May 1991, Paris

Leland MDP, Fish RS and Kraut RE (1988) Collaborative document production using Quilt. In: Proceedings of the Conference on Computer Supported Cooperative Work (CSCW-88), Portland, OR, September. ACM, New York, pp 206–215

Leung K (1987) Some determinants of reaction to procedural models for conflict resolution: a cross-national study. Journal of Personality and Social Psychology 53: 265–308

Leung K, Bond MH, Carment WD, Krishnan L and Liebrand WBG (1990) Effects of cultural femininity on preference for methods of conflict processing: a cross-cultural study. Journal of Experimental and Social Psychology 26: 373–388

Levins R (1966) The strategy of model building in population biology. American Scientist 54: 21–31

Lewis B and Hodges J (1988) Shared books: collaborative publication management for an office information system. In: Proceedings of the Conference on Office Automation Systems, Palo Alto, CA

Light P and Perret-Clermont A-N (1989) Social context effects in learning and testing. In: Light P (ed) Cognition and Social Worlds. Oxford University Press, Oxford

Light P and Glachan M (1985) Facilitation of problem solving through peer interaction. Educational Psychology 5: 217–225

Linde C (1988) Who's in charge here? Cooperative work and authority negotiation in police helicopter missions. In: Proceedings of the Conference on Computer Supported Cooperative Work (CSCW-88), Portland, OR, September. ACM, New York, pp 52–65

Litman DJ and Allen JF (1987) A plan recognition model for subdialogues in conversations. Cognitive Science 11: 163–200

Litman DJ and Allen JF (1990) Discourse processing and common sense plans. In: Cohen PR, Morgan JL and Pollack ME (ed) Intentions in Communication. MIT Press, Cambridge, MA

Lowe D (1986) SYNVIEW: the design of a system for cooperative structuring of information. In: Peterson D (ed) Proceedings of the Conference on Computer Supported Cooperative Work (CSCW-86), Austin, TX. ACM, New York

Luce DL and Raiffa H (1957) Games and Decisions: Introduction and Critical Survey, Wiley, New York

Luchins A (1942) Mechanization of problem solving. Psychological monographs 54(6)

Lynch M (1991) Ordinary and scientific measurement as ethnomethodological phenomena. In: Button G (ed) Ethnomethodology and the Human Sciences: A Foundational Reconstruction. Cambridge University Press, Cambridge, pp 77–108

Lyytinen K (1988) Stakeholders, information system failures and soft systems methodology: an assessment. Journal of Applied Systems Analysis 15: pp 61–81

Mabry EA (1985) The effects of gender composition and task structure on small group interaction. Small Group Behavior 16(1) 75–96

Macdonald AM (ed) (1981) Chambers Twentieth Century Dictionary (revised Edn). Chambers, Edinburgh

Mack RW (1965) The components of social conflict. Social Problems 22(4): 388–397

Mackay WE (1988) More than just a communication system: diversity in the use of electronic mail. In: Proceedings of the Conference on Computer Supported Cooperative Work (CSCW-88), Portland, OR, September. ACM, New York, pp 344–353

MacLean A, Young RM and Moran TP (1989) Design rationale: the argument behind the artifact. In: Proceedings of the Human Factors in Computing Systems Conference, CHI-89, Austin, TX. ACM, New York, pp 247–252

Malcolm N (1991) GroupWriter: a word processor for collaborative document production. Research Report 91/435/19, Department of Computer Science, University of Calgary, Alberta

Malone TW, Grant KR, Turbak FA, Brobst SA and Cohen MD (1987) Intelligent information-sharing systems. Communications of the ACM 30(5): 390–402

Mantei M, Baecker RM, Sellen AJ, Buxton WAS, Milligan T and Wellman B (1991) Experiences in the use of media space. In: Robertson S, Olson G and Olson J (ed) Proceedings of the Human Factors in Computing Systems Conference, CHI-91, New Orleans. ACM, New York, pp 203–208

Mantei M (1988) Capturing the capture lab concepts: a case study in the design of computer supported meeting environments. In: Proceedings of the Conference on Computer Supported Cooperative Work (CSCW-88), Portland, OR, September. ACM, New York, pp 257–270

Mantei M (1991) Computer supported meeting environments. In: Proceedings of the Human Factors in Computing Systems Conference, CHI-91, tutorial notes. ACM, New York

Maples MF (1988) Group development: extending Tuckman's theory. Journal for Specialists in Group Work 13(1): 17–23

Markus ML (1983) Power, politics and MIS implementation. Communications of the ACM 26: 430–444

Markus ML and Robey D (1988) Information technology and organizational change: causal structure in theory and research. Management Science 34: 583–598

Marx K (1847) Das Elend der Philosophie. Berlin

Maturana HR and Varela FJ (1987) The Tree of Knowledge. New Science Library, Boston, MA

McCall RJ (1989) MIKROPLIS: a hypertext system for design. Design Studies 10(4) 228–238

McCarthy JC, Miles VC and Monk AF (1991) An experimental study of common ground in text-based communication. In: Robertson S, Olson G and Olson J (ed) Proceedings of the Human Factors in Computing Systems Conference, CHI-91, New Orleans. ACM, New York, pp 209–215

McGrath JE (1984) Groups: Interaction and Performance. Prentice-Hall, Englewood Cliffs, NJ

McGrath JE (1991) Time, interaction and performance (TIP): a theory of groups. Small Group Research 22(2): 147–174

Mead GH (1917) Scientific method and the individual thinker. In: Dewey J, Moore AW, Brown HC, Mead GH, Bode BH, Stuart HW, Tufts JH and Kallen NM (ed) Creative Intelligence: Essays in the Pragmatic Attitude. Henry Holt, New York, pp 176–227

Mead GH (1964) The objective reality of perspectives. In: Reck AJ (ed) Selected Writings. University of Chicago Press, Chicago, IL, pp 306–319

Menzies-Lyth I (1988) Containing anxiety in institutions: selected essays. Free Association Books, London

Miles VC, McCarthy JC, Dix AJ, Harrison MD and Monk AF (1992) Reviewing designs for a synchronous–asynchronous group editing environment. In: Sharples M (ed) Computer Supported Collaborative Writing. Springer-Verlag, London

Milgram S (1965) Some conditions of obedience and disobedience to authority. Human Relations 18(1): 57–75

Minneman S and Bly S (1991) Managing a trois: a study of a multi-user drawing tool in distributed design work. In: Robertson S, Olson G and Olson J (ed) Proceedings of the Human Factors in Computing Systems Conference, CHI-91, New Orleans. ACM, New York

Moore CM (1987) Group techniques for idea building. Sage, Beverly Hills, CA

Moorhead G, Ference R and Neck CP (1991) Group decision fiascos continue: Space Shuttle Challenger and a revised group-think framework. Human Relations 44(6): 539–550

Moreno JL (1953) Who Shall Survive? Beacon, Boston

Morgan G (1986) Images of Organizations. Sage, London

Morris ME (1991) Phase 0 shared screen conferencing system: evaluation report, EuroCoOp Project Document, ECO-BNRE-91-1

Moscovici S and Zavalloni M (1969) The group as a polarizer of attitudes. Journal of Personality and Social Psychology 12(2): 125–135

Mudrack PE (1989a) Defining group cohesiveness: a legacy of confusion? Small Group Behavior 20(1): 37–49

Mudrack PE (1989b) Group cohesiveness and productivity. Human Relations 42(9): 771–785

Mugny G and Doise W (1978) Socio-cognitive conflict and structure of individual and collective performances. European Journal of Social Psychology 8: 181–192

Mullins LJ (1989) Management and Organizational Behaviour (2nd edn). Pitman, London

Mumford E (1983) Designing Participatively. Manchester Business School Press, Manchester

Nemeth C, Endicott J and Wachtler J (1976) From the '50s to the '70s: women in jury deliberations. Sociometry 39: 293–304

Neuwirth CM, Kaufer DS, Chandhok R and Morris JH (1990) Issues in the design of computer support for co-authoring and commenting. In: Proceedings of the Conference on Computer Supported Cooperative Work (CSCW-90), Los Angeles, CA, 7–10 October. ACM, New York, pp 183–195.

Newman M and Robey D (1991) A social process model of user analyst relationships (submitted). For further information, write to Dr M Newman, Department of Accounting, University of Manchester, Oxford Road, Manchester, UK

Newman M and Noble F (1990) User involvement as an interaction process: a case study. Information Systems Research 1: 89–113

Norman DA and Draper SW (1986) User Centred System Design: New Perspectives on Human–Computer Interaction. Lawrence Earlbaum, Hillsdale, NJ

O'Malley C (1989) Computer supported collaborative learning, NATO workshop, Maratea, Italy

O'Shea T, Evertse R, Hennesey S, Floyd A, Fox M and Elsom-Cook M (1988) Design choices for an intelligent arithmetic tutor. In: Self J (ed) Artificial Intelligence and Human Learning: Intelligent Computer-Aided Instruction. Chapman and Hall, London

Olson GM and Olson JS (1991) User-centred design of collaboration technology. Journal of Organizational Computing 1(1): 61–83

Olson JS, Olson GM, Mack LA and Wellner P (1990) Concurrent editing: the group's interface. In: Diaper D, Gilmore D, Cockton G and Shackel B (ed) Human–Computer Interaction: Proceedings of INTERACT '90. Elsevier, Amsterdam, pp 835–840

Olson MH and Ives B (1981) User involvement in system design: an empirical test of alternative approaches. Information and Management 4: 183–195

Olson MH and Bly SA (1991) The Portland experience – a report on a distributed research group. International Journal of Man–Machine Studies 34(2)

Opper S (1988) A groupware toolbox. Byte 13: 275–282, December

Owen WF (1985) Metaphor analysis of cohesiveness in small discussion groups. Small Group Behavior 16(3): 415–424

Pace RC (1990) Personalized and depersonalized conflict in small group discussions an examination of differentiation. Small Group Research 21(1): 79–96

Pasch J (1991) Dialogical software design. In: Bullinger H-J (ed) Human Aspects in Computing: Design and Use of Interactive Systems and Work with Terminals. Elsevier, Amsterdam

Patchen M (1970) Models of co-operation and conflict: a critical review. Journal of Conflict Resolution 14(3)

Pattison HE, Corkhill D and Lesser VR (1987) Instantiating descriptions of organizational structures. In: Huhns MN (ed) Distributed Artificial Intelligence. Morgan Kaufman, Los Altos, CA, pp 59–96

Pendell SD (1990) Deviance and conflict in small group decision making: an exploratory study. Small Group Research 21(3): 393–403

Perret-Clermont A-N (1980) Social Interaction and Cognitive Development in Children. Academic Press, London

Pettigrew TF (1986) The intergroup contact hypothesis reconsidered. In: Hewstone M (ed) Contact and Conflict in Intergroup Encounters. Blackwell, Oxford

Piliavin JA and Martin RR (1978) The effects of the sex composition of groups on style and on social interaction. Sex Roles 4: 281–296

Plant TA, Morris ME, Hughes PT and Benson ORK (1991) CoOpLab – computer supported cooperative working by evolution, UK Unix users group meeting, Liverpool, UK

Pliskin N (1989) Interacting with electronic mail can be a dream or a nightmare: a user's point of view. Interacting with Computers 1(3) 259–272

Pondy LR (1967) Organizational conflict: concepts and models. Administrative Science Quarterly 12: 296–320

Pood EA (1980) Functions of communication: an experimental study in group conflict situations. Small Group Behavior 11(1) 76–87

Poole M, Homes M and DeSanctis G (1988) Conflict management and decision support systems. In: Proceedings of the Conference on Computer Supported Cooperative Work (CSCW-88), Portland, OR, September. ACM, New York, pp 227–243

Price V (1989) Social identification and public opinion effects of communicating group conflict. Public Opinion Quarterly 53(2): 197–224

Priem RL and Price KH (1991) Process and outcome: expectations for the dialectical inquiry, devil's advocacy, and consensus techniques of strategic decision making. Group and Organization Studies 16(2): 206–225

Putnam LL (1983) Small group work climates: a lag-sequential analysis of group interaction. Small Group Behavior 14(4): 465–494

Putnam LL and Poole MS (1987) Conflict and negotiation. In: Porter LW (ed) Handbook of Organizational Communication: An Interdisciplinary Perspective. Sage, Beverly Hills, pp 549–599

Ramsay A (1988) Formal Methods in Artificial Intelligence. Cambridge University Press, Cambridge

Rapoport A (1974) Game Theory as a Theory of Conflict Resolution. Reidel, Dordrecht

Rauch-Hindin WB (1988) A Guide to Commercial Artificial Intelligence. Prentice-Hall, Englewood Cliffs, NJ

Raven BH and Kruglanski AW (1970) Conflict and power. In: Swingle P (ed) The Structure of Conflict, Academic Press, New York, pp 69–109

Reichman R (1984) Extended person–machine interface. Artificial Intelligence 22(2): 157–218

Reichman R (1985) Getting computers to talk like you and me. MIT Press, Cambridge, MA

Rein GL and Ellis CA (1991) rIBIS: a real-time group hypertext system. International Journal of Man–Machine Studies 34(3): 349–368

Renwick PA (1977) Effects of sex differences on the perception and management of superior–subordinate conflict: an exploratory study. Organizational Behavior and Human Performance 19: 403–415

Restivo S (1983) The Social Relations of Physics, Mysticism and Mathematics. Reidel, Boston, MA

Riddick J (1991) The implications of small-group interactions for understanding aspects of organizational culture. Construction Management and Economics 9: 219–229

Robbins SP (1974) Managing Organizational Conflict: A Non-Traditional Approach. Prentice-Hall, Englewood Cliffs, NJ

Robbins SP (1989) Organizational Behavior: Concepts, Controversies and Applications. Prentice-Hall, Englewood Cliffs, NJ

Robey D and Farrow D (1982) User involvement in information systems development: a conflict model and empirical test. Management Science 28: 73–85

Robey D, Farrow D and Franz CR (1989) Group process and conflict in system development. Management Science 35: 1172–1191

Root RW (1988) Design of a multi-media vehicle for social browsing. Proceedings of the Conference on Computer Supported Cooperative Work (CSCW-88), Portland, OR, September. ACM, New York, pp 25–38

Rosenberg D (1988) Knowledge acquisition for interaction with expert systems in manufacturing. Kingston Polytechnic CIM Centre Technical Report 067

Rosenberg D and Hutchison CS (1992) Patterns of talk as indicators of covert organizational structure. Kingston Polytechnic Kingston AI Group Technical Report 92-1

Rosenbrock HH (ed) (1989) Designing Human-Centred Technology. Springer-Verlag, London

Rosenschein JS (1985) Rational interaction: co-operation among intelligent agents, PhD thesis, report STAN-CS-85-1081, Department of Computer Science, Stanford University, CA

Rowbottom RW and Billis D (1977) The stratification of work and organizational design. Human Relations 30: 53–76

Saine TJ and Bock DG (1973) A comparison of the distributional and sequential structures of interaction in high and low consensus groups. Central States Speech Journal 24: 125–130

Sainfort FC, Gustafson DH, Bosworth K and Hawkins RP (1990) Decision support systems effectiveness: conceptual framework and empirical evaluation. Organizational Behavior and Human Decision Processes 45(2): 232–252

Scheifler R and Gettys J, with Flowers J, Newman R and Rosenthal D (1990) X window system: the complete reference to Xlib, X Protocol, ICCCM, XLFD (2nd edn). Digital Press

Scott B (1988) Negotiating Constructive and Competitive Negotiation. Paradigm, London

Sermat V (1964) Cooperative behaviour in a mixed motive game. Journal of Social Psychology 62: 217–239

Sharples M (ed) (1992) Computer Supported Collaborative Writing. Springer-Verlag, London

Shaw M (1976) Group Dynamics: The Psychology of Small Group Behavior. McGraw-Hill, New York

Shaw ME and Harkey B (1976) Some effects of congruency of member characteristics and group structure upon group behavior. Journal of Personality and Social Psychology 34(3): 412–418

Shaw MLG and Gaines BR (1988) A methodology for recognizing consensus, correspondence, conflict, and contrast in a knowledge acquisition system. In: Proceedings, Third AAAI Knowledge Acquisition for Knowledge-Based Systems Workshop, November 1988, Banff, Canada

Singer P (1980) Marx. Oxford Paperbacks, Oxford

Sloan S and Cooper C (1987) Sources of stress in the modern office. In: Gale A and Christie B (ed) Psychophysiology and the Electronic Office. Wiley, Chichester

Smith KK and Berg DN (1987) A paradoxical conception of group dynamics. Human Relations 40(10) 633–657

Smith R, O'Shea T, O'Malley C, Scanlon E and Taylor J (1991) Preliminary experiments with a distributed, multi-media problem solving environment. In: Bowers J and Benford S (ed) Studies in Computer Supported Cooperative Work: Theory, Practice and Design. North-Holland, Oxford

Spradley JP (ed) (1970) You Owe Yourself A Drunk: An Ethnography of Urban Nomads. Little, Brown and Co, Boston, MA

Sproull L and Kiesler S (1986) Reducing social context cues: electronic mail in organizational communication. Management Science 32: 1492–1512

Sproull L and Kiesler S (1991) Two-level perspective on electronic mail in organizations. Journal of Organizational Computing 2(1): 125–134

Stamp G (1989) Well-being and stress at work. ICIS Forum 19(1) Star SL (1983) Simplification and scientific work: an example from neuroscience research. Social Studies of Science 13: 205–228

Star SL (1983) Simplification in scientific work: an example from neuroscience research. Social Studies of Science 13: 205–228

Star SL (1985) Scientific work and uncertainty. Social Studies of Science 15: 391–427

Star SL (1989a) Regions of the Mind: Brain Research and the Quest for Scientific Certainty. Stanford University Press, Stanford, CA

Star SL (1989b) The structure of ill-structured solutions: boundary objects and heterogeneous distributed problem solving. In: Huhns M and Gasser L (ed) Readings in Distributed Artificial Intelligence 2. Morgan Kaufmann, Menlo Park, CA

Star SL (1990) Layered space, formal representations and long-distance control: the politics of information. Fundamenta Scientiae 10: 125–155

Star SL (1991) Power, technologies and the phenomenology of standards: on being allergic to onions. In: Law J (ed) A Sociology of Monsters? Power, Technology and the Modern World, Sociological Review Monograph. Blackwell, Oxford, pp 27–57

Star SL and Griesemer J (1989) Institutional ecology, "translations", and coherence: amateurs and professionals in Berkeley's Museum of Vertebrate Zoology, 1907–1939. Social Studies of Science 19: 387–420

Stefik M, Bobrow DG, Lanning S and Tatar DG (1986) WYSIWIS revised: early experiences with multi-user interfaces. In: Peterson D (ed) Proceedings of the Conference on Computer Supported Cooperative Work (CSCW-86), Austin, TX. ACM, New York

Stefik M, Foster G, Bobrow DG, Kahn K, Lanning S and Suchman L (1987) Beyond the chalkboard: computer support for collaboration and problem solving in meetings. Communications of the ACM 30(1): 32–47

Sternberg RJ and Soriano LJ (1984) Styles of conflict resolution. Journal of Personality and Social Psychology 47(1): 115–126

Strauss AL (1978) Negotiations: Varieties, Contexts, Processes and Social Order. Jossey-Bass, San Francisco

Strodtbeck F and Mann R (1956) Sex role differences in jury deliberations. Sociometry 19: 3–11

Swingle P (1970) Dangerous games. In: Swingle P (ed) The Structure of Conflict. Academic Press, New York

Tait P and Vessey I (1988) The effect of user involvement on system success: a contingency approach. MIS Quarterly 12: 91–108

Tang J and Leifer L (1988) A framework for understanding the workspace activity of design teams. In: Proceedings of the Conference on Computer Supported Cooperative Work (CSCW-88), Portland, OR, September. ACM, New York, pp 244–249

Tannen D (1991) You Just Don't Understand: Women and Men in Conversation. Virago, London

Tatar DG, Foster G and Bobrow DG (1991) Design for conversation: lessons from Cognoter. International Journal of Man–Machine Studies 34(2): 185– 210

Terhune KW (1970) The effects of personality in cooperation and conflict. In: Swingle P (ed) The Structure of Conflict. Academic Press, New York

Thimbleby HW, Anderson S and Witten IH (1990) Reflexive CSCW: supporting long-term personal work. Interacting with Computers 2(3): 330–336

Thomas K (1976) Conflict and conflict management. In: Dunnette MD (ed) Handbook of Industrial and Organizational Psychology, pp 889–935, Rand McNally College Publishing Co, Chicago, IL

Thompson L (1990) The influence of experience on negotiation performance. Journal of Experimental and Social Psychology 26: 528–544

Toffler A (1990) Powershift: Knowledge, Wealth and Violence at the Edge of the 21st Century. Bantam Books, New York

Trigg R, Suchman L and Halasz F (1986) Supporting collaboration in NoteCards. In: Peterson D (ed) Proceedings of the Conference on Computer Supported Cooperative Work (CSCW-86), Austin, TX. ACM, New York, pp 1–10

Tuckman BW (1965) Developmental sequence in small groups. Psychological Bulletin 63: 348–399

Tuckman BW and Jensen MAC (1977) Stages of small-group development revisited. Group and Organization Studies 2: 419–427

Tudge JRH (1985) The effect of social interaction on cognitive development: how creative is conflict? The Quarterly Newsletter of the Laboratory of Comparative Human Cognition 7: 33–40

Tudge JRH (1989) When collaboration leads to regression: some negative consequences of sociocognitive conflict. European Journal of Social Psychology 19: 123–138

Unger R (1990) Conflict management in group psychotherapy. Small Group Research 21(3): 349–359

Valacich JS, Dennis AR and Nunamaker JF (1991) Electronic meeting support: the GroupSystems concept. International Journal of Man–Machine Studies 34(2): 262–282

Viller S (1991) The group facilitator: a CSCW perspective. In: Bannon L, Robinson M and Schmidt K (ed) Proceedings of the Second European Conference on Computer Supported Cooperative Work (EC-CSCW '91), Amsterdam, September. Kluwer, Dordrecht

Volkema RJ and Bergmann TJ (1989) Interpersonal conflict at work: an analysis of behavioral responses. Human Relations 42(9): 757–770

Wahrman R (1977) Status, deviance, sanctions and group discussion. Small Group Behavior 8(2): 147–168

Wall VD and Nolan LL (1987) Small group conflict: a look at equity, satisfaction, and styles of conflict management. Small Group Behavior 18(2): 188–211

Wall VD, Galanes GJ and Love SB (1987) Small, task-oriented groups conflict, conflict management, satisfaction, and decision quality. Small Group Behavior 18(1): 31–55

Wastell DG and Cronin E (1988) Soft systems methodologies in the design of information systems: insights from hermeneutics and Habermas's theory of communication. In: Computers in Clinical Medicine. BMIS, London

Watabe K, Sakata S, Fukuoka H and Ohmori T (1990) Distributed multiparty desktop conferencing system: Mermaid. In: Proceedings of the Conference on Computer-Supported Cooperative Work, Los Angeles, CA, 7–10 October. ACM, New York, pp 27–28

Weinberg SB, Rovinski SH, Weiman L and Beitman M (1981) Common group problems: a field study. Small Group Behavior 12(1): 81–92

White P and Wastell DG (1991) Process support technology, cooperative work and information system development. In: Bullinger H (ed) Human Aspects of Computing. Elsevier, Amsterdam

Wilson P (1991a) Computer Supported Cooperative Work. Intellect, Oxford

Wilson P (1991b) An overview of computer supported cooperative work (CSCW): a new IT paradigm. In: Proceedings of the Conference on Advanced Information Systems (AIS '91). Springer-Verlag, London, pp 125–138

Wimsatt WC (1980) Reductionst research strategies and their biases in the units of selection controversy. In: Nickler T (ed) Scientific Discovery: Case Studies. Reidel, Dordrecht, pp 213–259

Wimsatt W (1986) Developmental constraints, generative entrenchment, and the innate-acquired distinction. In: Bechtel PW (ed) Integrating Scientific Disciplines. Martinus-Nijhof, Dordrecht, pp 185–208

Winograd T (1988) A language/action perspective on the design of cooperative work. Human–Computer Interaction 3(1): 3–30

Winograd T and Flores F (1986) Understanding Computers and Cognition: A New Foundation for Design. Addison-Wesley, New York

Witten IH, Thimbleby HW, Coulouris G and Greenberg S (1991) Liveware – a new approach to sharing data in social networks. International Journal of Man–Machine Studies 34(3)

Wood CJ (1989) Challenging the assumptions underlying the use of participatory decision–making strategies: a longitudinal case study. Small Group Behavior 20(4): 428–448

Young R and Simon T (1987) Planning in the context of human–computer- interaction. In: Diaper D and Winder R (ed) People and Computers III. Cambridge University Press, Cambridge

Zamarripa PO and Krueger DL (1983) Implicit contracts regulating small group leadership: the influence of culture. Small Group Behavior 14(2): 187–210

Subject Index

Name Index